WRITING-INTENSIVE

WRITING-INTENSIVE

Becoming W-Faculty in
a New Writing Curriculum

WENDY STRACHAN

UTAH STATE UNIVERSITY PRESS
Logan, Utah
2008

Utah State University Press
Logan, Utah 84322–7800
© 2008 Utah State University Press
All rights reserved

978-0-87421-703-2 (hard cover)
978-0-87421-704-9 (e-book)

Manufactured in the United States of America
Cover design by Barbara Yale-Read

Library of Congress Cataloging-in-Publication Data
Strachan, Wendy.
 Writing-intensive : becoming W-faculty in a new writing curriculum / Wendy Strachan.
     p. cm.
 Includes bibliographical references.
  ISBN 978-0-87421-703-2 (alk. paper)
 1. English language–Rhetoric–Study and teaching (Higher) 2. Interdisciplinary approach in educa-
tion. I. Title.
  PE1404.S835 2008
  808'.0420711–dc22
                            2007048503

In loving memory of my parents
RUBY MURIEL BEALE
and
SPENCER LAURENCE LITTLE

CONTENTS

ACKNOWLEDGEMENTS

Like many of my colleagues, I succumbed over the years to the dailiness of teaching pressures, the ongoing need for reports and documentation, the demand for new classroom materials, and the deadlines for conference presentations and articles about my work with faculty and students; writing a book was only a dream. I am immensely grateful, therefore, that I was given the opportunity and the time and that I was encouraged to believe that there was a contribution to be made both to the university and to the Writing Across the Curriculum/Writing-in-the-Disciplines (WAC/WID) field, by such a book. For this, I owe a debt to three people: to the Dean of the faculty of arts and social sciences, John Pierce, who included provision for a post-retirement contract in my agreement with him; and to both David Kaufman, director of the Learning and Instructional Development centre at Simon Fraser University and Bill Krane, associate vice president academic. They decided that the best way I could use a post-retirement contract would be to write a book about the preceding four years' work on implementing a writing-intensive learning curriculum. I owe thanks doubly to David Kaufman for providing me with a research assistant in the person of Johanne Provencal. Johanne was an invaluable resource and support for much of the writing period. Also a thoughtful reader and critic was my colleague and friend, Katharine Patterson, who highlighted loose ends and helped me talk through ideas.

The content of this book and the stories it tells, however, would not have been possible without the participation and contributions of the many faculty members with whom we worked over the years and, in particular, of the ones whose experience is directly reflected in a variety of ways in this book. They inspired and challenged us; any success we enjoyed in the work we did at the Centre for Writing-Intensive Learning (CWIL) and later, in the Writing-Intensive Learning Office (WILO), was due to their openness and their commitment to students and to teaching as well as to their discipline. I was also fortunate to have the support of my colleagues in CWIL: Kathryn Alexander, Adrienne Burk, Steve Marshall and Tara McFarlane, all of whom were excited by the prospect of documenting our collective efforts and progress in a public record. As I set out, they helped me think through the purposes for such a record and what it might accomplish. Along the way, their responses to my questions were always useful in extending or challenging my thinking. Toward the end of the process, the office of the associate vice-president academic offered corrections and redactions for the final chapter.

I thank Michael Spooner, director at the Utah State University Press, for his wise and thoughtful guidance; his care sustained me through some challenging periods. I thank the peer reviewers whose detailed comments and questions led me to re-consider some aspects of the book as a whole and some stories in particular. For the patience, energy, and commitment to reflective practice that fueled their stories, my deep appreciation goes to Erin Barley, Don DeVoretz, Robbie Dunlop, Karen Ferguson, Lee Hanlan, Phil Hanson, Andy Hira, Arne Mooers, Catherine Murray, Nancy Olewiler, Joan Sharp, and Richard Smith. I am also grateful to my family whose faith cheered me on, especially my husband, Richard.

FOREWORD

What exactly is a good education and how can universities best help students acquire one? These were the questions that guided a committee struck by the Vice-President, Academic, of Simon Fraser University to evaluate the undergraduate curriculum and make recommendations to improve it.

Following extensive reading and consultation, this committee, which I chaired, decided that the essence of a good education lies in the acquisition of the ability to write well (which entails thinking clearly and communicating one's ideas in ways that can be understood by others), the acquisition of quantitative abilities (which implies an appreciation for logic), and exposure to the ideas and modes of inquiry in the sciences, social sciences, and humanities. We believed that tax-payers who support universities have the right to expect students to acquire an expanded breadth of knowledge and an improved facility with numbers and words.

Some members of the faculty disputed the value of demanding breadth, and some disputed the value of demanding quantitative abilities (especially math) in the context of developing disciplinary and specialist expertise at the university level. But no one—*not one person*—disputed the value of all students in all disciplines becoming competent writers. The question that rose immediately was not whether to take measures to help students improve their writing abilities, but how to do it.

Fortunately for this initiative, there was expertise in our university on how to teach writing. I sought out Dr. Wendy Strachan, director of the Centre for Writing-Intensive Learning (CWIL), for advice and was struck immediately by her commitment to and persuasive articulation of writing-intensive learning. To be honest: my initial assumption was that we should teach writing in large composition classes in the English department. After all, that is (I thought) how I had learned to write. Wendy quickly disabused me of this wrong-headed assumption. She explained that the ways in which ideas are expressed varies across disciplines, and therefore, learning to write in the genres of disciplines is an exercise in epistemology. It contributes not only to students' writing abilities, but also to their understanding of how knowledge is organized in different disciplines. Students write—or should be required to write—in all disciplines. It makes sense, pedagogically and practically—for faculty in particular disciplines to assume responsibility for helping their students acquire the ability to communicate the ideas that define the disciplines in the ways and for the purposes that have evolved—for good reason—in those disciplines. Writing a poem is one thing, but writing a scientific report is quite another.

After deciding to adopt a writing-in-the-disciplines approach, we faced a host of practical and pedagogical problems, which are described in detail in this book. To guarantee that students received guidance in writing in disciplines, we set a university-wide requirement that all students take at least two writing-intensive courses. To ensure that appropriate writing-intensive courses were developed, we set criteria. To ensure that faculty and teaching assistants developed courses that met the criteria, Wendy and her colleagues at CWIL served as mentors. All of this—Senate approval of the writing requirement, the establishment of criteria, the agreement of programs to develop writing-intensive courses, and the actual development of effective writing-intensive courses—required thousands of hours of consultation and negotiation.

This book offers a record of the process that led to the implementation of the writing requirement at Simon Fraser University, and the development of courses designed to help students improve their writing abilities. It is a case study written by an "insider" who participated in every aspect of the endeavor and supplied invaluable guidance throughout. It is a case study that, I believe, documents for both our university and others, a record of what it was possible to achieve given conditions that subsequent events have demonstrated were essential. Inflicting writing requirements on students (and faculty) simply will not work. To be successful, writing courses must be designed in effective ways, faculty must be motivated to help their students cultivate the ability to write and students must be motivated to invest the time and energy necessary to achieve this goal. It is one thing to have informed opinions about which writing experiences have proven most effective in other contexts, as members of CWIL did, and quite another thing to work effectively with faculty to help them redesign their courses accordingly. Some faculty simply are not interested. Other faculty are interested, but either have no idea about how to proceed, or have wrong-headed ideas about how to help their students become better writers. Members of CWIL were able, on an individual–by–individual, course–by–course, discipline-by-discipline basis, to inspire a critical mass of faculty not only to redesign their courses in writing-intensive ways, but also to champion the value of this approach to their colleagues. They provided a model of professional development that was scholarly in its approach and respectful of disciplinary and individual differences.

But the way to significant pedagogical change is never smooth. Although all members of the committees who were charged with designing and implementing the new writing requirements valued the goal, they had quite different ideas about how to achieve it. Virtually every discipline, and many faculty entered the process with unique reservations. For example, on the one hand, some members of science departments feared that members of the Centre for Writing Intensive Learning were guided by a "soft-headed humanities" orientation. Words like "rhetoric" and "genre" turned them off. On the other hand, some members of Humanities departments assumed that they knew all there was to know about teaching writing, and were unreceptive to guidance. Try offering to mentor members of the English department about best practices in writing!

Equally significant for any such pedagogical change was the nature and form of administrative and institutional support that constituted an essential framework for efforts at the faculty level and that was forthcoming during the period documented in this book. Subsequent events notwithstanding, this book tells a story of success—success not easily achieved, mind you, but success all the same. I observed the growth of informed enthusiasm for writing first hand, and was delighted in the development of a set of innovative writing-intensive courses that preliminary reports indicate are benefiting students in significant ways. It is often said that the devil is in the details. I believe the full saying adds that angels are in the details also. The key to the success of endeavors such as the one described in this book is to invest the time, energy, and commitment necessary to refine the details, to overcome the inevitable obstacles, and to sustain one's commitment in the face of setbacks. No one invested more in this initiative than the author of this book and her colleagues in the Centre for Writing Intensive Learning.

Dennis Krebs
Professor of Psychology, Simon Fraser University
Chair, Ad Hoc Curriculum Committee 2000–2001
Chair, Undergraduate Curriculum Implementation
Committee 2002–2004

PROLOGUE

In the ancient Greek drama, the prologue constituted the opening. It set out the essential background to the events that would follow in the performance. It focused the interpretive gaze of the audience. In more contemporary use, the prologue becomes a peripheral space for the writer to position herself.

An itinerant, a scholar gypsy with "*one* aim, *one* business, *one* desire" (Arnold, *The Scholar Gypsy*) I wandered into international schools in thirty-five countries, over a twenty year period. I met with teachers of children learning their letters and with teachers of teenagers puzzling through Shakespearean plots or the mysteries of photosynthesis. I was the "expert" on writing, a consultant and director of National Writing Project sites. I went by invitation to do weekend workshops and teach alongside faculty from across the disciplines in their K-12 classrooms. I drew teachers to three-week summer programs in the Philippines, in Greece and in the south of France. It was heady stuff. It was a joy to watch the chemistry teacher discover an unexpected talent as a writer and to encourage Social Studies teachers to make a difference in the uses of writing among their colleagues. I was lucky to go back to many schools several times over a period of years to help sustain energy for the challenges of taking time for writing. An itinerant is just that, however, not a permanent presence, not engaged for the long haul, not responsible through bureaucratic tangles and shifts in personnel and administration. In any particular setting, there were no guarantees of continuity, of institutional effort, and of reflective practice: ideas about writing could be taken up and dropped when the people interested moved on to other places or a new passion took hold. In too few cases, did writing become everybody's business.

When I joined the English department at Simon Fraser University, I began working with the Centre for Research in Academic Writing and with its director, Dr. Janet Giltrow. Not only did I discover a whole new area of composing theory and new research methods, I was also placed to continue working with faculty on using and teaching writing in their courses. The difference for me in this new setting was that I was *in situ*. There could be continuity and sustained attention to thinking and learning about student writing and faculty practice. Although the principal responsibility of the writing centre was to assist the students, opportunities regularly arose to meet with the faculty who were preparing the assignments and marking them. No matter how effective the help from the writing centre, students' potential success or failure as writers traces back to the environment for the writing: the values, expectations, specificities, and ambiguities inherent in the discourse around the written assignments in the course. It was this environment that interested me. When the university began talking seriously about making a new commitment to improving writing and the teaching of writing, I was eager to participate.

The outcome of my participation is a story in this book. I became the director for the Centre for Writing-Intensive Learning (CWIL), the position from which I was able to contribute to what I regarded as a great adventure. It was an opportunity to do what I loved best, to work with teachers on writing, and to do so as part of an institutional imperative that held a promise of continuity and sustained commitment. It was something I believed in and felt strongly about, to which I could bring a lifetime of experience and in which I was willing to invest all my energy. My work is one part of the story. Depending on what needed to be done, I was often in the wings, behind the scenes. The actors were the faculty with whom I worked and this is their story as well. It is also the story of the administrative teams who developed policies that determined the direction and scale of the university's commitment to writing.

I embarked on the challenge of writing this book with some ambivalence. It meant withdrawing from the daily rush and exhilaration of working with faculty and sequestering myself in a mostly solitary undertaking. But it also meant an opportunity to record and to reflect on the contexts and complexities that had shaped our work. It allowed me to revisit and consult with the professors with whom I had collaborated and to reflect with them on what we had accomplished. While none of us would say the writing initiative had been nursed "in unclouded joy, and every doubt long blown by time away" (Arnold 1853), writing the book required an assessment of the initiative overall, giving all of us reason to take stock and consider future directions in a form different from the many reports and estimates CWIL had produced as part of ongoing evaluation and planning. The book was a means of bringing together many elements in a single project in a single portrait.

Although I have attempted to represent those many elements, this is a story that I tell from my own vantage point. There are things I did not and could not see from where I stood. There are things I did not understand

and could not explain from where I stood. But this account draws on all the resources available to me. I am immensely grateful that I was invited to write it and given a year to do it. Not only do I *not* walk away from the scene, as I had for so many years as a consultant, with no part in the outcomes, I also do not walk away with no evidence.

INTRODUCTION

The title of this monograph, *Writing-Intensive: Becoming W-Faculty in a New Writing Curriculum* points to what is clearly not a modest undertaking. We were latecomers, like most others in Canada, to the institutionalizing of writing at our university. But we gave serious attention to the reports of colleagues in other institutions, mainly American, which made it clear what would be involved if we also became serious about investing in student writers. Like others, we had noticed an increase in student literacy problems, and also like others, had begun to realize that laying the blame elsewhere, on the parents, the kindergarten teacher, the high school, or the TV culture, was not a solution. We could not ignore a growing student population that was different, both culturally and linguistically, from earlier decades. Investment in these students as writers might qualify, from some points of view, as a means to move them to more conscious and correct use of Standard English. From other points of view, however, investment in students as writers could set processes in motion that would affect their entire educational experience. Such processes would or could entail, I suggest, a cultural transformation at the university.

As David Russell and others have pointed out, approaching writing across the disciplines "asks for a fundamental commitment to a radically different way of teaching" (Russell 2002, 295), and encourages a new and articulated awareness of the role of discourse in the making of disciplinary knowledge. Correspondingly, there is new awareness of the learning and reconfiguring, perhaps re-inventing, of that knowledge by students. In the writing classroom, roles and purposes shift, new values emerge and adjust to new standards; relationships to subject matter are reconceived. New pedagogies in these classrooms may make a significant difference to the students in particular courses, but these pedagogies need to be part of much more widespread shifts in values, norms, and structures if they are to transcend individual behaviors. A new curriculum at the institutional level that applies across disciplines establishes the intention of a larger social purpose. Accomplishing it as a cultural reality in the scale of the institution is a more complex process than in the individual classroom. It would be achieved incrementally, and, in a university, by consent, not imposition.

The university is not a place where such shifts occur readily. In his account of reform in higher education, Richard E. Miller offers many cautions. He points out that the complications inherent in moving from a reform proposal to implementation require, beyond the fixed fiscal and material realities, an understanding that

> . . . intellectuals, administrators, and students are not different from anyone else who works in a large bureaucratic system: they need to be *persuaded* that change is necessary, they would prefer to exercise some control over how change is implemented and assessed, and they want to be certain that the proposed changes will not make their own work obsolete or more difficult. If those conditions aren't met—and they almost never are—then the affected parties offer public conformity and private resistance, engaging in what Scott calls an 'undeclared ideological guerilla war' that is fought with 'rumor, gossip, disguises, linguistic tricks, metaphors, euphemisms, folktales, ritual gestures, anonymity.' (Miller 1998, 137)

Miller's characterization of potentially obstructive bureaucratic and personal, relational elements finds its explication in the documentation of writing program developments across the country. These exemplify ways to bypass the emergence of 'guerilla war,' and illustrate the kinds of faculty interactions likely to be persuasive and pedagogically sound. They provide evidence that the use and teaching of writing can be constitutive in disciplinary pedagogies and become "everybody's business" (Fulwiler and Young 1990; Kipling and Murphy 1992; Monroe 2003; Segall and Smart 2005; Thaiss and Zawacki 2006; Townsend 2001; Waldo 2004). They also demonstrate Miller's caveat that, in spite of obstacles, "one finds a place where individuals acting alone and collectively have an opportunity to express their agency, albeit in the highly restricted realm of relative freedom" (Miller 1998, 8). As our university embarked on integrating writing in the disciplines, these pioneers were a *Guide Bleu* to consult about the territory, the pitfalls, and the options.

In joining this cornucopia of exemplars, this account confirms what have been marked as best practices, and offers fresh perspectives. The initiative at Simon Fraser University (SFU) and this book about it are distinguished from our predecessors in several ways. Set in motion by SFU's vice president academic, John Waterhouse, and led by his appointed Ad Hoc Committee, inquiry and discussion of the undergraduate curriculum drew participation from across the campus through surveys, department meetings, committee and sub-committee deliberation, widely distributed interim reports, presentations in Senate, and individual lobbying and information-seeking. Independent of this university-wide inquiry about the overall undergraduate curriculum, the dean of the faculty of arts and social sciences (FASS), John Pierce, set up the Centre for Writing-Intensive Learning (CWIL) in the Fall semester 2002 with two faculty members to assist professors, on a by-request basis, to use and teach writing more effectively in their content courses; that is, to make them writing-intensive. Concurrently, as CWIL's director, I was one of many people being consulted about how to improve student writing university-wide. Once the Ad Hoc Committee decided upon improving writing by instituting new requirements, and the decision became official through Senate, our unit, CWIL, moved from being dedicated to faculty support in FASS writing into becoming the principal resource for assisting instructors across all the faculties and disciplines in writing-intensive course (W-course) development. In the interim, we had developed a discipline-based pedagogy informed by new rhetorical genre theory that served as the framework for our approach to implementing the new writing curriculum.

Our view of genre was influenced by Carolyn Miller's original work in "Genre as Social Action" (1984/1994) and elaborated, among others, by a number of our Canadian colleagues who, through what Freedman has termed "Rhetorical Genre Studies" (1999/2001), have researched the learning and use of genres in both academic and professional settings (Artemeva and Freedman 2006; Coe 2002; Dias 1999; Freedman and Medway 1994; Giltrow and Valiquette 1994; Schryer 1993). Their work has demonstrated the significance and impact of rhetorical contexts, student motivation and relevance of the genre to course or situational exigencies, and invited reflection on the nature of genre pedagogies. Freedman's research into students' acquisition of legal discourse, for instance, challenged assumptions about the need for explicit teaching of genre features (Freedman, 1993). More recently, others have compiled classroom illustrations of genre pedagogy across disciplines and institutions (Herrington, 2005) or proposed approaches for such a pedagogy (Devitt 2004; Hyland 2004) that appear to counter Freedman's objections with some level of explicit teaching of genre. The account of our experience in this book represents the implementation of genre pedagogy at the course and curriculum level in a single institution. As a consequence, there was a theoretical consistency in the approaches we took in assisting in the development of the W-courses, but the particularities of local situations meant that this consistency did not lead to formulaic teaching across the disciplines.

Taking a new rhetorical genre perspective equipped us to engage our discourse analytic skills with the professor's intimate knowledge of the social action of their particular disciplinary genres. Together, we uncovered their often tacit knowledge, bringing it forward to a discursive level that helped us in identifying genres important for their students' initiation into the discipline, and in revealing the relevant textual regularities of those genres. New rhetorical genre theory anchored our stance, but rarely did we find it necessary to be explicit about that overarching theoretical framework. We suggested and developed strategies at a micro-level for communicating the features of the disciplinary genres to students. These strategies reflected criteria appropriate to a genre-based, process pedagogy. They included assignments and instruction offering rationales for, and explicit analyses of, the target genres, and structured engagement in writing processes with response and revision. The professors did not see themselves as writing teachers; they were teaching their subject matter with written work as a means of assisting and assessing student learning. They assigned writing for their own purposes in the genres they valued and that they themselves largely defined. By consulting with them, we largely avoided the concept of genre as formulaic, learning from them the fluid and evolving characteristics of the genres they knew as writers, and that they wished to encourage in their students as writers.

The new genre pedagogy had a significant effect on instructional processes and patterns of relationships in the classrooms. It also had the effect of creating and transforming the discourse around writing, providing a new context for discussing teaching and learning that the thinking about, and teaching of, writing had made more visible. The bringing together of faculty from across the disciplines created, in Wendy Bishop's words, "sites of terminology where far-flung constituents can meet and speak a second language" (Bishop and Ostrom 1997, xiii). The discursive space that was opened up contributed to constituting a community of faculty, who could share their experience as a basis for further action. In a 1994 revisiting of her earlier analysis of genre, Miller cites Joseph Rouse's argument about the ways in which "narrative has specifically the function of holding heterogeneity together" (Miller 1994, 75). Though they came from very different disciplinary cultures, the W-faculty were sharing in a common project. Their overlapping interests in this particular project made it possible for them to begin to construct what Rouse argues would be "a common narrative which gives common sense to everyone's endeavor" (cited in Miller, 75). Taking on a new discourse was a means of creating new and binding collegial relationships at what might be seen as a meta-disciplinary level.

Further, by taking a genre approach that was located in the disciplines, not in composition courses, we were working in the social and cultural contexts that could provide authentic exigences and make rhetorical demands that arose out of the course content and goals. By developing a genre pedagogy, we opened up opportunities for discussion about writing that were clearly situated in the disciplinary context and that helped reveal the work of learning to write as complex, multi-faceted, and deeply embedded in disciplinary knowledge and discourse.

The actual innovation itself was not seen as the introduction of a program as such, although the satellite and supporting services that were subsequently initiated may eventually constitute what could be defined as a program. The innovation was more in the nature of a project that had goals, but was perpetually in flux, responsive to, and learning from, the participants, both faculty and students. It proceeded on the assumption that the success of the new writing curriculum for students would largely depend on developing faculty's expertise and knowledge of their own writing and disciplinary discourse practices, and the consultants' willingness and skill in helping them articulate that genre knowledge and use it in their teaching. It remained to be seen whether and how the introduction of a new pedagogy and new curriculum would ultimately affect the climate for teaching and learning, rather than reflect a shift in the wind in a few sheltered places.

Few books address applications of new rhetorical genre theory to programs for teaching writing, and few offer comprehensive studies of developing a program at a single institution. Edited collections necessarily decontextualize. A distinguishing feature of this book is that it treats the curriculum initiative holistically, and illustrates the complex and nuanced realities of development. These include individuals' troubling uncertainties, as well as their sense of dynamism in their classroom practice. The chapters which follow illustrate and explain the ways in which the principal actors and stakeholders—the administration, the departments, and the instructors in the classrooms—are implicated in each event of the curriculum change. The sequence of chapters and topics is intended to reflect the institutional context within which the innovation took shape: the first two chapters address the inescapable complexities of the bureaucratic and administrative framework that both enable and constrain the work of the faculty; the next five chapters illustrate that work; the book closes with an assessment that returns to the administration; it considers the interactions of the administration with the faculty and the implications of those interactions for the future of the new curriculum initiative.

The opening chapter, *Forty Years On: The University Mission in a New Context*, traces the developments at the senior administrative and local department levels, two separate but related arenas that eventually converged in a symbiotic relationship out of which emerged the particular characteristics of SFU's *writing-intensive* requirements. The implementation of such requirements would have significant implications for the institution's teaching and learning culture, as well as for its budget and marketability: it could not be accomplished by administrative fiat. As such, the chapter also discusses the need for faculty collaboration and compliance, allocation of adequate resources, and the composing of a coherent, articulated vision that could be understood and shared by everyone affected by the innovation, including students. Finally, the chapter offers an examination of the local contingencies and contexts that helped to explain the pragmatics and rationale for the approach taken at SFU: (a) creating committees and consultative processes to investigate the case for change; (b) articulating departmental and faculty level concerns and needs; (c) negotiating the terms and purposes of the new requirement; (d) researching for precedents and exemplars to justify the pedagogical model being recommended; and (e) defining the role of the Centre for Writing-Intensive Learning in the implementation process.

Deciding to introduce writing-intensive courses (W-courses) to enhance student writing and learning was only the first step. Faculty who supported the initiative understood that it was essential to conceptualize "writing-intensive" as richly and fully as possible, and to encourage commitment to that conceptualization through effective communication of its meaning. The second chapter, *Criteria for Writing-Intensive Courses: Rules or Reasons?*, presents the ongoing and collaborative process of arriving at an understanding of how to implement W-courses within defined criteria, and the complex and varied forms of influence on those processes.

The chapter is divided into four sections. The first section sets out the array of vantage points from which the distinguishing details of a W-course were contemplated and critiqued by those involved in the pilot phase of the initiative. The second section provides an explanation of the development of the set of criteria put forward in light of those vantage points, and in response to the ongoing dialogues with departments and individual faculty members. The third section outlines the research and theory on which each criterion rests and could be justified. The fourth and final section describes the challenges posed by the certification process, as a new process had to be put in place to designate W-courses. The chapter reflects the multi-dimensional process of defining the criteria, and establishes the foundational role of the criteria in providing reference points for the future development of W-courses, a map to transcend disciplinary boundaries but also accommodate discipline-specific routes.

In recognition that change is not accomplished by fiat, nor without disruption, the third chapter, *In Defense of Stumbling: The Map is Not the Territory*, shifts the focus from the institutional framework to the classroom. It presents a candid discussion of the risks of undertaking a W-course: risks shared by the faculty member, the TAs, the students, and the writing consultant. Such risk-taking requires the transformation of the relationships among students, TAs, faculty, and consultants. A change in course materials and engagement with those materials are also required. The chapter acknowledges that if the course is to succeed, then it must try to satisfy everyone's needs and expectations, despite the demands of the new context, which in the W-classroom are demonstrably the deliberate choice of the professor. The chapter offers an exploration and analysis of the risks involved in undertaking a W-course and the inevitable stumbling; it presents both as key to navigating unfamiliar territory towards new understandings of the issues involved.

The context for this exploration and analysis is a third-year economics course taught by a senior professor with two teaching assistants (TAs) and a class of 97 students. The chapter traces the development of the course as a W-pilot course, from the first meeting of the writing consultant and the professor, through to implementation. Attention is given also to the contemporary student-as-customer culture of the academy and the initial challenge for the writing consultant with the professor and TAs to negotiate a pedagogy, and engender a level of trust and willingness to countenance the uncertainty of outcomes. Against the backdrop of student expectations and both institutional and departmental culture, the matter of developing trust and collaboration in a new setting played itself out in multiple ways during the course: in negotiations over course and writing objectives, in assignment planning, in grading and values assigned to student written work, in relations between the professor and the TAs, and in modes of feedback and tutorial interaction. The chapter describes each of these scenarios, and offers an analysis of both the stumbling and the insights, which make significant contributions to an understanding of what is entailed in implementing W-courses across disciplines.

Each of the participants involved in planning and teaching a W-course necessarily experiences the course differently, and different elements assume different degrees of relevance for their overall impressions and interpretations, as well as for their daily work with students. As with the economics course described in Chapter Three, the next chapter provides an account of processes and outcomes in a particular course; they need not be understood as particular to the course or discipline, however, and therefore what is contained in this chapter is widely relevant to attempts at pedagogical reform. Chapter Four, *What Happened in This Course? Reflections from Three Perspectives: Joan Sharp, the course instructor; Erin Barley, the TA; Wendy Strachan, the W-consultant,* presents the sometimes consistent and sometimes divergent reflections of instructor, TA, and writing consultant, in their collective responsibility for modifying an existing course to meet the writing-intensive criteria. The chapter opens with an outline of the course context and goals for a large (250 students) lecture/lab course and the two shared goals of consultant, instructor, and TA: first, to inquire into the feasibility of integrating new purposes and processes of writing instruction with a cohort of 14 TAs, most of whom were inexperienced in giving such instruction, and who required training and mentoring; secondly, to attempt to assess the outcomes of the modified W-course on student writing and learning. Through each of the three accounts, the chapter overall takes into account the key factors that affected the collaborative process: the size of the class, the number of TAs, the complex schedule of labs and tutorials, departmental skepticism about the process, the precedents for writing in the course, and the limited time and opportunities available for consultation and collaboration.

The chapter is divided into three sections. In the first section, the instructor explains what was entailed in revisiting the purposes and processes by which students learned from her challenging course material. For her, modifications brought a new understanding of the structure and design of the course, an enhanced awareness of student strengths and weaknesses, and a more collegial relationship with the TAs. In the second section, the TA contrasts her previous content-focused and question-driven practice in tutorial with her newly acquired pedagogy of using writing as a means of learning, and reflects on how this shift in focus repositioned her in relation to the students so that she became more engaged in their learning process, in skills development, and in their struggle to write. In the third section, the consultant/author offers a tentative assessment of the effect of the process on student writing and learning, including reference to student feedback surveys and to findings from analysis of writing samples on an essay exam in the course.

Chapters Three and Four exemplified engagement by faculty in economics and biology. Both included references to proposing and developing writing assignments that reflected genres appropriate to those disciplines in the context of offering their new W-courses. In the fifth chapter, *Taking a Genre Approach to Teaching Writing: The Consulting, Collaborative Process,* I take a more direct focus on genre. I explain how applying principles from genre theory effected a transformation in discourse about writing and in faculty understanding and recognition of the complex and subtle relationship between the features of text and rhetorical situation that gives rise to genres, and makes understanding their function in those situations so important in planning and implementing successful writing assignments. I use three examples from faculty with whom we consulted for W-courses in biodiversity, environmental economics, and philosophy. I demonstrate how the genre approach that CWIL adopted invited them to re-examine their assumptions and expectations for student writing, reconsider the sequences they planned for writing assignments, revise the ways they conceptualize writing and the teaching of writing, and consequently, their performance as writing teachers. Each example is framed by Coe's (2002) three basic principles for teaching with genre theory:

> Genres embody socially established strategies for achieving purposes in rhetorical situations.

> Genres are not just text types; they imply/invoke/create/(re)construct situations (and contexts), communities, writers and readers (i.e. subject positions).

> Understanding genre will help students become versatile writers, able to adapt to the wide variety of types of writing tasks they are likely to encounter in their lives (Coe 2002, 197–210 198–200).

Since our practice was to begin with existing course material and faculty goals and objectives, the examples described here explain the ways in which we assumed the role of interpreters and mediators between genre theory as our text and the faculty's own texts to enable changes in the ways faculty used existing materials to achieve their goals for student writing. The account begins with a detailed descriptive analysis of one particular course as illustration of the process and principles that directed our practice. The following two examples are briefer echoes of this approach with genre; I point out particular aspects that differentiated the applications of genre from one course to another, putting the focus on those particulars rather than accounting for them in the context within which they occur.

While examples of the planning and mentoring characteristic of CWIL's interaction with both faculty and TAs serve to illustrate the processes of the implementation of a new genre pedagogy, they were mediated in these first chapters mainly through my representation as the narrator. Except for Joan Sharp's and Erin Barley's pieces on the biology course, they do not represent directly the experiences of faculty or their reflections on those experiences. Chapter Six, *Am I Really a Teacher? Reflections and Discoveries from Across the Disciplines,* invites the stories and voices of individuals who participated as early adopters in the initiative. It draws on interviews with ten W-faculty from nine different disciplines, each of whom volunteered to reflect on and discuss their experiences of teaching W-course(s).

The first section of this chapter takes the form of faculty comments and observations (from the interviews) woven together to provide a detailed representation and analysis of how the faculty articulated writing as both a process of production and a means of engagement in social situations. The weaving of their perspectives, situating these in relation to the discourses in their fields, provides a unique illustration and affirmation of the rationale behind the university's decision to situate the teaching of writing in the discipline. The second section opens with clusters of observations the W-faculty make about being a teacher in a post-secondary institution, a role that, for some, is clearly secondary to being a researcher, and for others creates conflicts in their sense of identity. The observations are followed by a series of snapshots, each of which seeks to capture an aspect of the challenges that emerged for each of the faculty from the process of teaching a W-course. The significance of these snapshots is that although they present discipline-specific examples, they also transcend disciplinary contexts and boundaries, and, as a collection, testify to the valuable learning that occurs when faculty from across the disciplines exchange ideas and experience about teaching.

The faculty involved in the W-courses not only had views on their personal teaching experience, but also were deeply interested in and concerned about that experience in the context of the university-wide initiative. Chapter Seven, *Collected Wisdom and Expanded Horizons: A Forum Discussion,* brings the voices and perspectives of the faculty from Chapter Six into a shared forum to discuss the political, economic, historical, intellectual, and simply bureaucratic elements at the department and university levels that framed, and in some respects constrained, their work in the classroom.

By constructing an exchange of ideas among the participating faculty in the format of a forum moderated by the author, this chapter draws on observations and responses recorded during two small group dinner meetings, and notes from individual interviews. The forum is structured around the topics that reflect concrete indicators of what the group regarded as essential elements for successful W-implementation, including questions about: (a) the way teaching is valued at the university; (b) how it is, or might be, recognized, evaluated, and rewarded; (c) how W-teaching specifically might be made more visible; and (d) how the initiative needs to be communicated to, and understood by, students, TAs, and the general public. The forum affords insights, from the faculty perspective, into the larger contexts within which curriculum change occurs. The discussion also reflects the ambiguities, limitations, and range of vision that can be expected when people are brought together who occupy highly differentiated positions in the institutional hierarchy but who share a commitment to work together.

The final chapter, *Through Transition in Search of Stability*, reviews and assesses the preparation period. It draws on quantitative and qualitative data to assess the extent to which progress was made toward creating an environment that seemed likely to sustain and develop the writing initiative and its genre-based approach beyond that pilot period. At all levels of the administration, and within departments, the impending start date prompted a heightened state of activity and development (acceleration of course preparation and certification, and the creation of additional services, for instance), requiring considerable patience, collaboration, and consultation. In this chapter, I try to map out the varied and interdependent markers at the faculty, department, and administrative levels at SFU that signaled where we had made progress as well as what had been overlooked, or warranted more attention. Successful programs, whether designated Writing-in-the-Disciplines (WID) or Writing Across the Curriculum (WAC), tend toward characteristic features (Townsend 2001) and, also characteristically, appear to move through a series of four stages (Condon 2006) before becoming sufficiently integrated into the curriculum and into the university's sense of its mission to be self-sustaining. Using Condon's continuum of this staged process and Townsend's summary of characteristics as reference points, I detail the scene at the university as it appeared immediately before the semester of university-wide implementation (Fall, 2006). I conclude with an assessment of the prospects for the future of this ambitious curriculum venture.

I do not and cannot claim that the architects of the new curriculum requirements for writing at our institution were thinking in terms of cultural transformation. The purposes, as outlined in the documents describing the intended changes, were more pragmatic than idealistic, the implications for change in pedagogy more practical than philosophical. Nor indeed, would it be politically or ethically acceptable to the faculty to be informed that taking on a new writing curriculum meant endorsing a fundamental shift in their teaching and learning culture. That "writing disrupts the traditional pattern of classroom instruction" (McLeod and Miraglia 2001, 16) is not a rationale usually offered in plans submitted for Senate approval, nor is it an inducement to faculty participation in writing instruction. Neither, witness others' long experience, could any such outcome be predicted with any certainty. The process of change is a journey, as McLeod and Miraglia suggest, "not a blueprint." Embarking on a path toward a new pedagogy, however, in an activity as central to scholarship and teaching and disciplinarity as writing has the potential to unsettle and bring about fundamental cultural shifts.

1

FORTY YEARS ON
An Old Mission in a New Context

Historically, complaints about the quality of student writing have been as common and widespread at Simon Fraser University (SFU) as at any other university. Faculty responses to what are perceived as problems with students' abilities and performances have, also historically, tended to be piecemeal, intermittent, and often based on somewhat outdated ideas about writing, discourse acquisition, and learning. Instituting an in-the-disciplines writing requirement for all undergraduates suggested that the university was now ready to address systematically students' academic and professional literacy. It also created the opportunity to encourage discussion of writing development in more positive ways, as a desirable attribute of graduates, rather than as an indication of failings in students or their previous schooling. For the students who were targets of this new initiative and would need two writing-intensive courses (W-courses) before graduating, it would require a shift in expectations and an understanding of what they need as writers and learners in the discipline. Such shifts in student expectations and what could amount, through a new writing pedagogy, to a significant shift in the institution's teaching and learning culture cannot be accomplished by administrative fiat. This was particularly the case in a university with a history of valuing departmental autonomy.

In this chapter, I trace developments at the senior administrative and the local department levels, two separate but related arenas that eventually converged and led to the particular characteristics of SFUs writing-intensive requirements. In relation to these developments, I examine the local contingencies and contexts that help to explain the pragmatics and rationale for the approach taken at SFU. The overarching context at the senior administrative level was the university's review and evaluation of undergraduate curricula, which was set in motion by the vice president academic in the Fall semester of 2000. The local department level context was an approach to writing instruction developed in the faculty of arts by the Centre for Research in Academic Writing during the period 1996–1999, and later at the faculty level by the Centre for Writing-Intensive Learning (CWIL), which was created in the Fall, 2002.

CURRICULUM CHANGE: MAKING THE CASE

Although there are some variations in practice, curriculum development at SFU has tended to occur within faculties and departments. Since the university was founded forty years ago, each faculty and department has tended to set its own priorities, adjust course requirements, and to create new courses according to its perception of changing student demographics or changing disciplinary exigencies. Occasionally, more broadly representative committees have been established to make recommendations. During the 1990s, for instance, these committees addressed such university-wide concerns as the accessibility and efficiency of the undergraduate curriculum, the quality of undergraduate teaching, and the responsibility to provide good guidance and mentoring to undergraduate students (Ad Hoc Curriculum Committee, June 24, 2002, 12).

Recommendations specific to writing had been made as early as 1985 by the Ad Hoc Dean of Arts Committee, which proposed the creation of a task force to recommend practical ways of enhancing literacy. In 1993, The Senate committee on Instructional Methods and Organization (SCIMO) "recommended assigning appropriate amounts of written work in courses, providing adequate feedback to students, and not relying solely on multiple choice exams" (Ad Hoc Curriculum Committee June 24, 2002, 12.22). Although such general and specific recommendations and proposals moved through a process that led to Senate discussion and approval, historically they have not been catalysts for significant course or program revision. Consequently, the initiation and responsibility for curriculum change has remained local and particular. In the Fall semester of 2000, however, John Waterhouse, recently appointed vice president academic, put forward a unique proposal to Senate. He suggested that, "it is time for the University to examine whether undergraduate curricula are consistent with our commitments to a broadly based liberal education and are attractive when compared to curricula at other universities. The committee will examine SFU and other curricula and recommend principles and guidelines for curricular reforms, if necessary" (Waterhouse, November 2000). The proposal was quickly challenged in Senate as a "top-down" initiative that would not sit well with departments. Further, the actual need for any review of the curriculum was questioned. Senate members also voiced the opinion that the amount of work involved might not be justifiable (Grant 2000).

A number of external and internal influences, however, had converged to prompt the formation of what was to be the university-wide Ad Hoc Curriculum Committee. President Michael Stevenson identified these influences in the September 2001 statement of his agenda (Stevenson 2001).

He drew attention to competition, existing, anticipated, and increasing, on several fronts. In the first instance, he noted that the expansion of the college system in the province of British Columbia had increased competition for students, many of whom were able to access a growing number of distance education programs from their local colleges. There was also competition to be anticipated from private colleges, many of which were being established to teach English as an additional language, but also to offer traditional post-secondary programs, both professional and academic.

Such competition has implications for budgets and also for faculty recruitment. President Stevenson's agenda statement reminded the university community that 40% of current faculty and staff, under the existing terms of contracts, would be retiring within ten years. Since this phenomenon is not exclusive to SFU, the university would be seeking new faculty in what could likely be an employee's market. The university would need to offer attractive conditions to prospective applicants. These changes in conditions alone were indications of the wisdom of calling for a general review of what the university had to offer, and what it needed to do to enhance its programs. A further pressure originated from the provincial government. The government, looking for evidence of quality of performance, was indicating that the university, as a publicly funded institution, needed to be more visibly accountable to the province's tax-payers. Indeed, the new Liberal Government listed as its number one goal for 2001 the "best educated and most literate jurisdiction in the country" (BC Liberal Party).

If the university was to demonstrate that it indeed was accountable, then it first had to identify and/or determine what it would be accountable for, in order to avoid having performance demands thrust upon administrators, faculty and students that they were unable or unwilling to fulfill. Since its founding in 1966, SFU had always presented itself as innovative and unique, and clearly distinguished from sister institutions (Johnston 2005, 382). Although these perceptions seem to have been widely shared and acted upon more or less formally in SFU departments and programs when they were created, this vision of the university was not explicitly codified. In 1998, the then vice president academic, David Gagan, formulated and presented a detailed statement of nine purposes to Senate (Gagan 1998). Subsequently, President Blaney assembled a small committee to consult in group sessions with a cross-section of students, faculty, staff, alumni, and outside supporters, to uncover different views about future directions and "to capture, in one page and in few words, the essence of what . . . defines our University, now and in the future" (Blaney 1999). The one page outcome of the consultations was not a conventional mission statement. Rather, it set out SFU's "fundamental values and commitments." In a slightly revised form, the statement was approved by Senate on February 22, 2000. The values and commitments were as follows:

- We are an open, inclusive university whose foundation is intellectual and academic freedom.
- Our scholarship unites teaching and research: we relish discovery, diversity, and dialogue.
- Our students and communities can expect teaching that is personal and learning opportunities that are life-long.
- We champion the liberal arts and sciences and pioneering interdisciplinary and professional programs.
- We are a university where risks can be taken and bold initiatives embraced.
- Upon these foundations, we will engage all our communities in building a robust and ethical society (Blaney, 2000).

The process through which these statements were derived, the form that they took, and the intentions they proposed reflect the vision and character that SFU had long claimed for itself. In being formalized, these statements offered a point of reference for evaluation of future decisions and actions as well as for measurements of accountability. They represented the larger goals and objectives that were applicable to the university as a whole and, as such, could draw the entire campus community toward an articulated and coherent vision. In making the case for the curriculum review, for example, vice president academic, John Waterhouse, was able to point to this new statement of values and commitments as providing the motivation for an inquiry into whether the curricula available to students actually met these goals. In particular, Waterhouse specified that the committee would "propose strategies for enhancing opportunities for broad cross-disciplinary learning and ensuring that SFU graduates have the academic preparation for future success" (Ad Hoc Senate Committee 2002, 14). The rationale he put forward also reflected the need to maintain competitiveness with other institutions (as indicated by President Stevenson) and, in noting possible reforms, implied an encouraging commitment to change. In a comment on the 2001 Statement Agenda (mentioned above), Stevenson himself had also implied that the committee's recommendations could be expected to result in action, by commenting that he expected assessment of such key issues as program distinctiveness, innovative and effective pedagogy, student-centered learning, experiential learning, and research-intensive learning. These were all issues that reflected the thrust of SFUs values and commitments.

THE AD HOC CURRICULUM COMMITTEE: DETERMINING PRIORITIES

From its onset, then, the ad hoc curriculum committee can be seen as having taken on a somewhat innovative charge linked to newly articulated values. Accomplishing this charge would require that the committee be constituted by faculty of stature who could claim respect both in their departments and in the university at large. The VPA himself selected six members who met these criteria and in the interest of efficiency as well as what was considered adequate inclusiveness, the members of the Ad Hoc Curriculum Committee were drawn from the faculties of arts, education, science, business, and computing science. Rather than drawing on one faculty member from each of these, the faculty of arts, because of its size, was allocated two members: one from humanities and one from the social sciences. One of these, Dennis Krebs, professor of psychology, took on the role of chair. Krebs was ideally suited for this role. He had revised the undergraduate curriculum in psychology and social relations at Harvard University as well as the psychology undergraduate curriculum at SFU. He was also a recipient of one of Simon Fraser's Excellence in Teaching Awards, and widely respected as both scholar and colleague. Led by Krebs, the committee declared itself committed to respect SFUs culture of decentralization and the integrity and autonomy traditionally accorded to the departments. In order to allay any concerns, committee members assured colleagues that they would not examine the curricula of particular programs except as these seemed relevant to university-wide issues.

Over the course of the next year, the committee's actions were consistent with this stance. The members of the committee took a broadly consultative and collaborative approach to their mandate to review the whole curriculum. Initially, they sought to answer five main questions:

1. What are the main purposes of undergraduate education?
2. What methods do other universities employ to achieve these purposes?
3. How is the undergraduate curriculum structured at SFU?
4. How well are we at SFU doing?
5. What are the advantages and disadvantages of various strategies?

(Ad Hoc Curriculum Committee November 2001, 27)

The committee researched for information externally, reviewing the literature on curriculum change, examining the curriculum review processes at universities in both Canada and the United States, and identifying several that seemed comparable in their goals and process as a basis on which to compare and construct a plan for SFU. They consulted internally with departments and students through surveys and focus groups, and drew on the expertise of individuals in particular areas. The outcome of more than a year of research and consultation was reported in a December 2002 discussion paper (Ad Hoc Curriculum Committee November 2001, 27). The discussion paper, which followed the questions the committee had chosen to address, was the first stage in inviting response from the university community. The focus and concern with writing and the recommendations for changes in the ways writing was used and taught emerged partly through research of curriculum reviews of other institutions. Members of the committee found themselves in broad agreement with the claim that "the acquisition of communication and thinking abilities" was one of three "overlapping goals of undergraduate education." Communication and thinking abilities, they proposed, were the "foundational abilities" which enabled the achievement of the larger purposes of a university education and underlay life-long learning. They distinguished between communication and thinking, and defined these foundational abilities as both verbal and mathematical:

> *Communication Abilities (reading, listening, writing, and speaking)*: Communication abilities pertain to the ability to understand what is read and heard, and to the ability to communicate knowledge and explain new ideas to others, both orally and in writing. Communication may involve discussion, debate, collaboration, and teamwork.

> *Thinking Abilities (qualitative, quantitative, analytic, critical, synthetic, creative, interpretive, reflective, and aesthetic)*: Thinking abilities involve interpreting, organizing, and evaluating the ideas of others, creating new ideas, solving problems, and making decisions. These abilities provide the basis for advancing knowledge effectively, ethically, and productively (Ad Hoc Curriculum Committee November 2001, 27).

Although writing is here subsumed within communication, and thinking is separately defined, the committee selected writing as the communication ability most deserving of enhanced attention. In support of this claim, they cited Yale University's guidelines for under-graduate studies:

"It is axiomatic that educated men and women should be able to express themselves effectively in their own language. . . To suppose that anyone who cannot write clearly can think clearly is an illusion: words are the most basic tools of thought. Those who cannot use them skillfully will be handicapped not only in communicating ideas to others, but also in defining, developing, and understanding those ideas themselves" (Ad Hoc Curriculum Committee November 2001, 4). Having concluded that they would treat writing as one of the two foundational abilities (mathematics being the other), the committee next had to determine whether existing curricula and support for writing at SFU were adequate to achieve the goal of graduating competent student writers. In reviewing resources offered at other institutions, the committee found they could identify six approaches to supporting student writers:

> Admission requirements and entrance tests that assume students will have acquired foundational skills at the secondary level;
>
> Remedial assistance by means of dedicated courses to raise those skills to a satisfactory level;
>
> Skill development centres offering individual tutoring;
>
> Targeted workshops on such topics as academic writing, mainly with a remedial purpose;
>
> Stand-alone courses to develop foundational abilities such as academic writing, critical thinking, statistics, and so forth, and skill-intensive versions of existing courses that integrate the cultiva-tion of foundational abilities with the content of the discipline in which they are offered (courses in which writing is the skill that is integrated were, the committee noted, typically labeled "writing-intensive"); and
>
> Exit examinations, used by some to determine competency in foundational abilities (Ad Hoc Curriculum Committee November 2001, 27, III A).

Using these approaches as their basis for comparison, the committee undertook to characterize support for writing at SFU. SFU's admission requirements were based on academic performance overall, rather than on particular foundational abilities, with the exception of non-native speakers who were expected to have a sufficient command of the English language. Remedial assistance was offered for a very limited number of students who did not meet English language requirements through a ten-week "bridge" course. Other support, mainly outside academic departments, was offered by the library on such topics as research and essay writing, and by Student Services on generic topics such as study skills. The writing centre, which had provided tutoring to any registered student on a one-on-one basis, had already been dismantled. The English department offered two stand-alone courses in academic writing and a few other professional writing and rhetoric courses. The engineering department had several well-established general technical communication courses and a dedicated one-credit writing course attached to a third-year engineering course. The faculty of business administration offered a small though successful program of training writing mentors who, on appointment and drop-in bases, assisted undergraduate students taking business courses. Apart from such programs and clearly identified writing courses, it proved to be very difficult, if not impossible, for the committee to estimate how much, if any, and in what forms, writing instruction might occur in regular subject-specific courses. The committee could only acknowledge that some students in some courses were learning to write, and to write well. Overall, the attempt to characterize support for writing made clear that it was largely ad hoc, unevenly dispersed across a limited number of classes, and largely invisible. The committee decided, therefore, that "the most promising way to enhance the writing abilities of students is through discipline-based writing-intensive courses" (Ad Hoc Curriculum Committee November 2001, 27, VIII B.1). While the example of other institutions contributed to this recommendation, the more persuasive case derived from experience and expertise internal to SFU, which had developed mainly through the unit that in 1996 became the Centre for Research in Academic Writing, located in the English department.

LOCAL CONTEXTS FOR WRITING: THE ENGLISH DEPARTMENT AND WRITING

Although writing was not a significant element in their overall academic program, which has focused mainly on literature, the English department had historically treated writing instruction as an important responsibility. A decade before the introduction of the university's new writing requirements, the English department had informally been using the label "writing-intensive" in reference to its first-year English courses. Up until 1996, students in these courses had been required to write three papers per semester and receive instruction in writing in six scheduled writing labs.

These labs were supplementary to the regular tutorials in which there was discussion and review of the literature. Depending on the individual TA and the instructor's level of supervision, the quality of writing instruction and even actual tutorial time given to writing nonetheless varied greatly.

Cuts to the TA budget planned for the Fall semester of 1996 prompted a rethinking of this structure in the English department. Since the department did not wish to abandon its commitment, it looked for an alternative approach to filling the recognized need and the acknowledged weaknesses in the existing approach to writing instruction. In a memo, Carole Gerson, Undergraduate chair of the English department, reminded faculty members that even those students with excellent grades in high-school English needed instruction in academic writing. The writing that students would be expected to do at the university would make demands on them that would be different from what many of them expected. Furthermore, it was preferable, she pointed out, that they were taught by people with expertise rather than "by graduate students still in training" (Gerson 1996). Faculty in what was then called simply the writing centre were then charged with becoming more involved in the direct instruction of students in the first-year courses.

THE ROLE OF THE WRITING CENTRE
IN THE ENGLISH DEPARTMENT

Since the mid-1980s the functions of the writing centre were mainly in the hands of two faculty members: Dr. Janet Giltrow and Michele Valiquette, both of whom taught academic writing, held one-on-one consultations with students in their offices, and pursued inquiries into writing in the disciplines. Their work was supported in the English department by successive chairs, and assisted by Dr. Richard Coe, the only tenured professor of rhetoric in the department at the time. Indeed, Coe claimed that the support for writing reflected the department's long-standing "willingness to share responsibility, to make its expertise available, and to enter into partnerships with other departments, schools, or faculties" (Coe 2000).

In her submission to the department's External Review committee in 1997, Giltrow characterized relations between SFU's then-renamed Centre for Research in Academic Writing (usually abbreviated to the "writing centre") and the department's program of literary studies as a "productive partnership" (Giltrow 1997, 6). This relationship was reflected in joint publications between literature and writing faculty, literature courses taught with an emphasis on stylistics, and Coe and Giltrow's regular teaching of literature as well as writing courses. Such a collegial relationship as well as the new departmental mandate and the established record of involvement in cross-disciplinary tutoring and inquiry positioned the writing centre to expand its faculty and to make an argument for a designated workspace for workshops and expanded one-on-one tutoring services. It also formally positioned the centre as the site of scholarly investigation into writing across the university as well as a resource for course-based instruction in the department. External reviewers in 1997 congratulated the English department for the redesign of the writing centre as a research unit, and urged a university-wide mandate. They contrasted the SFU writing center model favorably with "the tendency evident almost everywhere else to make the study and teaching of writing a peripheral or trivial feature of the department's mandate" (Monkman et al. 1997, 6).

SETTING PRECEDENTS FOR WRITING INSTRUCTION IN THE CENTRE FOR RESEARCH IN ACADEMIC WRITING

At SFU, Janet Giltrow and Michele Valiquette together established teaching and research practices grounded in New Genre Theory, and developed an innovative approach to application of a think-aloud methodology. New Genre Theory draws attention to the regularities of situations and the regularities in structure, purpose, and wordings of texts associated with those situations (Bawarshi 2003; Berkenkotter and Huckin 1995; Christie and Martin 1997; Cope and Kalantzis 1993; Devitt, Reiff, and Bawarshi 2004; Dias 1999; Freedman and Medway 1994; Freedman and Medway 1994; Giltrow and Valiquette 1994; Herrington and Moran 2005; Miller 1984). It examines the ways in which genres represent cultural and social values. At the university, those values are very much derived from disciplinary cultures. Students who succeed will be those who can participate in disciplinary ways of thinking and acting, and can show that they have appropriated the values as their own. Successful students will be able to demonstrate their ability to participate partly, or in some disciplines almost entirely, by virtue of *what* they write about and the *way* that they write.

In drawing on New Genre Theory as the foundation of their practice, Giltrow and Valiquette insisted on recognition of differences in what would be expected in writing across and even within disciplines. At one level, it may seem rather obvious to note such differences. It does not take much discernment to see that the literary essay is not a scientific report or that a philosophical treatise has little in common with an economics brief. What is perhaps less obvious, however, is what such differences mean for understanding what is entailed in the writing, and thus, what is entailed in teaching and responding to student writing. Unitary notions of writing imply that there is a set of rules and conventions for writing that can be applied across all texts (and by "texts," I refer here to anything written down). The assumption underlying this notion, termed by Mike Rose "the myth of transience" (Rose 1985, 355) is that if you can learn the rules and conventions of writing, then you have learned to write and you are able to take those transferable skills to any writing situation. Writing instruction for such skills might be understood as, and principally focused on, teaching usage and correcting usage errors. Understandable as this assumption and purpose may be, many student writers clearly lack adequate facility with the basic tools of grammar, vocabulary, and spelling, which limits its effectiveness as an approach to teaching writing. Genre theory challenges these unitary notions by drawing attention to the differences in social and cultural contexts that inhere in disciplinary genres. Knowledge of these contexts is acquired by immersion, by reading, writing, listening, speaking, experimenting, performing, collecting, or doing whatever it is that characterizes the practices of that social and cultural context, be it of the context of the biologist or the philosopher. Parroting information is not participation. Participation in, and gaining entry to, a social and cultural community (in this case, the disciplinary community) becomes possible by being able to communicate in the ways respected and valued by the community. This is true of the street gang or the lawyer's office. Without the language and the ability to use it appropriately, in the genres that both represent and enable the purposes and attitudes held in the community, one is not a participant in its culture.

Giltrow and Valiquette (1994) took this understanding of genre to their work with students in one-on-one tutorials. They recognized that a consultant in the writing centre could not create the social and cultural context in which the genres of the discipline function. A consultant can, however, help the student writer understand what is meant by genre and disciplinary differences, and show how those differences need to manifest themselves in the writing. Of course, this is assuming that the consultant is aware of the specific differences and is able to make them explicit. Much genre knowledge is tacit. It functions at the level of what Giddens calls "practical consciousness," not "discursive consciousness" (Giddens 1984), and most successful practitioners do not need to consult their conscious or discursive knowledge. Realizing that writing consultants need to articulate disciplinary differences to student writers, and in order to inform themselves for that work, Giltrow and Valiquette sought the help of faculty from across the disciplines. Applying a think-aloud protocol method

(Waern 1988), they invited faculty participants to voice their thinking as they read aloud both student papers and professional journal articles. As they read and paused to express their responses and thinking, the professors, as disciplinary experts, revealed their expectations and thereby made explicit the features of the respective genres. The transcripts from these protocols were a source of immensely valuable information about such genre-specific features as appropriate uses of technical language, structure of argument, what constitutes common knowledge and does not require explanation and reference, what can be presupposed, and where it is conventional to hedge or modalize claims.

Giltrow and Valiquette took the same think-aloud model to their consultations with student writers. As they read the student papers aloud, they voiced their own thinking and meaning-making processes, and articulated their expectations. From the think-aloud approach to these readings, students were able to listen in on how the consultant, standing in for the TA or professor, was likely to respond to and interpret what was on the page. As writers, the students could then make adjustments in what they had written to better communicate with the reader, often with help from the consultant. They might rearrange the order of information they had included, add examples to illustrate a point, make connections between ideas explicit, embed quotations in contextualizing information, or correct errors in grammar and usage that impeded the reader's comprehension. In each of these encounters with text, a well-informed consultant would stand in as a representative for the disciplinary culture. If the consultant herself was uncertain of disciplinary conventions, she could consult the student. Just by asking a question about conventions, the consultant would be alerting the student to become more conscious of genre and disciplinary differences.

This approach to response to student writing and its underlying theory became the foundation for practice in the newly constituted Centre for Research in Academic Writing. Janet Giltrow, promoted to associate professor in the English department, became director of the centre. In consultation with the department chair, Kathy Mezei, and Roger Blackman in the Dean of arts office, Giltrow proposed a new vision for the centre that would expand its services campus-wide, make it more visible, enhance its professional appearance, and create a lively community for scholarship on the teaching and learning of writing. More faculty would be needed, as would a designated space and some equipment. Giltrow made a successful application to the Academic Enhancement Fund (AEF), which provided for the hiring of one additional full-time faculty member, a half-time instructor, and a half-time position for technical support. The Dean of arts allocated a bright, spacious room, and money from another grant by the AEF was allocated for renovations, furniture, and computer equipment. Heather Skibenyecki was brought in from the English department staff as half-time administrative assistant.

Within a few months of its expansion, the potential of the writing centre was radically enhanced. While, as noted earlier, the expansion was primarily motivated by the needs of the English department, support for the centre was also driven by widespread recognition of the need to give more attention to writing. Because of the work of Giltrow and Valiquette and because the English department resisted taking general responsibility for writing instruction, the attention would be located in the disciplines themselves.

Although English 199, the department's flagship academic writing course, attracted students from many disciplines, it was required by none, nor was it intended to substitute for in-house, discipline-specific instruction. Departments and individuals concerned about the level and quality of student writing were always free to develop their own solutions. As the Ad Hoc Committee was later to discover, though few departments systematically addressed writing, there were some exceptions. Dennis Krebs revised a first-year Psychology course in 1996 to better prepare students for writing research papers in the field of psychology. The Business Administration Faculty and engineering department established communication and writing support for their students at about the same time. Such initiatives notwithstanding, the Dean of arts office, the English department, and the 1997 External Review committee were all aware that the university was long overdue in developing and supporting a flourishing and adequately funded writing centre to which faculty could send students or from which they themselves could seek assistance.

The new name—Centre for Research in Academic Writing—made a strong claim about the centre's purpose and mandate. The significance of the name for later developments lay in the interplay of research and practice, which were the hallmarks of the centre, and which enabled a dispersal and growth of understanding and new awareness about writing and writing expertise across the disciplines. By engaging faculty in reflection on their own discourses, the centre encouraged an intellectual and theoretical stance toward writing. Such a stance helped foster understanding and/or appreciation of the complexity and situatedness of any writing task. It helped transform assumptions about *deficits in students* to acknowledgement of *deficits in teaching*. The new centre embarked on an ambitious agenda of workshops, appointments with students about their writing, in-class and tutorial collaborations with English 100-level course instructors, a writing-centre internship program, TA preparation, materials development and cataloguing, and ongoing scholarly inquiry into writing in the disciplines.

DEVELOPING OUTREACH ACTIVITY IN THE CENTRE AS THE "ADDITIONAL FULL-TIME FACULTY MEMBER" (1996–1999)

As the new full-time faculty member, I brought fifteen years of K-12 experience consulting on writing with teachers from across the disciplines. Consequently, I was immediately drawn to this aspect of work at the centre. My particular interests were in understanding how writing was being used and taught in other disciplines, and in collaborating with faculty to enhance student learning and writing. Since the more pressing matters, from the department's point of view, clustered around class- and course-based teaching, that interest could usually be indulged only intermittently and was usually limited in scope.

At the request of individual faculty members, many outside the English department, I helped develop assignments for courses in different disciplines or worked on such aspects of writing as structuring text, citing sources, or giving feedback to peers, sometimes in the form of workshops in a tutorial, sometimes as materials for use by the TAs. All such forms of assistance were tailored to meet whatever the faculty member identified as a priority for his or her course, and were often preceded by consultation and inquiry into what was required according to the particular genres of the assignments. In a more extended project, I partnered on a semester-long project with a new lecturer, Katharine Patterson, in her first-year poetry course.

It would be naïve to presume that faculty participation in this activity reflected a general belief that writing needed to be taught in the context of the discipline. Instructors who requested assistance usually did so because they identified problems with student writing and either felt ill-equipped to address those problems themselves, or felt they could not afford the time to do so. They came to the writing centre as a resource, responding to our offer to provide a particular kind of consultation and/or service. The approach of the centre to that consultation and service affirmed the centre's theoretical framework: we made every effort to ensure that writing instruction was contextualized. We avoided practices that might suggest that acts of writing required the simple application of a set of transferable generic skills. But we could not assume that the theory on which our practice was based was shared, nor did we presume to explain our reasoning unless requested to do so. Because our interventions, however useful and effective, were typically one-off and brief, we were only scattering seeds at random, and not cultivating a terrain that could yield a significant transformation in practice across the university. We did not have the mandate, nor did we have the resources for movement toward such widespread transformation.

In Spring 1998, however, an opportunity arose that would provide a cornerstone point of reference when it came time for the ad hoc undergraduate curriculum committee to consider alternative and more substantive approaches to supporting student writers. Steven Davis, a senior professor of philosophy, decided that he wanted to find a way to improve student writing in his first-year philosophy course. He came to the writing centre, and then requested funds through the associate dean of arts, Roger Blackman, to buy some of my time to work with him. Blackman had long been a strong supporter of the writing centre and actively encouraged faculty involvement in writing instruction. He had been instrumental in securing Academic Enhancement Funds for the expansion in 1995. With a vision for strengthening the teaching of writing in the faculty of arts, Blackman went to work again, and found funds for some of my time, and a little later, funds for a research assistant who would work with Steven and me. Steven Davis was a highly respected, soon-to-retire professor and vigorous advocate of the inherent association of his discipline with enhancing intellectual development and critical thinking. He was well placed to test a writing-in-the-disciplines approach, as he was professionally and personally committed to the university, to his department, and to students. In his view, finding a way to improve their writing would leave a legacy he could be proud of; it was a way to give back to the university. In my view, this was a chance to engage in a carefully planned and theorized project with someone whose response to it could be taken seriously because that response was based on direct experience. It held promise of setting a convincing precedent, if indeed it achieved our purposes.

PHILOSOPHY-100: A TEST CASE FOR WRITING-INTENSIVE LEARNING

Steven Davis and I began talking together in the Fall of 1998. We had two purposes. Our first purpose was to improve student writing and understanding of philosophy. Steven felt that students have to do more careful thinking, and that they lacked skills in expressing themselves in writing.

Our second purpose was to develop a model for integrating writing into an existing course by drawing on expertise in the discipline and on expertise in writing.

Our reason for choosing a first-year course was that the philosophy department offered these as service courses to the university. Although not required by any program, they were offered to first-year students as electives and were highly recommended by several departments. Few students in these courses went on to major in philosophy. As service courses, they attracted high enrolments Typically, 250 students enrolled in both the Fall and Spring semesters and were divided into sections of 17–20 students for tutorials led by graduate student TAs. Any model for integrating writing would need to take account of these numbers and the use of TAs. We agreed to use the 1999 Spring semester to develop the course and to implement our plans in the Summer 1999 semester, when the course would have a smaller and more manageable enrolment of about sixty students, and would not include TAs. In this way, we could make any necessary substantial revisions for the next time the course would be offered (in Spring 2000) and also prepare for including TAs in the new process.

In preparing to modify philosophy-100 ("Knowledge and Reality") as a W-course, we drew on methodology and theory now well-established in the writing centre. We began with inquiry into the discourse. Using the think-aloud protocol as our tool, we taped Steven's readings of samples of successful student and professional writing in philosophy. These readings had the advantage of helping me as the consultant instantiate what it meant to "make an argument" in philosophy. I then did a discourse analysis of the samples and followed up with Steven to confirm what I identified as significant features of the genre. In this way, we were able to determine and agree on what features were valued and sought in student writing at the first-year level, and equally importantly, what kinds of deviation from conventions of expression and reasoning would attract penalties from a marker in philosophy.

Identifying these features functioned as a way of articulating and illustrating the criteria that might be used in evaluating student writing. They could be communicated to students and used as a guide by a marker. Since we would be team teaching the course, and it was Steven's intention to fully integrate writing as a way of learning the philosophy, as well as helping student improve as writers, we collaborated on thinking through the pedagogical aspects of the course. At every stage of the course, we planned to model and illustrate what was required of students in their assignments, in participation in-class processes, and in work with peers.

Since the pedagogy Steven was embracing was both new and interesting to him, we did not stint on the details in planning. While we recognized that in actually working with a group of students we would need to adjust as we went along, the process of planning in advance helped us both because it meant discussing and agreeing on a rationale for each stage of the course development. Planning included selecting, composing directions for, and sequencing of ungraded and graded writing assignments; identifying uses and ways of responding to ungraded writing; developing materials and handouts specific to graded writing assignments that would illustrate key features expected in the writing, and that could be used to demonstrate both how to read and how to respond to writing in philosophy; and drafting tentative criteria for evaluation of writing. We drafted out a schedule to allow in-class time for practice in aspects of the drafting, feedback and revision processes, including workshop time for peer response. To encourage an atmosphere of trust and collegiality for that peer cooperation, we decided that everyone, including instructors, should learn the names of all students in each tutorial group (Strachan and Davis 2000, 5).

From the outset, Steven entered enthusiastically into the planning process, and our collaboration in advance of the course led smoothly into team teaching in the Summer semester of 1999. Both of us were present at lectures and tutorials. In lecture, the focus was principally on philosophy and in tutorials the focus was on writing about the philosophy, and writing itself. Steven lectured on the philosophical content during the two lecture periods each week, and I worked on writing with the three tutorial groups. Since there were just two of us involved in teaching, we were able to coordinate lectures and tutorials by means of frequent consultation. We made our structure and methods explicit in an attempt to ensure that students were informed about, and understood the purposes for the various activities of the course.

Although we had engaged in detailed preparation, teaching the course nonetheless involved further daily development of materials and the collection of data. We wanted to be able to document and assess the effects of changes to the course on student writing. We prepared a short survey to capture information about students' expectations and attitudes toward writing at the beginning and end of the course; collected and analyzed a selection of student papers including drafts and final copies to identify the kinds of improvement prompted by the revision process; and identified a study group of 12 students who agreed to offer more detailed feedback and response to the writing activities.

In the next two iterations of the W-version of the course—the second in Spring of 2000 with a class of 203 and three TAs, and a third in the Summer 2000, with an enrollment of 60 students—the materials and strategies developed for the first trial were revised in light of experience, and in keeping with the orientation of the two different writing centre faculty members who worked alongside Steven each time. The follow-up iterations were essential to making any argument in favor of improving student writing through a writing-in-the-disciplines approach to instruction. The service courses at the 100-level would always draw on TAs to support the lecture component in tutorials, and we needed to know how practical that would be, and what preparation the TAs would require for new responsibilities of teaching and marking the students' writing. The graduate student TAs would have to be competent writers themselves, but that did not mean they could effectively assist their students. We soon learned that across the disciplines, the competence of the TAs themselves as writers, and often as English speakers, would be quite problematic.

In reporting on our experimentation with the course to the Dean of arts and subsequently to the Ad Hoc Curriculum Task Force, Steven and I were able to provide evidence that this admittedly labor-intensive model had achieved the intended outcome for students, and, equally important for any curriculum change, had shown us what successfully taking on such a model would entail. Students' evaluations and survey responses indicated their high levels of satisfaction with being taught how to write in the context of the course subject matter. They reported being confident of having improved across a range of dimensions in their writing. Dropouts in the course in the first few weeks were much lower than usual, and attendance at both lectures and tutorials was high throughout the semester with none of the usual dropping off at the end. No student failed the course because of plagiarism, and there were none of the usual problems with flagrant plagiarism. Student writing, which was the object of this effort, had clearly improved. While we had no means of comparing writing for this course and writing in previous classes, Steven had been marking student writing in courses at this level for the previous thirty years. He felt well able to assess the overall quality achieved by teaching, rather than simply assigning, writing. Further, with the subsequent instantiations of the course, he was confident in attributing what he regarded as significant improvements in thinking, sophistication in expression, and maturity in organization to the instruction in writing (Strachan and Davis 2000, 9).

SENIOR ADMINISTRATIVE AND LOCAL LEVEL DEVELOPMENTS BEGIN TO CONVERGE

On the basis of this experience and on our review of the literature on developing W-courses, Steven collaborated with Dennis Krebs, chair of the Ad Hoc Curriculum Committee appointed by John Waterhouse, vice president academic, to prepare and submit a proposal for consideration to that committee in May, 2002 (Davis, May, 2002). The proposal set out essential principles and features of a program for W-courses (see Appendix 1 for the full text). The proposal opened by asserting that:

> Universities that have implemented successful writing-intensive programs have insured that the university community (a) understands the value of writing as a fundamentally important tool for learning, especially as it relates to the acquisition of knowledge in disciplines and the cultivation of critical thinking abilities, (b) is receptive to recommended initiatives and (c) collaborates in the creation of the program (Davis, May, 2002).

Further, the proposal set out the following as critical features of successful writing-intensive programs:

They are adequately funded.

They are widely supported by faculty, students, and administrators.

They are phased in relatively slowly, over a period of at least 3 years.

There are no quick fixes; a long-term commitment is necessary

Participation by faculty is voluntary.

The distinctiveness of writing in different disciplines is respected.

Departments are actively involved in the process, deciding how great an emphasis to place on the acquisition of critical thinking and writing abilities in their disciplines, and whether to focus on the development of such abilities in lower- or upper-division courses.

The effectiveness of initiatives is assessed at appropriate times.

The remainder of the proposal outlined a process and possible models of implementation. The Krebs/Davis proposal was the culmination of three years of involvement, and then reflection and evaluation of an actual implementation of a model for a W-course. In addition to our jointly produced report on the course, the implementation represented part of Steven Davis's legacy to the university, fulfilling before his retirement his strong commitment to contribute to the development of an improved pedagogy for student writers.

By the time Krebs and Davis submitted their May 2002 proposal in support of W-courses for SFU, the Ad Hoc Committee had already spent a year researching other institutions and consulting widely across the campus. The committee was coming to a decision on its recommendations for writing that echoed those in the Krebs/Davis proposal. Also by this time, the Centre for Research in Academic Writing, which had been the force behind Davis' work, had been dismantled. For a variety of reasons not related to the Ad Hoc Committee survey of the undergraduate curriculum at the university-wide level, the new Dean of arts, John Pierce, decided a year earlier in Spring 2001 to remove the Centre for Research in Academic Writing from oversight in the English department. He convened a cross-disciplinary faculty of arts Ad Hoc Committee to review the mandate of a writing centre and make recommendations for a new structure. The centre's cross-disciplinary work as well as one-on-one tutoring of students was thus suspended until decisions could be made. Faculty who had been consultants in the writing centre were re-assigned to teach additional regular writing courses.

Pierce's decision to restructure the former Centre for Research in Academic Writing did not signal a lack of commitment to writing support and instruction. On the contrary, he saw the need for a freshly imagined centre, notwithstanding the recognition in the 1997 departmental review of the successes and excellence of the previous unit. While what was being proposed for the curriculum at the broader university level would have an impact on Arts as on everyone else, his obligation and concern was adequate support for student learning and faculty teaching in the faculty of arts.

THE EMERGENCE OF THE CENTRE FOR WRITING-INTENSIVE LEARNING (CWIL)

Dean Pierce was attracted to the concept of *writing-intensive learning* and, influenced by the philosophy department experiment, saw the potential for a new centre, which would work not with students but with faculty to help them modify their pedagogy to use writing as a method for improving learning. So persuaded was he by this concept that his presentation to department chairs tended to emphasize writing to learn rather than learning to write.

By Spring 2002, Dean Pierce had abandoned the idea of reinstating a centre to assist students with writing through one-on-one consultations. The English department seemed satisfied to manage without workshops or other support for writing in its 100-level courses. The Interim chair was concerned with other priorities. Discussion of writing, which had been so prominent in departmental planning a few years earlier, now fell silent. At the Faculty level, however, the Dean put forward his idea for a new centre dedicated to faculty support in using writing as a means of learning. He initiated discussions with me about such a centre, and in June 2002, I agreed to take on the role of director of what Dean Pierce named the Centre for Writing-Intensive Learning or CWIL (pronounced, appropriately enough, as "quill"). CWIL was to be housed in the faculty of arts, and would work with instructors and TAs in that Faculty. In August 2002, Kathryn Alexander was hired as a limited term CWIL lecturer. With a PhD in education, a background in teaching university writing, and over a decade of experience of the university as a student, Kathryn was well suited to cross-disciplinary work with Faculty. In Fall 2002, she and I set out to invent and adopt processes that would help create an environment to encourage Faculty participation and innovative practice in using and teaching writing.

Since the creation of CWIL would anticipate Senate's final approval of the proposed new curriculum requirements by a year and a half, this unit laid much of the groundwork for its eventual mandate to help develop W-courses university-wide. It was an initiative which reconfirmed and helped to anchor the approach the university seemed intent on taking toward supporting and improving student writing at the undergraduate level. While creating CWIL did not mean opening the floodgates of pent-up demand for help in developing W-courses, the philosophy course that Steven and I worked on together had attracted some interest in a few departments, and there seemed to be sufficient support for active steps to improve writing. Over the first eight months of the formation of the centre, seven faculty members in five departments collaborated with us in adapting their courses to include more writing and writing instruction. These were the early days of pilot efforts to create practices and a momentum on which to grow.

The sequence and timing of these events would prove consequential, even somewhat prophetic of the institutional hazards to come some years later. From an institutional point of view, the former writing centre housed in the English department had, if peripherally, been successfully involved in and taking responsibility for supporting writing across the disciplines. That activity, however, had been curtailed by the closing down of the centre just ahead of the time when a university-wide requirement for writing in the disciplines was emerging as a likely commitment. A more favorable confluence might have fore-grounded that writing centre as the potential agent in achieving the goals of a university-wide curriculum, and prompted a broader discussion about its re-invented functions and status, thereby achieving a convergence not only of goals but also of structures. But the writing centre as it had existed in the English department had lost its former director to another institution and the faculty dispersed. There were, therefore, no voices able to speak to the broader context for writing support and to advocate for the logic of creating a centre that would centralize writing initiatives. Furthermore, the move to restructure in the faculty of arts was in keeping with the traditional practice of developing curriculum initiatives at the local level and, in the absence of any coherent, programmatic, and university-wide attention to writing, a local initiative was consistent with accepted practice. It was also the case at the time that the Ad Hoc committee's likely recommendations could not be guaranteed Senate acceptance.

It was in this context that CWIL found itself awkwardly positioned as a resource with the necessary expertise and experience but with a structurally limited profile. For most of the pilot period leading up to Fall 2006 when it was eventually agreed that the undergraduate writing requirement would take effect, the significance of that structurally limited profile receded in relation to the more immediate demands for expertise and experience in developing W-courses. CWIL's roles oscillated between the needs of faculty and courses in the faculty of arts and the demands of the implementation process of the new writing requirement. One of the first priorities of the implementation was to determine what would constitute a W-course, which is the subject of the next chapter.

2

CRITERIA FOR WRITING-INTENSIVE COURSES
Rules or Reasons?

The introduction of an in-the-disciplines writing requirement for all undergraduates created an opportunity to encourage discussion of writing development as a desirable attribute of graduates, in contrast to a writing-as-remedial approach to address the concerns of faculty and the university administration. The W-initiative invited a shift away from the complaint of, "why hasn't someone taught them this before," which tends to reflect a belief that writing is only or mainly a matter of learning transferable generic skills. The concept of writing in the disciplines held out a promise that could transform such perceptions: it presented the possibility of understanding writing as socially situated and deeply implicated in, if not constitutive of, knowledge-making in the disciplines. Such an understanding of writing, however, could not remain merely an abstract concept if it was to have consequences for student writers.

Understanding writing in this way had implications for how to use, teach, and respond to writing as part of a pedagogy through which students could better learn the subject matter of their courses. Yet, adopting writing-intensive courses did not necessarily indicate that this particular view of writing was widely shared or even recognized as a worthy goal either by individual faculty or at the departmental level more generally. When Senate gave final approval in May 2004 for the new curriculum initiatives in writing, breadth and quantitative reasoning, it was responding, in the case of writing, to the generalized feeling that student writing was not meeting a university standard and generalized agreement that something needed to be done. Further, there also seemed to be a consensus across departments and the administration, that W-courses would be a sound approach for the university to take to improve student writing. The details of what those W-courses would be like, what concepts of writing they would embody, and how they would be distinguished from other courses had yet to be worked out. The term "writing-intensive" as it appeared in the early discourse about the new curriculum was mutable, transparent, unattached, open. There was still much to be discussed and worked through.

This chapter attempts to represent the complex and varied forms of influence on the working-through process, and what eventually became the application of the W-criteria to the undergraduate curriculum. The chapter is divided into four sections. In the first section, I begin by setting out what seem to me to be the array of vantage points from which the distinguishing details of the W-course would be contemplated and critiqued by those involved in the pilot phase of the initiative. In the second section, I then explain the development of the set of criteria put forward in light of those vantage points, and in response to the ongoing dialogues with departments and individual faculty members (as this also accompanied and informed that development, modifying the substance and wording of each criterion). The third section outlines the research and theory on which each criterion rests and could be justified. By the time the criteria had been drafted and adopted, a new process had to be put in place to designate courses as W-courses. The fourth and final section describes the challenges posed by the certification process.

W-COURSES: STARTING POINTS

While making their recommendations, the Ad Hoc Committee gave few details about what would constitute a W-course. The November 2001 discussion paper specified that "The crucial element seems to be to ensure that students write a good deal, get frequent and intensive correction of their work, and are encouraged to rewrite and receive further correction" (Ad Hoc Curriculum Committee, November 2001, 27). Elsewhere, in the same document, the committee suggests that:

> Writing-intensive courses emphasize careful reading and extensive writing, providing frequent opportunities for re-writing, criticism, and further re-writing. The style and formal standards of such courses are those of the departmental discipline. Writing-intensive courses are designed to increase students' critical reading and writing abilities. (Ad Hoc Curriculum Committee November 2001, 27)

These early descriptors made no claim to precise definition or theoretical framing. They were generic and general indicators of the kinds of activities and purposes expected in a W-course. In the June 2002, Ad Hoc Committee Final Report, the description was somewhat elaborated to indicate that:

By W-courses, we mean specifically designated courses in which:

- Students write multiple drafts and receive feedback on each draft.
- Writing is associated with critical thinking and with problem-posing and problem solving through assignments that require arguments.

- Samples of writing are available for analysis involving recognition of typical structures, modes of reasoning, use of evidence and technical language, and modes of audience address. (Ad Hoc Curriculum Committee 2002, 12)

Although these general descriptors were a starting point for justifying a writing requirement, they were much less specific than those proposed by CWIL in Fall 2002 at the invitation of the Undergraduate Curriculum Implementation Task Force (UCITF), again chaired by Dennis Krebs. CWIL's first draft of the criteria listed ten characteristics. These characteristics were not only more numerous than those of the Ad Hoc committee, they also represented the view that writing is a means of learning as well as a means of demonstrating learning; that writing can and needs to be taught (so use of samples was linked with instruction), and they referred to such features as frequency of opportunity to write and the importance of purpose (Strachan 2002).

To establish the credibility of the principles embedded in their criteria, CWIL had validated their principles against criteria adopted by the well-established and reputable writing programs at George Mason University, University of Missouri, University of Minnesota, University of North Carolina at Charlotte, and the University of Georgia, institutions roughly comparable in size to Simon Fraser University. Some of these institutions defined criteria according to quantity of writing: by number of pages or number of words. Some also defined criteria in terms of pedagogy: use of informal writing to learn, and other instructional practices which both taught and coached students and which ensured feedback and revision during the process.

Since CWIL's discipline-based practice was grounded not only in process but also in New Genre Theory, their criteria included assigning writing that would enable students to engage in the kinds of thinking typical of the discipline, as well as in writing in the genres typical of professional practice. The UCITF, however, was trying to draft criteria for the new Q (quantitative reasoning) and B (breadth) courses as well as for the W-courses. They were motivated to define courses in ways that would be comprehensive and meaningful, but would not impose demands likely to alienate faculty. They compressed CWIL's ten W-criteria to five, but retained the key elements.

CWIL's starting point for developing criteria was embedded in practice as well as research and theory. "CWIL" in the Fall of 2002 was a centre with two people: Kathryn Alexander and me. We started with the charge from the Dean of arts to develop "W-ness" in existing courses. Our process from the outset was targeted to the specific local contexts and needs of individual professors and courses. We worked to build on precedents established by the earlier writing centre, and on the example of the philosophy-100 course. Reflection on that course had led Steven Davis and me to define what we thought had made it successful. In taking those precedents and examples to work in CWIL, we were disposed, when starting out, to use them as the basis for our practice in this new context. In our early work with professors, however, we were not in a position to impose rules.

We soon discovered the folly of making any pronouncements about the amount of writing, for instance, which might distinguish a writing-intensive approach, and took it as our goal to find professors willing to experiment and to take some steps toward engaging more with writing. We were consultants with expertise in how to use and teach writing, and we suggested strategies and provided materials. The fact that those strategies were grounded in research and theory, and could be signaled as criteria emerged in our process of discussion with faculty about the rationale for adopting particular teaching strategies. The emphasis was on alternative pedagogies, not on a list of rules requiring compliance. Just as one does not need to know that a particular word in a sentence is functioning as an adjective in order to use adjectives, faculty also neither needed, nor were necessarily concerned, to associate a practice like revision with criteria for an as yet non-existent W-course. What eventually became official criteria were initially the elements that we encouraged according to what an individual faculty member was able and willing to accommodate. The early pilot courses overall represented all the elements that we would identify as foundational to effective practice in teaching writing, but in very few courses were all of the criteria present.

Faculty members positioned themselves across a spectrum of starting points in their views of writing and its role in their courses. For many professors in the Arts and social sciences, the "writing-intensive" label simply acknowledged that their courses included substantial amounts of writing. For many in the Physical Sciences, the concept as applied to their courses could, at first glance, easily be interpreted as irrelevant, although Science faculty wished, even longed, to read better student writing, and agreed with the initiative to improve it. There were individuals in every discipline who recognized writing problems but wanted no part of addressing them: some regarded them as outside their expertise or area of responsibility; others thought students should be held more accountable, be better prepared in high school, or not admitted at all if they lacked the requisite language skills for university writing. Such views influenced not only receptiveness to, but also constructions of, the meaning of W-courses.

In Spring 2003, the UCITF sent out the compressed list of five criteria that they proposed would define a W-course. Sensitive to the need to respect the autonomy of departments and programs and the academic freedom of professors, the wording was left open to interpretation:

A W-course is one that fulfills the following conditions:

- Students have frequent opportunities to use writing as a way of learning the content of the course and are taught to write in the range of forms and for the range of purposes that are typical of the discipline.
- Students receive appropriate feedback and response to their writing.
- Exemplary samples of writing within the discipline are used as a means of instruction about typical structures, modes of reasoning, the use of technical language, the use of evidence, and of modes of address.
- Revision is built into the process of writing for "formal" assignments.
- A significant amount of the course grade is based on the quality of students' written work, which is evaluated according to explicit criteria.

(Undergraduate Curriculum Implementation Task Force 2003, 1).

Such a list can itself conjure up images of clipboards and boxes to be checked off. Designating criteria can tend to invite simplified questions: *Has that been done? Has that element been added? Has that aspect been deleted?* Designating criteria, however, is always a deceptively complex process. It requires not only the identification of distinguishing hallmarks, but also attention to the implications of the simple questions of *what has been done, what element has been added, and what aspect has been deleted?* While criteria can simplify a process—in this case, the process of designating a W-course—by identifying discrete (and implicitly unrelated) parts, criteria can also be very useful if understood synecdochically, as an efficient shorthand for richly contextualized phenomena. Stripped of context and reduced to checklists, however, criteria can become mere tokens, marking conformity to unsituated and perhaps arbitrary expectations.

The committee, recognizing the almost inevitable conundrum posed by a list, emphasized that it was a draft in their request for responses from departments. It was a first step toward making progress in reaching broad agreement on how a W-course would be defined. Incidentally, but importantly, it was also a first step in raising awareness of the implications of the writing-intensive requirement, and in encouraging departmental conversations that would articulate values about writing that the criteria would represent. The draft criteria went out to thirty departments with questions about faculty expectations of entering and graduating students' writing; existing or planned courses that could be designated as W-courses; resources that departments would need to assist implementation; and an invitation to comment on the draft criteria.

Only ten of the thirty departments offered any comments on the criteria. Of these, two expressed approval and four criticized them as "vague," "inadequately defined," or "not sufficiently inclusive" of what would be needed to learn to write. Of the remaining four departmental comments, one thought the criteria might have an unwelcome impact on their existing pedagogy, one recommended the addition of reading, one challenged "writing in the discipline" as difficult to achieve in their multi-disciplinary department, and one referred to the need for course development. Apart from one concern about the requirement to write in the discipline, the criteria aroused no comment on such basic principles as using writing as a means of learning, including feedback and revision as part of the writing process, and assigning a significant proportion of the course grade to written work. Nonetheless, observations that the criteria were vague or inadequately defined presaged the kind of challenges to come when the abstractions embodied in the principles would need to become evident in concrete actions and classroom practice.

The challenges were not slow in coming once departments gathered for focused discussion of the criteria with members of the UCITF and with CWIL. A meeting with Science faculty was particularly informative. These faculty members wanted precise specifications. "What does 'appropriate' mean in relation to feedback?" they asked. "How much is a 'significant amount of the course grade'? We need that quantified." We explained that the committee was caught between needing to define what distinguishes a W-course and not wanting to be overly prescriptive. By meeting to discuss W-course development in terms of the W-criteria, we learned that what had been set was, in many respects, a no-win situation. As noted earlier, while criteria can be very useful if understood synecdochically, they can also become arbitrary tokens. We were meeting with researchers and scholars for whom the matter of writing and its evaluation seemed to be, fairly transparently, about correct usage and conventional form. What makes good writing seemed to be taken for granted, common knowledge about which everyone had opinions and practices and expertise. All of the faculty members, after all, were writers. As teachers, they read student writing and graded it. Certainly, they were, for the most part, dissatisfied with the student writing they saw, and they wanted better from their students, but they did not feel responsible for doing what might be required to improve it. They were not English teachers, they protested. Nor did they wish to be. We were called on, moreover, to justify the absence of grammar and usage as key elements in the W-criteria. What some professors saw as the main writing problem was that "students can't write in complete sentences." Some faculty objected as well to being expected to teach the forms and structures of their discipline. They felt this required them to do what they saw as remedial work. They would like students to come prepared with the necessary writing skills, and apply these skills to writing in the discipline.

In the sciences, writing was not typically represented as a means of developing understanding and learning. Writing was generally seen as a matter of writing up or writing down what had already been formulated. Indeed, that view is indicative of commonly held and long-established disciplinary values and epistemologies, and it would have been surprising if objections had not been voiced in this context. The new requirements were positioned to make inroads that might challenge such objections and assumptions, inviting reflection on, and revision of, what had previously been taken for granted. But a discussion of the criteria that was ungrounded and was at a remove from the contexts of use that would give them meaning in the classroom proved quite unproductive. It seemed to engender more resentment and resistance than understanding and appreciation. Certainly, a large group meeting did not seem to be the place to launch into an esoteric, and probably unconvincing, explanation of the possible causes of poor sentence structure, and the importance of understanding writing in the context of disciplinary discourse and culture.

However, the questions raised at that first meeting and the reactions we encountered were salutary cautions. They alerted us to the kinds of concerns the UCITF and Writing Support Group (WSG) would need to be mindful of, and work to address in planning the implementation of the W-initiative. For us, in CWIL, the concerns reinforced our own sense that pedagogical change does not begin with imposing rules to follow. The criteria provided the map, but we had to negotiate the territory in which they were to be instantiated. While the criteria would underlie our approaches as points of reference, we would always be working at the ground level, starting with the instructor's goals and contexts, and finding spaces to root new approaches to writing that would reflect the criteria. The list of criteria, however, as an object in itself and a constituent of the program, still had to be negotiated at the administrative level if courses were to be identified and the new requirements put in place for entering students in 2006. The Writing Support Group (WSG) took up this task of refining the wording and clarifying the meaning of the criteria.

NEGOTIATING THE CRITERIA: PRAGMATIC AND POLITICAL ISSUES

The five criteria presented as part of a document circulated by the university administration did not, as noted above, attract much comment or response from the university community. It was through face-to-face meetings that the full implications of each criterion could be articulated. Members of the WSG as well as Kathryn Alexander and I in CWIL learned, through informal coffee line and hallway conversations and scheduled meetings, the concerns and questions being raised by faculty and departments. Not all the criteria aroused the same level of concern. The discussion in the WSG of how to rephrase each criterion required finding wording and meaning that would demonstrate responsiveness to faculty while not undermining the intention of that criterion.

In this next section, I list the original and revised wordings and review the changes that were made in each criterion and the rationale for those changes. Some were simple shifts and additions of phrases, others required exhaustive discussion and review of their theoretical basis as well as their pragmatic import.

Original criterion #1:

"*Students have frequent opportunities to use writing as a way of learning the content of the course and are taught to write in the range of forms and for the range of purposes that are typical of the discipline.*"

Revised criterion #1:

Added to the end of this first criterion was the phrase: "*in ways that are clearly distinguished from remedial and foundational skills courses.*"

The first part of the criterion about writing as a way of learning was apparently not contentious, or its implications were not yet apparent. But the second half had caused some alarm, and it was not only professors in the sciences who saw such instruction as remedial. Others who shared this view asked questions about the university's responsibility to teach "unprepared" students who had nonetheless been admitted. For some at the university, teaching disciplinary forms or genres became an ethical issue as well as a pedagogical, personnel, and budgetary one. It was argued that the university should not admit students whom it was not prepared to teach effectively because they lacked the prerequisite skills. Resources for such remedial teaching did not currently exist, and securing them would be at considerable cost. The objections were both practical and political: the university did not want to turn away students who showed exceptional ability in math and science but whose reading and writing abilities fell far short of what was assumed would be needed to succeed in a W-course. Nor did the university want to see such students fail. Making a distinction between a W-course and some form of foundational skills course reflected the decision to develop two related new initiatives: (1) changes in entry requirements and (2) a commitment to develop a pre-W Foundations in Academic Literacy (FAL) course.

Original criterion #2:

"Exemplary examples of writing within the disciplines are used as a means of instruction about typical structures, modes of reasoning, styles of address, and the use of technical language and of evidence."

Revised criterion #2:

The word "exemplary" was omitted on the grounds that it would infringe on professors' academic freedom. Some professors, for example, might wish to illustrate points about writing using failing examples as well as strong ones. This criterion had already been relieved of such technical terms as "discourse analysis" that appeared in the much earlier versions and was left as proposed in the draft.

Original criterion #3:

"Students receive appropriate feedback and response to their writing."

This criterion was one of those identified in the faculty responses as "too vague." The WSG had to decide on the nature and purpose of feedback, and on what would make it appropriate. They could not require any particular form of feedback such as comments on papers, nor could they prohibit the use of shorthand keys to indicate usage and grammar errors. The key factor, it was agreed, was that students needed to know what the marker was looking for in his/her feedback, and that clarity on this question could be reached with explicit criteria. It was observed that some marking appeared to be a way of justifying a grade on the paper rather than assisting student writers in becoming more knowledgeable and competent. While not everyone agrees on what will help a writer, it seemed important to draw attention to this purpose in the criterion.

Revised criterion #3:

The WSG therefore added the qualifying phrase: "*that is based on explicit criteria and is directed at improving the quality of their writing.*"

Original criterion #4:

"*Revision is built into the process of writing for 'formal' assignments.*"

This criterion had been highly contentious from the outset. While most professors recognized that revision was a necessary part of their own writing process, requiring it of students brought protests about such issues as:

- feasibility in a semester system;
- students' willingness to take the time to revise;
- the typical failure of students to take advantage of opportunities to revise when faculty offered to read drafts if they were submitted early enough;
- the time and expertise needed to respond effectively;
- alternative ways of improving writing that did not involve rewriting any particular piece of writing.

The WSG and indeed the UCITF were fully aware that to require revision would mean more work for students, instructors, and TAs, and would be challenging in all the ways that professors had identified. The WSG was unwilling, however, to omit this requirement. The wording was modified to accommodate those courses in which a standard assignment, like a lab report or a critical reading response, was repeated throughout the semester.

Revised Criterion #4:

The phrase "*usually in terms of revisions of the same paper, or alternatively, in revisions accomplished through successive similar assignments*" was added.

The concerns about workload and expertise that this criterion aroused were addressed through the provision of extra funding to allow adjustments to the size and number of tutorial groups assigned to TAs, to the size of classes that would warrant TA support, and through a program for TA training, mainly offered by CWIL.

Original criterion #5:

"*A significant amount of the course grade is based on the quality of students' written work, which is evaluated according to explicit criteria.*"

This criterion also proved highly contentious but it was the view of the WSG that a course could not be distinguished as a W-course if, in fact, the actual amount of writing and the value attached to the written work was not significant enough to affect an overall grade.

The committee resisted making it possible for students who obtained extremely high scores in multiple-choice exams yet barely managed the written work, to complete a W-course with a C+ or B grade because written work had constituted only a small percentage of the whole. That concern would be addressed by having written work constitute at least 50% of the course grade. But the other part of this criterion that seemed more difficult to resolve was the focus on "quality" of written work. That focus seemed to imply a content/style dichotomy, which would conflict with the purpose of teaching writing in the discipline. Omitting attention to quality, however, seemed to leave the way open for an argument that essay answers on an exam could be included as part of the writing for the course grade. Such exam answers, the committee agreed, were not part of the instruction in writing and should not qualify. They decided that the important factor was whether or not students would get feedback. If it was the case that mid-term exams, for instance, were returned with instructor feedback, the WSG agreed that the written work on the exam could constitute part of the required percentage to qualify the course as a W-course.

Revised Criterion #5:

"*At least half the course grade is based on written work for which students receive feedback (see Criterion 3).*"

Finally, to answer arguments that courses that already based most of the grade on written work should automatically qualify as a W-course, the WSG pointed out that:

Postscript:

"*On these criteria, courses that require written assignments but <u>do not</u> provide explicit instruction on writing would <u>not</u> qualify as W courses.*"

After more than a year of consultation and revision, the finalized W-course criteria read as follows:

Criterion 1: "*Students have frequent opportunities to use writing as a way of learning the content of the course and are taught to write in the range of forms and for the range of purposes that are typical of the discipline in ways that are clearly distinguished from remedial and foundational skills courses."*

Criterion 2: *"Examples of writing within the disciplines are used as a means of instruction about typical structures, modes of reasoning, styles of address, and the use of technical language and of evidence."*

Criterion 3: *"Students receive appropriate feedback and response to their writing that is based on explicit criteria and is directed at improving the quality of their writing."*

Criterion 4: *"Revision is built into the process of writing for 'formal' assignments, usually in terms of revisions of the same paper, or alternatively, in revisions accomplished through successive similar assignments."*

Criterion 5: *"At least half the course grade is based on written work for which students receive feedback (see Criterion 3)."*

MORE THAN MATTERS OF WORDING: THEORY AND RESEARCH GROUNDING FOR THE CRITERIA

Although the discussion and negotiation over the criteria seemed largely to deal with finding pragmatic solutions to logistical problems, the criteria themselves constituted a commitment to epistemic uses of writing, and assumptions about the making of knowledge as dialogic. The criteria implied that the uses and teaching of writing occur in a complex social context in which the interplay of readers, writers, and texts is conditioned by the relations among classroom discourses, syllabus construction, assignments, grading practices, teacher and student expectations, and the differentiated novice status of students at varying stages in their undergraduate careers. The criteria thereby attested to the situatedness of writing instruction, to the demands of disciplinarity, and to the comprehensiveness of literate practices. Underlying each criterion are theories of composition and learning, as well as empirical research, both qualitative and quantitative. In this section, I provide some reference to the body of theory and research in which it is grounded.

WRITING AND LANGUAGE LEARNING

Acquiring the knowledge of a discipline is partly a matter of learning its language: its vocabulary, conventional sentence structures, patterns of organization and reasoning, modes of audience address. Further, as Charles Bazerman explains it, knowledge of a discipline requires learning the substantive matters of what "issues it addresses, the purposes it serves, the concrete objects it manipulates, the questions it has excluded or already answered to the satisfaction of the community, the things that can be left unsaid. . . or the things that might be said to accomplish its objectives" (Russell 2002, 13). There is no content that can be learned in a discipline that does not depend on language: even dancers learn a language to name and describe their movements. Disciplinary knowledge is constituted by its written language, even when the knowledge may also be communicated orally and with some graphic illustration.

In order to learn the language of the discipline, students need practice in its use. They need opportunities to participate with guidance from expert others who intervene to provide instruction. According to Vygotsky, such guidance occurs most usefully in what he terms the "zone of proximal development." That is to say, when what is to be learned can be connected to what is already known, and understanding can be advanced to a higher level "under adult guidance or in collaboration with more capable peers" (Vygotsky 1978, 86). James Wertsch, Jean Lave, and Etienne Wenger developed this concept and applied it to all forms of learning in communities of practice, suggesting that novices move from the peripheries of practice within a community toward the center and toward expertise through a process of what they term "legitimate peripheral participation" (Lave and Wenger 1991, 138; Wertsch 1998, 203). That is to say, by participating at whatever level and in whatever ways that allow the learner to engage in the actual activity of the community, the learner can move from a novice status toward the more expert and knowledgeable status.

Writing has particular advantages over oral communication, particularly in academic work. Writing is visible and permanent; it can be consulted later and changed. Writing allows the development of extended lines of argument and the bringing together of a wide variety of sources in ways that very few people can or need to hold in memory. As the research on writing and learning indicates, however, not all writing activities appear to achieve these objectives (Applebee, 1984, 577–596). Writing is most likely to assist learning and/or understanding when it occurs in a context that is meaningful and purposeful for the writer and when it involves composing to make meaning, as distinct from copying or parroting information from other sources.

WRITING AS COMPOSING

Composing, as Berthoff reminds us, is an act of forming, a dialectical operation. When we compose we set ideas in relation and make meanings. When we write, we see those ideas and the relation we have constructed, and can engage in dialogue with them to modify, change, limit, or discard our ideas altogether, examine what we mean, and adjust those meanings to make a new meaning and to form concepts. Further, as Berthoff explains, "forming concepts is the way you see/explain relationships; as you form concepts, you are making meanings, and that is the purpose. . . of composition" (Berthoff 1978, 88). Language itself provides a form to think with: words in sentences and sentences in paragraphs. When you think, you find the form in language, and its structures signal different kinds of relationships, which is why it is important to write in sentences. Lists and bullets name parts. As a means of putting those parts into relation, sentences indicate an intended meaning. Thus, if we want to show a relation of comparison, we would use a structure like: "Just as . . . , so. . .," or a relation of consequence: "but if you consider . . . , then . . . ." (Berthoff 1978, 81). When students are invited to write in ways that allow them to draw on the structures of language and to compose concepts, they are provided with opportunities to make meanings that explain what they are learning. When they are asked to write in sentences, they are clearly being asked to do something quite different from what they do in making a list. Both can be useful, but certainly they have different purposes and different outcomes in concept formation and the development of understanding.

WRITING AND LEARNING

What connection writing has with learning also depends on student and teacher beliefs about what learning is. If learning is understood as knowing things, and having factual information imprinted in memory, then writing things down—the way we write lists for our grocery shopping—may serve as a mnemonic, but writing is not thereby being used for depth of understanding. Using writing as a mnemonic, we may agree with Plato, who (despite the fact that his own philosophical treatises depended on writing) famously argued through Socrates that writing destroys memory and weakens the mind. But it is precisely because the memory is not able to hold on to all that is heard in a lecture, for instance, that writing things down is so important. While it is a practical matter that students can refer to lecture notes, the work of active thinking occurs when they construct meaning by making their own connections across ideas.

If the work of connecting ideas occurs only in test situations or in the writing of one paper per semester, the context for the writing indicates that its principal purpose is for testing and evaluation, rather than learning, and students do not have sufficient opportunities in those cases to practice putting things together. There is also little opportunity for practice if students have most of the course information pre-digested or processed in the form of detailed course notes and outlines or PowerPoint presentations. In such cases, the instructor has usually done a lot of the thinking for the students by abstracting concepts from the evidence, and arguments from the cases. Indeed, central to the issue of using writing as a means of learning is the way in which the instructor conceptualizes her role. She may function as a lively substitute for a textbook, offering students an alternative medium to reading: listening. But if she sees her role as a guide to ways of thinking about the subject matter, she will require not only listening, but a stance of inquiry, ideas to *think with* as much as *think about*. To enable understanding, as distinct from learning and remembering facts, writing needs to be conceptualized as a mode of inquiry through which ideas and information are tentatively put into relation for critical reflection, leading to meaning making and meaning construction. This does not imply the making of new knowledge in the sense that the academic researcher makes new knowledge to contribute to the field. Rather, it implies that in any composing, as described above, the writer makes meaning and knowing for herself.

Writing as a mode of inquiry appears to be what students recognize as valuable in their courses. Students in the Hilgers *et al.* study of the writing-intensive initiative at the University of Hawaii at Manoa reported that upper-division students

> demanded more WI courses in their majors . . . and it was almost as if doing writing assignments in the major involved making an investment in who the student desired to become; writing, in other words, seemed to be part of professional identity building . . . whatever the major, students clearly preferred writing experiences involving its courses . . . and 91% claimed that by completing their focal writing assignment, they learned about the topic or subject. (Hilgers, Hussey, and Stitt-Bergh 1999, 345)

In his extended inquiry into undergraduate education, generally, Richard J. Light reported that "Of all skills students say they want to strengthen, writing is mentioned three times more than any other" and "students relate the intellectual challenge of a course to the amount of writing it requires. More writing is highly correlated with more intellectual challenge" (Light 2001, 56). Light observed that:

> The relationship between the *amount of writing* for a course and *students' level of engagement*—whether engagement is measured by the time spent on the course, or the intellectual challenge it presents, or students' level of interest in it—*is*

stronger than the relationship between students' engagement and any other course charac-teristic. It is stronger than the relation between students' engagement and their impressions of their professor. It is far stronger than the relationship between level of engagement and why a student takes a course (required versus elective; major field versus not in the major field). (italics in original; Light 2001, 55–56)

In another study, Nancy Sommers examined the role that writing played in learning in her four-year (1998–2002) comprehensive study of undergraduate writing at Harvard University. Sommers found that first-year students "repeatedly refer to 'something more, something deeper' required of them in college writing." In an interview about her work, she quotes one of her students, Shames, who is doing a joint concentration in social studies and women's studies, who says,

I feel like I really make the subject matter my own when I put it into a paper. And that's not something I do as well in tests or multiple-choice exams. I have to go through the material enough so that I can put it in my own words, and find the key ideas—and the key flaws—in the texts we read, and somehow synthesize all of that into my own argument. (Shen 2001)

While researchers have largely been unsuccessful in finding experimental data to support arguments about the relationship between writing and learning (Ackerman 1993; Applebee 1984; Bangert-Drowns, Hurley, and Wilkinson 2004; Newell and Winograd 1989; Penrose 1989), the reasoning and qualitative research cited above provided sufficiently convincing grounds for including writing as a means of learning as one of the criteria for W-courses.

WRITING AND DISCIPLINARY GENRES

The key distinction here from business-as-usual is that there is a focus on how students must be *taught* and not simply assigned to write. The emphasis on teaching students to write in discipline-specific forms and purposes challenges the assumption that learning to write involves acquiring a set of skills that can be applied to any writing activity, or that writing ability depends mainly on intelligence, perseverance, or natural talent. The criterion acknowledges that writing effectively in a new situation requires understanding that what is acceptable style and form in history is not likely to be acceptable in biology and, beyond that, knowing what to do differently in order to communicate in the new situation. In other words, *knowing how* as well as *knowing that* different situations make different demands.

A writing-in-the-disciplines approach also distinguishes W-course instruction from remedial and foundational courses. The latter might deal generically with such concepts as organization, argument, use of secondary sources, citation, and standard English usage. A W-course, however, would approach concepts like organization from the perspective of what is conventional in such disciplines as biology or English literature, or explain argument as it is made in philosophy or political science. Such structural matters in texts would be addressed as ways in which the discipline's methodology, and its norms, values, and ideology are constituted by its genres. Even such general similarities in structure as introduction, data and discussion, and conclusion show up differently in different disciplines. As MacDonald *et al.* have pointed out, ideas in the Humanities are introduced through particular cases that are used for discussion of general conclusions, whereas in the social sciences, introductions focus on general principles that are then examined in light of a particular dataset and conclusions drawn in terms of the general principles (Madigan, Johnson, and Linton 1995, 429). Even the use of tenses distinguishes disciplinary epistemologies. In English, for example, the present tense is always used to refer to what a writer says in a text, regardless of whether he or she is alive, but in History, the past tense is used if the writer is dead, the present if alive. Such meaningful conventions and patterns, whatever is typical of the discipline or profession, would be the ones that students might be taught to write: lab reports in chemistry, policy briefs in economics, case studies in Anthropology, and critical reviews in Contemporary Arts.

The actual forms and conventions are, of course, not new, nor is the expectation that students will be assigned to write in these forms. There is no limit or restriction on the genres that might be included and that a faculty member might identify as typical for particular audiences or purposes. What is new with the W-requirement is that students are not simply exposed to whatever kinds of texts they are asked to write, but that distinctive features are pointed out so that they can more readily recognize them, produce them, and ideally, be aware of the rationale behind them. Further, the W-requirement implies that instruction in how to write in these genres engages students in the kinds of thinking and processes necessary if they are to participate in the culture of the discipline.

NEW RHETORICAL GENRE THEORY

New rhetorical genre theory, by its attention to evolving but recognizable forms and purposes of non-literary forms of communication (memos, editorials, and field notes) is distinguished from the more traditional association of genre with the well-defined and relatively stable character-istics of literary texts. Thrust into expressivist and process-oriented discussions of writing by Carolyn Miller's landmark analysis of genre in 1984, genre studies have repositioned non-literary forms of written text as forms of social action, and have focused on the social dynamics within which they function (Miller 1984). Researchers and theorists have examined the ways in which the forms and structures of written texts both construct and maintain social situations and human interaction.

Students in all disciplines are exposed in various ways to the genres of their discipline. Indeed, it is difficult to make a distinction between the genres of the discipline and the knowledge of the discipline. As noted above, however, students may be quite unaware of *how*, or even *that*, knowledge is constructed and organized to define and embody disciplinary meanings and values. Yet, as Hyland observes, "it is *how* they write rather than simply what they write that makes the crucial difference between [disciplines]. . . different appeals to background knowledge, different means of establishing truth, and different ways of engaging with readers" (Hyland 2000, 3). When reading and listening, students are most likely to concentrate on understanding and remembering information. In order to become successful participants, however peripherally, in the discourse community represented by their discipline, students need to understand the demands being made upon them as writers and they need help to recognize the *how* of text construction and the social context that produces it. Admonitions to be clear and concise, or to explain more fully, or provide supporting evidence is generic advice that will be interpreted by a student in terms of his/her prior knowledge and experience, which may or may not be transferable to the new situation. The use of annotated samples to illustrate how such features are instantiated in particular genres provides students with ways of reading and seeing how texts function and why. It is one means of making disciplinary genre demands explicit.

It might seem like common sense to provide examples of the target genres in which students are expected to write, but unless there is a lively awareness on the part of the instructor, disciplinary genres may seem taken for granted and not seem to require explanation. There may also be some resistance to the idea of using samples as models, since novice users tend toward rather unsophisticated imitation. Research on the effectiveness of model texts had been fairly sparse (Hillocks 1987, 71—82) despite the fact that model texts are commonly used in workplace as well as in school settings. Charney and Carlson studied the effects of using models for student writing of methods sections in a Psychology course and concluded that "model texts are a rich resource that may prove useful to writers in different ways at different stages of their development. . ... It seems likely that early experience in evaluating and drawing from models will be of lasting value" (Charney and Carlson 1995). What seemed clear from the Charney and Carlson study and others (Smagorinsky 1991, Werner 1989) is that timing, choice of sample, subject matter, writing task, student knowledge, and method of presentation all affect the ways that students read and make use of models. Hillocks' 1987 meta-analysis of writing research led him to conclude that "teachers are most effective when they use their own awareness of task-related knowledge to design and sequence activities for students to engage in, with explicit attention to specific procedures and their purposes" (Smagorinsky 1991, 341). In Smagorinsky's view, the use of samples and genre analysis was integral to course design. His 1991 study compared different approaches to teaching 11th grade American Studies students to write definitions. His findings corroborate the conclusion that multiple factors affect the usefulness of model texts. He observed that, "students . . . who combined the study of models with instruction in task-specific procedures improved in thinking more purposefully and critically about their task and topic."

WRITING, RESPONSE, AND RUBRICS

"All writing" claims Alberto Manguel, "depends on the generosity of the reader" (Manguel 1996, 149). No doubt many readers of student writing would describe themselves as needing to be generous. Giving feedback and response can be very demanding, but commentary nonetheless continues to be a primary method of instruction in writing. Early research on commentary strongly suggests that comments on writing have little or no impact on the quality of writing when not accompanied by instruction and opportunities for revision (Hillocks 1982, 261–277; Knoblauch and Brannon 1984; Sommers 1982). Twenty years on, however, while developments in both theory and research on composing generally support Hillocks' early landmark conclusions (Hillocks 1987) about the need for inquiry strategies to foster writing development, they have also led to a more refined and sophisticated understandings of what is entailed in assisting student writers. More recent research probes into the kinds of feedback and response that appear to be effective. For example, from his review of studies between 1980 and 1995, Richard Straub was able to identify a wide range of principles that researchers and teachers judged to be essential for effective response (Straub, 1997). He also reviewed studies of what students had to say about teacher comments. He found agreement among students in three general areas:

1. Students do read and make use of teacher comments (Beach 1979; Burkland and Grimm 1984; Lynch and Kleman 1978).

2. Students are able to discriminate among different kinds of comments, and find some more helpful than others (Land and Evans 1987; Odell 1989).

3. Students appreciate comments that reflect the teacher's involvement in what they say, and that engage them in an exchange about the writing (Beach 1989; Land and Evans 1987; Sitko 1992; Straub 1997).

Of these three general responses from students, the first would probably be the most reassuring to instructors, who may often feel that their efforts are ignored, while the second and third responses offer no surprises. In keeping with the purpose of W-courses, the kind of feedback that would be considered appropriate is that which the students define as comments that reflect the teacher's involvement in what they say, and that engage them in an exchange about the writing. Both students and instructors would see the writing as an invitation to a dialogue about what is written and about how the way it is written affects the meaning and the reader's response. While this is not the only form of feedback that research shows to be useful, nor the only form to adopt, it is particularly appropriate in W-courses where the main emphasis is on learning the course content. professors are generally not eager to be grammar hounds.

The choice of this kind of commenting, however, rests on the assumption that the student's writing is a means of communication to a reader/audience. If the purpose of writing is to communicate, then the writer has to write in a way that will prompt the teacher/reader to engage in an exchange. To write in such a way in a discipline-based academic course, the writer needs to understand her reader: to anticipate what the reader expects and will react to, what the reader is likely to agree and disagree with, what evidence or line of argument will be convincing, and what level of details is needed. Further, the writer will need to relate these particulars and provide evidence of careful study and reflection on topics and in ways that are judged interesting and relevant in the discipline (Thaiss and Zawacki 2006, 5–7). These are not particulars that a general, educated reader is likely to recognize and respond to; instead, they are particulars for a more qualified reader who writes the discourse as a "mother tongue" (McLeod 2001, 155).

Feedback from a qualified reader can take a variety of forms, and, as suggested above, research offers no simple answers on what form will be most effective under what conditions. Setting explicit criteria, along with instruction, contributes to the likelihood that students will understand what is expected, and that instructors will focus their commentary on shared expectations.

Explicitness seems particularly important in discipline-based courses because students often bring prior knowledge and attitudes about writing from English courses. They expect, and also resist, the kinds of commentary and attention to the technical aspects in their writing that they associate with these courses. They may protest that "this is an economics class, not English class." The teacher needs to be able not only to articulate what constitutes good writing in economics (or political science or biology), but also to help students distinguish between good and bad writing in the discipline. Instructors need to use their criteria and their feedback to explain how to change bad writing into good.

A rubric can be a very useful tool in both standardizing feedback and customizing it. It has the potential for helping a teacher *formatively* assess a student performance during the teaching/learning process by clearly establishing the standards and quality expectations. A rubric also assists in customizing the student feedback: what a student has done well; what weaknesses exist; and how or what might be done to correct or improve the performance. It also helps the students in the fair and honest opportunity for self-assessment of their work, and allows them the opportunity to set, monitor, and achieve their personal learning goals. Finally, rubrics also provide teachers with the option to later *summatively* evaluate their students' performances with a higher degree of consistency. Information obtained from the summative use of rubrics can be used to report student progress toward the agreed-upon learning goals or outcomes.

REVISING, REWRITING, AND RETHINKING

A requirement for revision is a necessary corollary to the requirement for feedback that will help improve the quality of writing. If students get feedback but have no occasion to act upon it, it is unlikely that their writing will improve in either the short or long term since the feedback will not appear to have any consequence or significance. While research suggests, as noted above, that students do read teacher feedback, feedback in itself does not lead to improved writing unless students both know how to apply what they are told, and have a reason for doing so.

The W-requirement treats writing as a thinking process: writing is think-ing; re-writing is re-thinking. Giving students the opportunity for revision, prompted by the types of feedback described above, promotes an inquir-ing, questioning, probing, and speculative attitude toward what is written. It demonstrates that writing is a means of opening, not of closing off discussion and thought. Offering the chance to get feedback and revise as a choice, however, can imply, "you are having problems and if you were a better writer you wouldn't need me to see your draft." Requiring revision constructs the task of writing as a process and reflects what professional writers do. Studies of the habits of professional and novice writers report that professionals revise, novices do not (Sommers 1980). Professionals take advantage of the fact that what they write, unlike what they speak, can readily be reconsidered and changed. Novices seem to associate the need to revise with failure, and this understanding is attributed to the way they conceptualize writing.

Historically, and until quite recently, the ability to write was considered to be an innate ability or a matter of inspiration. After all, completed and published written texts show their faces with no hint of the messy bits and pieces process secreted in the back room. The advice to "*think before you write*" could, until recently, make it seem that good writing is the product of prior thought: if you know what you want to say, it will emerge fully formed on the page. It is perhaps no surprise, then, that students who understand writing as a more or less faithful transcription of their think-ing, a visual representation of what they know or remember would indeed correctly interpret the need to revise as a failure: whatever they "knew" or were thinking has not produced a satisfactory text. The end product, what is written, must apparently and accurately represent what is known. Requiring revision, however, constructs the writer as engaged in a process of constituting ideas and understanding in visible linguistic form. By writ-ing, a writer stores ideas outside her mind. She then has them available as possibilities to consider and reflect upon if, as a novice writer, she can come to see useful outcomes of such reflection in the process of revising her writing. As John Bean suggests, what teachers hope is that when they revise, "our students learn most deeply both what they want to say and what readers need for ease of comprehension; revising means rethinking, reconceptualizing, 'seeing again'—for in the hard work of revising, stu-dents learn how experienced writers really compose" (Bean 2001, 242).

As is the case in many of the claims to be made about writing as a means of learning, revision does not necessarily bring with it enhanced understanding or improvement of a particular piece of writing. Whether revision serves these purposes depends on a complex of factors embedded in such aspects of the context of the writing situation, including the clarity and purposefulness of the assignment, the student's sense of that purpose, his/her confidence and attitude toward writing, interest in and knowledge of the subject matter, genre knowledge, time, and understanding of expectations. Studies of revision show a broad spectrum of outcomes from fairly trivial tidying up of non-standard spelling and punctuation to transformed conceptualizing of topics and arguments. The nature and purposes of revision of a particular paper can only be decided upon within the specific local contexts of that particular piece of writing.

These reasons for including a revision requirement for W-courses do not apply in cases where successive similar assignments substitute for rewriting a particular paper. There is no reason to suppose that ideas and claims and arguments could not be revisited and refined in a revision of any written assignment, but there would seem to be diminishing returns for students, as well as instructors, to revise every lab report, for instance. How frequently a particular genre is used attests to its significance in the ways of thinking and learning in a discipline. Writing in a given genre would then be deeply embedded in the disciplinary context and the pedagogy associated with the course, and as such, the writer would have multiple opportunities to understand the expectations, and the assignment and its purposes would be clear. Under these conditions, frequent practice in writing in a particular disciplinary genre may accomplish more for a writer's learning and understanding of how to participate in the discipline than rewriting a single paper. This would especially be the case if the explicit feedback could be applied on a next iteration and even more clearly the case if the feedback was able to scaffold expectations to provide for gradual increase in sophistication over the semester.

The criterion that at least 50% of the grade be for written work in the course ensures that a course designated as writing-intensive would demonstrate the importance of writing through its weight in the grading and, as noted earlier, that satisfactory performance on the written work would be required for a passing grade to meet the requirement.

CRITERIA AND THE CERTIFICATION PROCESS

The introduction of the certification process in Spring 2004, centralized and administered by the WSG, and the UCITF, was the vehicle through which the meaning and interpretation of the criteria were codified and standardized. During the early pilot phase, before the concept of writing-intensive learning was adopted as part of the new curriculum requirements, criteria for W-courses were embedded in practices adopted in courses as an outcome of collaboration between faculty members and consultants from CWIL. As already described above, there were occasions, mainly at the committee level, when an explicit list of criteria was negotiated. In CWIL's day-to-day consultation with faculty, however, the criteria were a code that represented assumptions underlying strategies being discussed in planning and teaching writing. For faculty who experimented with new strategies, the criteria did not represent rules to follow. The economics instructor might adopt a strategy like "quickwrites" (for instance, asking students to write what they understood about pollution) as a means of identifying misconceptions that students held. The writing would serve the purpose of writing to learn, and would therefore meet what later became the first criterion. But the writing was motivated more by the context and purposes of the course content, than as a means of meeting the requirement. Students experienced writing instruction as an alternative way of learning in the course; faculty as an alternative way of teaching their material.

With the need to integrate W-courses into the undergraduate calendar for the Fall 2006 semester, however, the characteristics of W-courses had to be brought to the forefront, specified, and standardized if students were to meet the W-requirement. Faculty planning to teach the courses needed to show that they could and would meet the criteria. That need set in motion a long and complicated process that included many people's ideas and many committee hours. There were decisions about dates for calendar entry, decisions about flexible or permanent W-designation, decisions about W-course distribution across departments and levels, decisions about levels of funding support, decisions about acceptance of college transfer courses and decisions about the kinds of information needed for the decisions about certification itself. In this section, I briefly describe the evolution of this complex and somewhat fraught process, and I try to assess its effect on university-wide implementation and its effect on CWIL's practice in particular.

The main difficulty associated with the certification process was a matter of communication. As bare statements, however precisely worded, each criterion was simply a skeleton. Each could be larded and styled in many different ways. This meant that writing and/or instructional practices could be interpreted and applied in ways that would accurately reflect epistemological and cultural differences across disciplines. There was, however, equally the risk that adherence might be to the letter, to the bare bones, rather than to the spirit of the criteria, which could mean token compliance and the likely marginalizing of the initiative as a serious enterprise and likely its eventual demise as a force in transforming the educational experience of SFU students. The certifying of courses was, of course, only one piece of that intended transformation, but for better or worse, it was at its core. The challenge, therefore, was to communicate the meaning and significance of the criteria for certification in ways that kept faculty and departmental frustration and resistance to a minimum, and instead encouraged reflection and thoughtful course planning.

Just as the sources and responsibility for curriculum change were traditionally dealt within departments (see Chapter One), the university was also without a policy that applied generally to course outlines or syllabi. While all instructors were expected to prepare outlines and submit these for distribution to students, they would take individual responsibility for providing more detailed syllabi or course descriptions and notes for students. Each department had its own process and these differed widely. The English department, for instance, decided that students in all first-year literature courses would write two papers. All instructors teaching those courses would be expected to comply with this stipulation. The History department, on the other hand, had no such guidelines and no process for inspecting how many or what kinds of assignments were required in any particular course. With the introduction of the new curriculum, the requirement to submit course proposals to a central and multi-disciplinary body represented a significant departure from the tradition of local decision-making that was based on local values and local appraisal. It seemed that there was little if any resistance to the need for a proposal process: it seemed clear and understood by faculty that if funding were to be allocated for changes to the teaching of a course, there would need to be some accountability. What did create problems, however, was clarifying and communicating what would be expected of faculty in a W-certification proposal.

The WSG was charged with reviewing proposals and forwarding them to the UCITF for funding decisions. Initially, proposals were for pilot courses, preceding their submission for certification. The interval provided valuable time for refining the proposal forms for the approval process, and for learning what information was needed and how to communicate that to faculty. The WSG received the first six proposals for review on February 6, 2004 and each of the seven members of the committee had copies of the proposals. As chair, Roger Blackman invited discussion and clarification of the role of the WSG at this stage. He advised that the committee could not overstep faculty authority and autonomy. It could not presume to make judgments about the course content and about the specific nature of the assignments. But it did have to determine whether the course met the W-criteria. It needed to be aware of whether the course would help meet the university-wide demand for W-seats. It also needed to consider whether or not the course seemed to use resources appropriately and efficiently. That is, was the course sustainable? The committee could not recommend proposals that requested support at the level of one TA per ten students, for instance. Successful implementation based on that kind of support could not be used as a general benchmark.

The first proposals aroused some very basic questions. Which assignments are to be revised? What percentage of the grade is for written work? How do oral presentations fit into a writing requirement? How does the proposed instructional plan address writing? How is writing being used as a means of learning? All the first proposals were recommended for funding, but their omissions and lack of explicit response to topics and questions led the committee to begin revising the form. The form went through several iterations, with an explanation added for each criterion. A set of tips on how to complete the form was put out as a separate document. Finally, the committee added an elaborated illustration of each criterion with examples from across the disciplines of what we needed to see. Faculty responded to all documentation with some impatience. The documentation that was meant to clarify seemed instead to make the task onerous. To assist in the process, CWIL offered a three-hour workshop titled, "Streamlining the Process: Preparing Your W-course for Certification" during which instructors worked with their own proposals and got them well underway for submission.

The process certainly was not simple since, taken seriously, it required the kind of thinking that typically goes into rewriting a course. That aspect of completing the form could be seen as a bonus from the point of view of effective implementation of the W-initiative: the questions themselves prompted reflection on purposes and pedagogical decisions. Instructors, many for the first time, were being called on to make their objectives and their teaching methods explicit, to articulate the basis on which they planned to evaluate their written assignments, and the means by which they intended to prepare for and monitor TA tutorial instruction and marking of student writing. As the forms improved and samples gave examples of how to complete the form, the issues that caused problems for the WSG became more refined as well. There often seemed to be a need for more information about instructional methods, but partly this was a consequence of higher expectations. By March 2005, it was not enough, for instance, to say that there would be some revision of writing. The committee wanted to know how much revision, and an explanation. In the case of a French course, for example, the committee wanted to know how comments on the mid-term exam could provide usable feedback to students. In the case of a third-year Psychology course, the committee wanted clarification of the term "corrections" as it applied to drafts of student writing. Proposals that prompted this level of question were typically given approval pending clarification by the instructor. But some were sent back, with a request for more information before the course could be approved.

On the one hand, the process could be looked at as an invasion by the administration into pedagogical matters that had previously been left to the discretion of the instructor and fell under the protection of academic autonomy. On the other hand, the certification process was one of the ways by which writing and writing instruction were being made more visible and it also established the credibility of a writing-intensive approach to improving writing. Until the university endorsed the criteria, CWIL was often in the position of having to defend the practices the centre advocated as effective ways to use and teach writing. For the first year, the reality of CWIL's status was that there were two people making assertions about the teaching of writing, and claims about its uses, that not everyone wanted to accept or were motivated to consider. Being able to refer to the university's criteria for courses that met institutional requirements enabled CWIL faculty to act as agents of the university's policy around writing, rather than as individual spokespersons for their own beliefs. With the criteria providing endorsement, CWIL practice and pedagogy could be seen as illustrating and exemplifying their meaning, and CWIL's expertise became relevant and situated in a context of more widely recognized and accepted need. As the next chapter illustrates, however, being agents of university policy did not allow us to make assumptions about individual cases nor diminish the need for sensitive negotiation around the ways in which the criteria might be instantiated.

3

IN DEFENSE OF STUMBLING
The Map is Not the Territory

"So, we'll see what the new TA (teaching assistant) is like. If I don't think he can handle it, we'll have to drop the idea. I'll call you right after I see him." I nodded. "Okay, let's hope it works out. Talk to you later." I sighed and left Don DeVoretz's office. It was August 20th and classes in economic development were to begin on September 3, 2003. Don was still not able to confirm that he would experiment with making his third-year economics course a pilot W-course. He was willing. We had first met earlier in the summer and developed a few ideas about ways to integrate writing and writing instruction in his course. In the Spring, he had commented on a faculty-wide survey that he was concerned about writing. I had followed up on that comment, and by August 20th was ready to work closely with him and his TAs, whom I was yet to meet, in a consulting and mentoring role throughout the thirteen-week semester. At that particular point, however, my availability seemed almost irrelevant. The immediate stumbling block was the matter of TAs. He wanted to be sure that they were themselves competent writers. Taking on the teaching of a W-course entailed risks for him as the faculty member as well as for the TAs and the students. Like a captain and crew washed ashore with passengers on an island, they would be transforming their relationships with each other and with their course materials. If they were to survive successfully, they would have to satisfy everyone's needs and expectations to some degree, despite the unfamiliar demands of the new context, which in the W-classroom, are not the consequence of an accidental running ashore, but the deliberate choice of the professor as captain.

The W-course also entailed risks for me as the CWIL writing consultant, particularly at this pilot stage before the new writing requirements became official. A failure might not be seen as the failure of one individual consultant. Instead, it could be construed as the failure of CWIL to be a useful resource for faculty in the W-courses (each of us at CWIL would *be* "CWIL") and possibly also it would be read as a failure of the processes and purposes of the W-initiative. We knew from reading about other such initiatives that the path forward to a transformation of the teaching and learning culture could easily reach a dead end. We would all have to be constantly aware of the elements in our surroundings as well as know where we wanted to go. The map is not the territory.

The map and the territory of this chapter draws on my experience of collaborating with Don Devoretz and his TAs, and offers an exploration and analysis of the risks involved in undertaking a W-course for the first time, the inevitable stumbling involved, and the need to overcome obstacles and move forward into next attempts and next collaborations.

OVERCOMING THE FIRST STUMBLING BLOCK: APPOINTING AND TAKING ON TAs FOR THE COURSE

Transforming Economics 355 into a W-course would mean more student writing. More writing would mean more marking for the TAs, and thus a workload that required more hours than were available in their usual contracts. Leaving Don's office that August afternoon, I had felt quite discouraged. CWIL had a small budget that I was using to add TA support for professors who decided to do pilot W-courses. If Don took this on, the budget would give him an extra TA. It was, however, not just a matter of extra hours for marking. In some departments, like economics, the nature of the TA job changed. The TA needed to be able to give some writing instruction and respond to and grade writing, qualifications that were not normally required of them. Both economics department policy and the Teaching Support Union contracts required that entering graduate students be allocated to TA positions in their first semester as a way of assisting them financially. The longer they were graduate students and the more TA-ships they took on, the lower on the hiring priority scale they moved, since the way was kept open to support incoming students. As Don saw it, the department chair had conceded one experienced TA, Kevin, for Don's course. Kevin was a mature student, strong writer, native English speaker, and excellent teacher, but being low on the hiring priority scale, he could not be assigned the majority of the six tutorial sections. The other TA-ship would be assigned to whichever new graduate student was next in line; he or she would not have to demonstrate competence in writing to satisfy the department. It seemed the chair felt he had no license to change the hiring rules and suggested that if Don could not work with the system, he had the choice of waiting until another semester and seeing if he was satisfied with the TAs at that time. It would be up to him to decide.

Don's own standards, however, also created an obstacle. He was unwilling to embark on this new venture without being confident in his TAs' competence in writing and overall English language abilities. "How can

TAs read and comment on students' writing unless they have skills themselves?" he asked. I appreciated Don's concern but was eager to proceed anyway. We had planned that I would work with him and the TAs throughout the semester, and I thought consultation and some instruction could compensate for the lack of experience. Being a skilled writer, after all, was not a guarantee of skilled response to student writing. His caution was legitimate, however, since he knew better than I that being a capable writer of academic or professional English was not a prerequisite for being accepted in the department's graduate program. Nor indeed, was a high level of sophistication and fluency in spoken English.

Over the past twenty-five years, the department's hiring and teaching emphasis, and thus its expectations of graduate students, following trends in the field, had shifted toward employing more technical statistics and highly abstract theoretical models in its empirical work. The use of writing, previously a common and expected means of assessment, had been moved outside the typical framework of economics courses and was often ignored and even actively excluded. Developments in the field have led to changes in the classification of what counts as the study of economics, and the change is reflected in course textbooks and assignments. The current focus privileges mathematical models as means of explanation and has led to different measures of evaluation of student performance. Multiple-choice exams have replaced written work and verbal explanations. It has become quite possible for an economics student to graduate without having learned to write in such typical professional forms as proposals, research reports, or policy briefs. Class sizes, a stumbling block in this context as elsewhere, have grown enormously: Don's upper-division 355 course, which he has taught every year for the past thirty-five years, has grown from groups of 30 to 120. Lower division courses regularly have 300 or more students. Budget constraints have increased pressure on departments to increase enrollments and classes grow in size, while no corresponding increase occurs in available teaching faculty. These constraints set bounds on what pedagogies can readily be accommodated.

But there are also faculty with an interest in policy development and in the public implications and consequences of economic decisions who resist the dominant trends, both theoretical and practical. They believe that students should be able to write well and critically about economic matters. When the opportunity arose to enhance instruction with writing, Don Devoretz stepped forward. Don's request that he be supported in the as yet unofficial W-course initiative clearly positioned him outside what had become typical departmental expectations of faculty teaching practice. His status, however, as an internationally distinguished senior professor in a large economics department, five years from retirement, gave him the kind of security he needed to challenge departmental norms. At the same time, he had to accept departmental constraints. The chair's discouraging response regarding the TA allocation reflected the hierarchy of departmental values that Don also could not, or was unwilling, to violate.

Don felt that the chair's response indicated a lamentable indifference to his efforts in the department, but nevertheless we had scheduled a meeting on August 20th and, notwithstanding the prospect of not having the kind of TA he wanted, we went ahead and reviewed some of the logistics that would be involved. We talked as if a suitable TA would arrive, and as if the course would go ahead as writing-intensive. Fortunately, the day after that meeting, Don interviewed Bryan, the novice TA assigned to the course, who turned out to be an enthusiastic and skilled writer. We were able to begin the collaboration optimistically. Following policy, Bryan was assigned to four tutorials with 70 students, Kevin, the experienced TA, to two tutorials with 34 students. Don would prepare lectures twice a week and post notes and assignment details on his website. I would attend lectures, meet with the three of them weekly to discuss the writing and tutorial activity, and assist in any way I could with the writing instruction. Exactly what forms that assistance would take and how it would be received and acted upon would be worked out among the four of us. With our roles identified, however, we could begin.

MAPPING THE TERRITORY OF ECONOMICS 355

The aim of Economics 355 was the study of "the sources of growth or retardation in poor countries." Individually, students gather data on one of about 125 poor countries, and examine the impact on that country's development of such forces as globalization, trade, debt, and migration, topics that Don discusses and illustrates in his lectures. Applying sophisticated theoretical models, students were expected to make a case to explain why their country remains poor or, alternatively, is developing. When Don and I first met for about an hour in June, we discussed the goals of the course and Don's concerns. He told me that a majority of the third-year students were "unable to marshal a sustained argument," and tended to rely on assembling lists of facts that they mistakenly assumed would speak for themselves. He wanted them to provide evidence and argue a case, not merely represent it symbolically and mathematically. In order to help them understand how to take a position on a key topic and how to make an argument, he had tried using Oxford-style debates. Although these debates were popular and required students to make an argument, the debates involved too few students in the thinking Don wanted to foster, and participation was minimal. Most students simply sat and listened to the speakers and had no questions. Don felt frustrated with what he saw as a failure in this aspect of his course. Large classes had led him to abandon the research paper he used to assign when his classes were smaller and he was now assessing students by means of a mid-term exam worth 40% of the grade and a final exam worth 60%. Both exams still required some verbal answers in the form of short paragraphs and a short essay inviting an argument, but any in-class writing was voluntary and took the form of ungraded notes for exam preparation and for a debate topic that was conducted orally.

Although this first meeting was ostensibly intended to orient me to the course and Don's interests, it was also, of course, his opportunity to decide whether it was worth his time and effort to engage in rethinking his course and whether or not I had anything to offer him. I took up his debate idea. As a way of enhancing the debates and engaging all students in thinking about the issues and taking a defensible position, I suggested that he ask for some informal writing about the resolution before the debate took place. Writing to explain and argue a point of view, I suggested, is a means of encouraging thoughtful reflection. To create dialogue, we could structure the assignment so that students exchanged papers with someone who had taken an opposing view, and get a written response from them. I suggested that if students not only wrote, but were challenged by someone who disagreed, they were likely to get engaged and respond more knowledgeably to the arguments made during the debate. Don liked the idea and agreed to make time and space available for students to write, to exchange papers during his lecture time, and get some response. We would work out the details later, but his immediate positive response signaled both his commitment to make changes and his willingness to countenance the uncertainties attendant on a new role for writing in his course.

The next issue we needed to consider at that time was how the students would respond to a change in course description. According to the published outline, no marks were attached to writing assignments. Don agreed that this would need to change and he was confident that as long as he announced his plans to students at the first class, he would not be challenged. He decided to reduce the value of the exam grades to 30% and 45% for the mid-term and final, respectively, and allocate 25% of the grade to participation. The 25% was to be distributed across various writing assignments, as yet undefined. While 25% did not locate the written work at the heart of the course, as was intended by the criteria being proposed for W-courses, it would be a radical change and represented a critical, and in this department, risky first step. Recognizing this, Don wanted to wait until he was certain he had two TAs and would be making this a trial W-course before going further with plans.

We had crossed into a new area through the exchange in this first consultation, creating what Mary Louise Pratt calls a "contact zone." In this liminal space, we could anticipate that the traditional lecture–tutorial model might well be transformed. Don, the TAs, the students in the class, and I would all be located in positions of potential and possibility, but also of uncertainty, everyone stumbling together. Each of us would need to negotiate our relationships with each other and with the course content. Don, the TAs, and I would each be situated differently in relation to students in the course, and in relation to departmental practice and expectations of instructors and TAs. As an outsider to the discipline, I was clearly a cultural anomaly. We were not in positions of equal authority or responsibility for the success of the course: Don, as the instructor, was responsible, and it was up to him to decide what he could take on, what he preferred to forego, and what he thought would be effective for students.

From my point of view, the object of our collaboration was the transformation of his practices around the uses and teaching of writing at the site of the classroom, with him as a forerunner of future departmental transformations, which in turn reflected on the university as a whole and its proposed new curriculum. From his point of view, the object was at the site of the page: the improvement of students' writing in economics. I, of course, shared his wish to see improvement in students' writing, but more than that, I hoped our collaboration would affect how he thought about assignments and about response to writing; that it would affect his teaching beyond this one course or these particular students. So, what was my role there? The course was his territory. I was in his cultural space, an outsider. I would need to work on his terms. I could suggest strategies for solving what he identified as the problems. I could do such things as propose forms of instruction in writing; find samples of the genres he chose to assign; suggest guidance for reading; suggest a schedule for appropriate and timely feedback and built in opportunities for revision. But we were just setting out. This was a course in economics, not in writing.

POSITIONING WRITING IN THE ECONOMICS 355 COURSE

By agreeing to assign 25% of the course grade to written assignments, Don opened up a space that would crowd out more familiar practices, challenge student expectations, and potentially create anxiety and even hostility toward him and his course. Fortunately, as a securely tenured professor, Don's position in the department would not be threatened by negative student evaluations. However, negative assessments could undermine any claims he might make about the value of writing in his course, and thereby buttress resistance by colleagues and the department to an anticipated institutional imperative that was seen as a directive of the university administration. We were all committed, therefore, to enabling students' successful experience with writing as far as we could.

Since we had not yet done the detailed thinking and planning that ideally would have occurred months before, in the previous semester, we began this process at our first meeting in the first week of the semester. We needed to consider logistics, resources, and attitudes. As the writing consultant, I proposed processes for discussion and acceptance. We were not simply trying to add writing, but to teach students as well. That meant we would need to schedule timing for drafts, feedback, and revision cycles if we were going to make this a pilot course that met the criteria being proposed for eventual W-courses. Although the university senate committee had not actually given formal approval of the initiative or of the criteria at this point, the framework we had developed at CWIL served as a generally accepted reference for planning W-courses. Neither Don nor the TAs challenged the precepts of our working criteria, agreeing as they did with the purposes they embodied. We therefore did not have to argue about reasons for making space for drafts and feedback but could concentrate on the purposes, topics, and possible genres of writing assignments and how and when they would fit into the lecture structure of the course and the content. The logistics were the main challenge. We agreed there would be short pieces that would give students opportunities to practice writing and that these would lead to a longer paper toward the end of the course; all of these papers were intended to help students use data to construct economic arguments addressed to academic or non-academic readers. We hoped to initiate the students into thinking in terms of the interests of different readers and to develop an awareness of how to be persuasive in making a case by means of well-substantiated claims.

We were somewhat at cross-purposes when it came to the matter of evaluation of the writing. I saw the early short pieces as informal and probably ungraded; these pieces, I suggested, could accumulate in the grade as credit, be given some feedback, but not be formally graded on a scale. Don and the TAs argued that students would not do the writing if it was not graded, and they felt very strongly that it was important to distinguish satisfactory from unsatisfactory work: "doneness" was not sufficient to get credit. For them, as for the students, the concept of assigned in-course writing was most commonly associated with evaluation, and not to evaluate was to be negligent or would suggest that the writing was not really important. In economics, they insisted, students worked for grades and if we wanted the work done and effort put into it, it would have to be graded. Theirs was a pragmatic response from a context in which required work was graded. In this new situation, they were being consistent with traditional practice and also with the disciplinary culture of cost–benefit thinking. Their position could also be understood as consistent with a consumerist culture evident in university rankings, which frame educational value in terms of "is the professor doing his job and are you getting your money's worth?" But they patiently heard me out, acknowledging that teachers have a coaching role and that practice in preparation for testing events helps promote success.

We resolved the issue by allocating a few marks to the first two short assignments (two and three marks, respectively) and crudely distinguishing performance as inadequate, adequate and good responses. Subsequent assignments would be worth five and ten marks each and assessed on more specifically defined criteria. In arguing for grades, the TAs and Don made the further point that the idea of writing in economics would be unusual for most students. They suspected that many would resist and possibly resent having their grades affected by their ability to write, instead of by their ability to use computational skills and apply theoretical models to problems in graphical representations. These uncertainties around anticipated student responses made them all a little anxious.

WRITING AND THE LECTURE CONTEXT

The lecture itself was not a site of anxiety or uncertainty for anyone. It followed a familiar and predictable structure. Students in the lectures received information aurally; PowerPoint notes appeared on the screen, and Don drew graphs to exemplify trends and their relationships. Occasionally he asked questions but did not invite answers from students. "They pay me to do the talking and ask the questions," he responded to a raised hand, establishing the tenor of the social setting of the lecture and the lines of authority. But he seemed eager to see that students were attentive and responsive, and he paced across the front of the room as he spoke, looking for eye contact. Since he was a generally engaging and lively speaker, with a sense of humor that most students seemed to appreciate, lectures were usually well attended.

Don proposed to outline the process of writing and its purposes in the course at his first lecture. I requested that students also complete a confidential pre-course survey (see Appendix 2) intended to give us some background information on the students' attitudes and beliefs about their writing ability. Don agreed, and from this survey, we learned that more than half the students reported speaking a language other than English at home, and of those, the great majority were from Asia. In a class of 106, thirty-two of the students checked "need lots of help" with language correctness on a scaled question (1–5) and five said they "worry about" grammar in response to a question inviting comments on how they felt about writing. No one openly voiced unwillingness to write, which was encouraging, since the difficulties the students reported having with writing ran the full spectrum of possibilities. The fact that the course would include writing instruction seemed to be received positively at the outset, allaying some of Don's initial anxiety that student response might prove an intractable obstacle.

Over the course of the semester, Don's references to writing typically occurred when writing assignments were to be explained or papers returned. He did not attempt instruction in writing, confining himself to admonition and explanation of the reason for the choice of genre, its purpose, and audience. As he stressed on those occasions, "I'm not looking for opinion; I'm looking for research results to be addressed to a question, in a field of interest in economic development. I'm looking for evidence to support your answer to a question and for a conclusion." While these were not new expectations—he had always wanted the students to apply and analyze the usefulness of theory in specific contexts—he explained that he was not satisfied with the results and wanted to see them do better. He expected that the change he was making to use more writing would mean that the students would need to understand and be able to explain situations and offer some interpretation and critical analysis. Each short writing piece would require them to use data to make a point about an aspect of their country's development or lack of it. Recording data and being able to recite it would no longer suffice. While the focus on applying theory would not be new in the course, what would be new and potentially problematic was the process by which students would be assisted to do it more successfully.

Don made it clear to students, however, that the new demands were his demands and he wanted to see the students engage seriously with the writing. This positioning of himself as the person making the decisions about including writing and about the genres chosen, while not, at the same time, claiming expertise in teaching them how to do the writing was important for his relationship with the students and with me and the TAs. My presence on the teaching team required some adjustment for the students. They had to make space in their thinking for an outsider whose influence was clearly affecting the nature of the course, but who was not there to help them. I was often at the lectures: I felt I needed to understand the context for the assignments, the details of which we were refining as we went along. I also needed to grasp the discourse and the concepts students would be dealing with, since I would be talking with the TAs about responding to how students handled the discourse and concepts in their writing. During the lecture, Don occasionally referred to me directly, usually by way of suggesting good humouredly that "Wendy will correct me if I'm wrong," but his handling and representation of our relationship helped to avoid ambiguities about the place of writing in the course and the source of ideas for assignments.

THE TUTORIAL AS THE SITE OF ACTION

The site of the change in pedagogy was largely in the tutorials, led by the TAs, though clearly endorsed by Don, the instructor. Bryan, as a new TA, had no prior teaching experience and, because he arrived just before the start of the semester, no opportunity to take the university's class management and teaching skills workshops, which would have oriented him to a teaching role. Kevin had highly developed teaching skills and took on the idea of giving instruction in writing confidently. The TAs and I developed the actual assignments at our weekly meetings. That collaborative process, along with six hours of workshop sessions, which I planned for both TAs around writing theory and pedagogy, provided a context in which we could strategize processes and plans for the tutorials. I would write an outline following our discussion and make up handouts they could use, and it was up to them what they did, or did not do, or what they organized to do with the students in the fifty minutes of the tutorial. Bryan, in particular, had a lot of demands on his time in all his new courses, and while he did not need to be convinced of the value of writing instruction, he was quite open about his predictable difficulty with organizing time in the tutorials. We were all stumbling to some extent, figuring out what was possible and desirable to do with students in this course and in this discipline as well as in our relationship.

Economics 355 was a third-year course, and students had expectations from their experiences of how tutorials function. Their TAs in this course were no longer only answering questions and explaining concepts from the lectures. They were introducing and monitoring writing activities. They were putting themselves into a new relation to their students. They were quickly learning what the students understood and what was giving them difficulty. By the end of the fourth week of the thirteen-week semester, the TAs had read and responded to two short pieces from each student and had graded a revision. The first graded assignment took the form of a letter to the editor in which students were to respond to an article that referred to their country as "developed." They were to explain why they agreed or disagreed with this assessment, taking account of both economic and social indicators in their 400–500 word explanation. For the second assignment, they were to make a case, in 400–450 words, "FOR or AGAINST the adoption" by their own country of one or two of China's population control policies. Tutorial instruction for this second assignment included examples of reasoning to make the argument and some wordings to illustrate verbal interpretations of numbers and statistics. (e.g. "*The Population Reference Bureau indicates that Malawi's population growth rate is 4.05% per annum and that 43% of the population is under 15. What this means is that there is enormous pressure on parents, schools, the government and the health system. Parents have responsibility for . . . etc.*") Both the assignments required the application of new concepts, and though worth a maximum of two and three marks, respectively, Bryan and Kevin conscientiously gave students feedback about their economic reasoning and their language. We reviewed sample responses together at our weekly meetings to check for consistency in marking, and both TAs were disappointed by what they judged to be students' lack of writing skill, rather than lack of understanding. They felt they could not tell whether an under-elaborated idea was a consequence of lack of understanding or lack of knowledge of how to explain it or perhaps, why to explain it, since they were not yet positioned to grasp the exigence prompting use of the genre. The TAs also were not sure how students interpreted the fact that they were being given some guidelines. Did they see these as useful and important clues about how to write, or just as more "noise?" Revised versions showed some improvement on the drafts, but as we discussed the writing, we wondered whether students were engaging in the writing in a perfunctory or a serious manner. The decision not to make success in the course dependent on the written work had been intended to reduce risk for the students as well as for Don, not to trivialize its importance. But, we decided against making any hasty conclusions; it was still early in the semester; we were embarked on an experiment and could wait and watch and learn what to take account of another time.

In the third and next assignment, students would need to apply a theory about foreign aid to an explanation of their own country's needs. This assignment was also worth more: five marks. In the fifth week, Don followed his usual practice of lecturing on the topic of the week and providing a structure for thinking about it, which included reference to relevant theories and to examples of policies that would illustrate how those theories applied to a selection of countries. That particular week, the topic was foreign aid and the issues it generates around the conditions, characteristics, and effects of aid as a means of supporting development in poor countries. To assist the students in tackling complex analytical tasks, Don always gave examples, set out terms, explained implications, and elaborated on what conditions are necessary and sufficient to justify a theory's claim to explanatory power in a particular context. By way of preparing them for the next assignment, he proposed alternative analyses for particular cases and explained how to assess the applicability and strength of different theories. For this assignment, we devised a real-life scenario:

> You have been asked by your boss, Mr. Peter Harder, who heads Canada's Aid Programme (CIDA) to outline an argument to justify why x/your country is deserving of a portion of Canada's $100 billion aid package. Using one economic, social, or demographic indicator, outline a case for this country.

The paper was to be not more than 500 words and would take the form of a memo to Mr. Harder. Since it was to make an argument, not simply offer information, we took time at our weekly meeting to discuss the features that would need to be included, and I drafted some wording, which the others reviewed and commented on before Don presented it at the next lecture to the students as a guide for writing. He also posted it on the course website: see Appendix 3 for details.

The scenario asking students to make an argument in their memo to Harder would be similar to an item that would appear on their mid-term exam. We decided that the exam link with the assignment would help motivate thoughtful participation in a formally structured peer review process that we would schedule during the tutorial. The students would use the time in the tutorial to see how they could improve their presentation of the issues addressed in the memo and to make sure they understood how to explain their reasoning and be convincing to someone who could give money to their country. I wrote directions for this peer process, which I reviewed with the TAs, and they took it to students in their tutorials. Through this assignment, we introduced students to writing in a professional genre, we gave them a staged process with response and revision, and we prepared them to explore the course content in a way that could foster understanding, not simply information recall. We were taking our experimentation a step further by adding another element. We could not predict how students would respond. Nor could we know what impact the TA or peer suggestions and revision opportunities would have on their writing, but we hoped the process was building on the experience given by the first two short pieces and that we had begun to create expectations about response and purpose that students would value.

One of the goals of the writing in the course was to invite students to think of themselves as economists and to write in ways that would be expected of them if they took up economics professionally. This third assignment turned out to be pivotal in ushering students toward that goal. It repositioned them in the discipline: they were to respond in the role of economists, and to shift from being spectators of the discourse to appropriating it for themselves. They would be finding that economics was not only a matter of retaining content and being able to use formulae; it was also a matter of putting this knowledge and skill into service for their needs as economists. It was an experience of using writing as a means of learning: the assignment required the students to synthesize information and understand it well enough to reformulate it in a second setting on the exam. They were also beginning to acquire a language for talking and thinking about writing. Not only were they to respond to each other's drafts by reading them and making comments, they were to write notes on their own draft about the changes that they saw they needed to make. In so doing, they had to take a stance, which put them in the position of assuming some responsibility for the meaningfulness of their texts from the reader's point of view.

Not only were the students being repositioned as writers and students in economics by this assignment, the TAs were also repositioned. They assisted in a new process that required them to relinquish some authority and observe students trying to imitate the response the TAs had modeled for them on previous papers. They were in the role of coaches here, rather than graders. The grading would come later and would be a separate activity. For Don also, this assignment led to a shift in role. When he looked back on the course later, he noted that there was a change at this point in both student attitudes in the course and in the papers. He reflected that at this mid-semester point, "they began to get the hang of it, and I think that indicated to me it was sort of like 'we get it' . . . and I started getting a lot more e-mails taking it more seriously . . . e-mails that go beyond the usual 'what's on the exam' to asking me things like, 'How would I go about structuring news and reviews or response?' Or something like that" (Post-course interview December 3, 2003).

We had some data on this change in the form of anonymous feedback as a follow-up to the third assignment. We asked the students to comment on the process so far, tabulated their responses, and showed them the results (see Appendix 4 for details). For example, one question read as follows:

> You have now completed three short writing assignments and got careful and detailed feedback on these from your instructor and from a classmate.
>
> Please respond to the following:
>
> 1. Based on what you see in the feedback, what are 4 or 5 ways you can improve what you write in your next two papers?
> 2. How does writing affect your knowledge and understanding of economics?
> 3. Any suggestions and general comments on the writing assignments and your own progress?

Students identified 12 different aspects of writing that they thought required their attention, and 76 percent claimed that writing was "significantly" helping them understand the economics material; 5% said "not at all." The following is an example of one student's response:

> Writing I find to be very helpful in economics. Without constant work, the concepts can pass me by. By doing regular writing assignments, I felt up to date with the course. Also, it helps to organize my thoughts in my head to make sure I truly do understand. It is easier to think I understand than actually write about it.

The most common general comment at this point was about workload, and some students suggested there be fewer assignments, less restriction on length, and even more feedback. We knew the writing was taking a lot of time and energy and, from their point of view, it must have seemed out of balance for the marks attached to it. At the same time, if the writing was the more difficult part of the course and they could succeed in the mathematical and statistical applications, it was probably better for their grade point averages not to have too much depend on writing. We also knew it was difficult to discuss complex issues in such short papers. But longer papers would mean less feedback and fewer pieces, and we had decided practice was important. The request for more feedback was, we hoped, indicative of its quality, since they were not saying the feedback was not useful and that they needed something different. We all felt quite encouraged that the students were not rejecting the attention to writing nor complaining that they were not getting enough time in tutorials to discuss the economics content. We would have to wait, of course, until the end of the semester to see what judgment they would pass on the course overall.

The remaining two assignments for the course were, first, a short piece in which the students were to take a position in favor of or against the debate resolution; and secondly, a longer paper in which they used the arguments about development from an article by Nobel Prize-winning economist, Joseph E. Stiglitz, as the basis for analyzing the process of development in their own country. The short debate piece was handled as Don and I had agreed earlier. The students wrote out reasons for taking the "for" or "against" position they were assigned, and then, during the lecture period, they exchanged papers with someone who had taken the opposing position. On their classmate's paper, they wrote a response critiquing the other's claims. In this way, each person witnessed the subsequent oral debate having thought through both points of view. These pieces were collected and graded fairly generously—they had served their purpose and no TA response was necessary. The longer paper entailed an instructional process that included guidance in analysis of Stiglitz' points, cues on applying his reasoning to their own country's development, and a drafting and response cycle with peer and TA feedback before the final draft was submitted.

REFLECTIONS ON THE COLLABORATION AND ON WRITING IN THE ECONOMICS COURSE

As the CWIL person in this course with expertise in teaching writing, I was always in the role of novice. I acquired something of the discourse, but in the zone we created through contact between the two disciplines and through an interaction characterized by asymmetrical power relations, I had to become alert to openings and potential cues for changes in the ways students might better be initiated into that discourse. I was not in the position of being able to insist on any particular strategy or indeed to impose my thinking and beliefs on how students in economics could become economists. This was not my course. I learned to put myself into a place of uncertainty about my role and about both the nature and the value of my contribution. I was well aware that I could not bring appropriate metaphors or analogies that derived from their discipline to explain concepts about writing. Bryan showed himself to be adept at this. Frustrated by students' struggle to develop strong arguments, he created a clever statistical/econometric analogy on thinking.

He set out the thinking process required in working through a basic multiple regression equation, linking each step in working through the mathematical problem with its corollary in a verbal argument, and suggested that students who understood this mathematical process might apply it to formulate ideas in writing. Unfortunately, we did not find out how, or whether, students used the analogy, which he e-mailed to them and also posted on the course website. But I was impressed; this was not an analogy that would have occurred to me but it clearly could resonate for students in this discipline.

Respectful of their insider, naturalized knowledge of the discipline, I learned to trust that Don's and the TAs' own experiences and reflections would lead to new perceptions of writing and to an eventual transforming of practice that was coherent with, and could emerge out of, their own values and beliefs. Our inevitable stumbling around in our planning meetings did not seem to me to be a disadvantage. Though we did not name it that way, we were in fact taking advantage of the potentialities in uncertainty. We did not start out sharing a discourse that could ease our transactions or serve as a shorthand for the pedagogy they were trying to understand and to implement. We were all novices in different ways, and our relationship was characterized by mutual recognition of our different areas of expertise. As graduate students, the TAs deferred to Don's knowledge of the field, but he deferred to them as teachers. They all deferred to my expertise in teaching writing, but did not shy from clarifying disciplinary values that I needed to understand. Although we stumbled about in our attempts to arrive at processes and strategies, we had a common goal and trusted that we would find ways to move toward it.

Student responses to the course on the post-course surveys confirmed that we had got some things right and that we also needed to keep working to improve our practice if students were to become more capable and competent writers. In order to make a comparison between the self-ratings at the beginning of the semester and the end, we averaged the responses to questions from pre- and post-course surveys to determine change. Table 1 shows the number of responses on a question about overall writing skills.

On the basis of the rating scale below, 92 students self-rated their writing skills at an average of 5.76 at the start of the course. At the end of the course, 62 students rated their writing skills at an average of 6.17, a change of 7.1% by the end of the course.

TABLE 1

Pre-and post-course survey comparison

SURVEY QUESTION	Compared to other students at this university, how do you rate your writing skills overall?			
Self- Rating	Pre-Course Survey		Post-Course Survey	
	# of Responses	Rating x # of Responses	# of Responses	Rating x # of Responses
1.0 Poor	1	1.0	0	0
2.0	1	2.0	0	0
3.0	5	15.0	6	18.0
4.0	7	280.0	6	240.0
5.0 Adequate	32	160.0	13	65.0
6.0	14	84.0	10	60.0
7.0	20	140.0	15	105.0
8.0	9	72.0	11	88.0
9.0	2	18.0	3	27.0
10.0 Excellent	1	10.0	2	20.0
TOTAL	92	530.0	66	407.0
Average Rating		5.76		6.17

We saw the most encouraging changes in student's increased confidence in several areas that we had targeted for instruction. The survey asked them to rate themselves on thirteen specific writing skills before and again after the W-course. They checked descriptors on a continuum of 1–5 with 1 indicating "need a lot help" and 5 indicating "very confident." The responses were weighted by the number of students in each level on the continuum. The averages for the number of students responding to each question showed changes in ratings between the pre- and the post-course surveys. Table 2 summarizes the averages. The most marked differences in student estimates of their own skills were in the first six skills listed in the table to which we had paid particular attention.

In general, how do you rate yourself on the following writing skills:

TABLE 2

Student responses to individual questions

	Pre-course	Post- Course	% Change
(1) Editing and rewriting drafts	2.70	3.24	0.199
(2) Getting papers in on time	2.91	3.29	0.165
(3) Paraphrasing things in my own words	3.02	3.48	0.153
(4) Writing good introductions	2.90	3.20	0.122
(5) Writing good conclusions	3.0	3.33	0.111
(6) Voicing my own opinions appropriately	2.93	3.26	0.11
(7) Making an argument effectively	2.87	3.15	0.098
(8) Using correct grammar and punctuation	2.85	3.12	0.096
(9) Summarizing others' ideas	3.17	3.50	0.09
(10) Deciding on a topic and focus	3.05	3.29	0.076
(11) Spelling	3.20	3.44	0.076
(12) Organizing the material for the paper	3.25	3.49	0.075
(13) Avoiding procrastination	2.65	2.71	+ 2.4%

In the post-course survey, we were also interested in how students were responding to the purposes and processes in the W-course. They were asked whether they "generally agree or generally disagree" with the statement "There are anticipated advantages for taking a course that pays attention to writing as well as content." Approximately 90% of the students affirmed the value of feedback and opportunities for revision. Approximately 80% seemed also to recognize that the writing was helping them learn the course content. A majority of students expressed negative responses only to the added work required by a W-course and to the quality of feedback from classmates (Appendix 5).

Despite the fact that the students seemed to value what they had learned and their self-ratings on skills implied a sense of their improvement as writers, they expressed some ambivalence about taking the W-course. They were asked to "generally agree or disagree" with six statements of opinion about the W-course. Table 3 indicates that although a majority thought there were direct benefits of the writing experience, 86% said they would not want to take another W-course.

TABLE 3

Student responses to W-courses

	Valid Responses	% Yes	% No
(1). The writing-intensive process gave me skills I can apply to other courses	61	68.9%	31.1%
(2). I think that the writing emphasis worked well in this course	61	60.7%	39.3%
(3). The emphasis on writing in this course improved my writing skills	58	55.2%	44.8%
(4). I think the writing emphasis would be better in another course in my area	48	43.8%	56.3%
(5). The writing focus in the course was well- timed for me in my program	58	39.7%	60.3%
(6). I would like to take another writing-intensive course because I saw my writing improve with this approach	58	13.8%	86.2%

Their responses to a following question about recommendations for changes in the course gave some insight, however, into why they would not elect to take another W-course. The greatest number of students responding suggested fewer assignments or more credits for the W-course. Since this particular course required a great deal of writing for only 20% of the grade, students probably reacted to that imbalance. Whatever the reasons, the distribution of responses and the suggestions for change offered some guidance for our own thinking as we reflected on the process.

Finally, we were interested in knowing what resources students considered most helpful to them in their development as writers. Among the numerous resources they identified were friends, e-mail responses, the in-class debate, the internet and the professor. By a significant margin, they named their TA as a helpful resource (Appendix 5).

In an interview at the end of the course, Don identified insights he had gained to take forward into his next iteration of Economics 355 as a W-course. Like other professors making a shift from a focus on delivering content in a lecture course to teaching students how to write about that content, he was aware there might be some trade-offs in making time for writing instruction. For him, a "eureka" moment was about keeping the balance, despite a bit of stumbling, and not falling into either trivializing attention to writing or sacrificing too much content:

> There's a delicate balance that has to be recognized between restructuring the course and changing the course content. In my case, I pulled out modules that were always supposed to be applications of what they had learned so there was no trade-off, the things have just been shifted around. . .. I went through the textbook to sort of pick and choose what I would cover [on the final exam] and it was pleasant to realize that in fact, I really hadn't lost the essence of the course, you know, I hadn't skipped things, which was a good confirmation, and I haven't rushed things either. (post course interview, December 3, 2003)

As we reviewed the course and the use of writing together, we discovered new resources and connections that we had not had time to explore in this first iteration. In working with the TAs to plan in helping students read the textbook, I had consulted the text quite extensively. Don had been using editions of this text for many years. He originally selected it for features he valued but he seldom needed to consult it. He commented, however, on what he noticed as he reviewed it for the exam:

> I've realized how much of the textbook you've involved to exemplify things about writing and positioning, and I'm pleased I can say yes, the textbook is no longer something that they hold in their hand and say "Okay, if I memorize this, then I'll pass." . . . There's stuff in there which I'll use more of, essays on particular countries for example, that I now realize, with the writing component of the course I could say, "Read the essay on China, read it on the Ukraine, and then tell me, is it worthwhile to give up personal freedoms to experience Chinese growth?" You know, these kinds of questions, right out of the textbook. . . . I'll use those essays that are in the textbook, not the technical material but the essays that are in that textbook and use those like news and reviews, like the New York Times articles and Stiglitz, as examples of how to write them . . . My goal is to want them to take the course, I don't want them to say "Oh shit, we've got to do writing so which one of these four could you get away with, with the least amount of work?" You know, "Where's the template so that I don't have to do anything?" I want people to say, "Oh

gosh," you know, "Don Devoretz' course is great" and "He gets you to debate" and it's all real. (Post course interview December 3, 2003)

As noted earlier, one of the first ideas that Don took on enthusiastically, though he could not anticipate the exact outcome, was having students write to a debate topic individually, and respond to an opposing view, again in writing. He saw this as an additional resource that connected with his goals in the course. He observed that:

> What that meant was that the quality of questions from the audience for the debaters in the second part of the sessions was bang on. Before, you know, I'd always have one or two eager people, partially informed about the issue, who would either blabber on or make almost good points, you know, and I was constantly redirecting their questions. But now with the written component, they really have their position on this issue and they want to get their point out so they ask specific questions: "Why didn't you include that other argument," for instance. For the first time, after years of doing these debates, I had to intervene and say, "Okay, that's all the time we have . . . that's enough questions." (Post-course interview, December 3, 2003)

The "trends" we noted from the pre- and post-course student surveys were not dramatic, but they were positive. The implementation of the W-ness in the course was somewhat haphazard, in keeping with a first attempt, but the experience had convinced Don that modifying his course was a doable and worthwhile venture. He was able to report encouragingly on his work to the department and to colleagues from other disciplines. The territory had not proved too hostile. We had overcome the obstacles: department policy, TA levels of preparedness, the uncertainties about students' responses and about marking and grading, fears about workload, concern about watering down or losing course content, and, importantly, uncertainties about our relationship in working together. We had resolved enough of the uncertainties about the "hows" of a W-course for Don to move forward to a next iteration with confidence and commitment to its purposes. We would continue to explore.

4

WHAT HAPPENED IN THIS COURSE?
Reflections from Three Perspectives

Joan Sharp, the Course Instructor
Erin Barley, the TA
Wendy Strachan, the W-Consultant

"I've been doing this for years," said Joan Sharp at one of our first meetings, reminding me that she had introduced an essay assignment into the first-year biology course in the early 1990s and had given students feedback on drafts if they submitted them early enough. An enthusiastic and dedicated teacher, Joan is the sort of person who sends you e-mail messages at 1:00 in the morning, who is constantly on the move from one appointment to another across the wide range of her activities both at the university and outside it, and whose passion and fascination for all living things is inexhaustible. When we first began talking about working together to make her biology 102 a W-course, I was well aware that I had given up formal study (such as it was) of science over forty years ago, and that my recollection of Grade 10 biology was limited to covering leaves on a plant with bits of paper to learn about photosynthesis. Working with Joan and her TAs would clearly be a collaboration. All my questions seeking clarification about topics and directions for assignments would be absolutely genuine ones. I would be the novice learner in biology, Joan and the TAs the experts. And, since she felt she had already created a role for writing in the course, I could not be sure exactly what she would need from me.

We began thinking about the course where Joan identified the greatest need: in the training and preparation of the TAs to assist in writing instruction in the tutorials, in responding to drafts, and in grading revised writing. That focus on the TA training led us to examine details in the syllabus, the wording of lab questions, and the structuring and preparation of the main writing assignment, all of which would form the new elements needed in the delivery of the course that would most affect the work of the TAs. Joan would be lecturing on course content, and the TAs would follow up on those lectures in their tutorial sections, responding to questions that arose from the lecture material or text book, and guiding students through the various writing assignments intended to help them learn how to write about biological content in discipline-specific ways and how to begin to think like biologists.

Our shared goal in the course was to improve student learning and writing in biology. We also hoped to demonstrate that learning had not only taken place, but had been enhanced by the strategies and practices that we introduced in making this a W-course. Despite these shared purposes, we necessarily brought different perspectives and expectations for our individual roles. These affected how we experienced and interpreted what we did together and individually. Each of us had a different story to tell: Joan as the instructor for the course, Erin as one of the TAs, and I as the writing mentor.

This chapter opens with Joan's detailed account of how she views science and approaches teaching, how she and I worked together, and how she worked with the TAs. In the second section, Erin offers the perspective of a TA with experience in teaching, but no previous experience of W-courses. She describes and reflects on what she learned from this experience, how she dealt with the new expectations, and how she interacted with students in her tutorial sections. In the final section, I comment on our collective experience and our assessment of the outcomes. We used a variety of measures, including TA interviews, pre- and post-course student surveys and course evaluations, student writing samples, and a quantitative comparative analysis of writing on an exam question. Together, these data would help us determine what changes needed to be made as well as assess what seemed to be successful.

THE INSTRUCTOR'S PERSPECTIVE: TEACHING GENERAL BIOLOGY 102 AS A W-COURSE (JOAN SHARP)

Students taking BISC 102 are a diverse group. Most are first-year students in their first or second semester at university. A small number are upper-division students taking the course either as a required laboratory science course or out of individual interest. A significant number are college transfer students. A General biology course is inherently interesting but can be intimidating for a first-year student. BISC 102 covers the "macro-topics" in biology: the origin and diversity of life on Earth, ecology, behavior, genetics, natural selection, and macroevolution, with a unifying theme of evolutionary change. The volume of new information, vocabulary, and ideas can be overwhelming. biology has a difficult and specialized vocabulary, and it is often claimed that students in a first-year biology course learn more new words than first-year language students do. Many biological terms have familiar, everyday meanings that are different from their biological definitions. Consider the term *fitness*. This term conveys a sense of general health, vigor, strength, or intelligence. A student may find it hard to grasp the idea that any trait that increases an organism's relative reproductive success—even if it is a trait that hastens the death of the individual—increases, in biological terms, its evolutionary fitness. In contrast, some biological concepts, such as chemiosmosis, are both unfamiliar and inherently difficult. Some important biological ideas, such as the role of chance in evolutionary change, are counterintuitive. Also, the meaning of biological terms changes over time, as our understanding increases. Even expert knowledge is incomplete and rapidly changing.

I first studied biology at McGill University in 1968. Ten years later, I looked at my old textbook and was amazed to see how much of the information I had learned was incorrect or incomplete. The living world cannot be divided into plants and animals. Cell membranes are not sandwiches of protein and lipid. The central dogma of molecular biology, that information flows unidirectionally from DNA to RNA to protein, is sometimes violated. In a first-year biology course, students need to be introduced to science as a process, rather than as a set of information. If we teach biology as a body of facts, we do students a grave disservice. Although the living world is fascinating, a course full of inert facts about living processes is boring. Students need to learn that facts are important only in the context of the concepts that give them meaning. I encourage them to develop and nurture a curiosity about living things. I want them to question what they see and hear, to ask when concepts or examples are not clear, when there are aspects of the material that arouse their curiosity, or when they wish to know more about current biological knowledge of a particular topic. It is especially important to tell students that biologists do not have all the answers to biological questions. Each course should introduce students to questions that are the focus of current biological research, questions whose answers are incomplete or controversial.

As an instructor, I provide opportunities for students to actively explore and develop their own understanding of biological concepts through writing. Students must do more than merely learn definitions: they must understand the concepts related to each new term, relate each new concept to others, master examples that illustrate each concept and use the concepts to pose or solve problems. Faced with these challenges, many students adopt memorization as a learning tool, often fail to understand the significance of the details they are learning, and have difficulty building connections between concepts. Assignments that require students to "write biology" can be effective tools to help students' master biological concepts and develop and demonstrate biological understanding. Such assignments help clarify for students what they understand and what they do not understand and, equally importantly, provide them with an occasion to use the terms in context themselves, which is something they have little opportunity to do if they are only taking notes from an overhead in a large lecture or downloading outlines from the course website. By reading what they themselves have written, I gain insight into their understanding and I can use written work as a starting point to address areas of misunderstanding.

REVISING BISC 102 AS A W-COURSE

When Simon Fraser University (SFU) embarked upon the new curriculum initiative that would require students to take one lower and one upper-division W-course, I was an early supporter. I volunteered to work on the implementation team to encourage university-wide participation in the W-initiative and to chair the WSG. I sought approval from my department's undergraduate curriculum committee to run a trial of BISC 102 as a W-course and welcomed the opportunity to work with faculty members in SFU's CWIL. I was ready to modify my course assignments to meet the W-course criteria, to train TAs to respond effectively to student writing, and to develop meaningful rubrics for marking writing assignments.

I had already dramatically transformed my teaching of BISC 102 in 1991, a number of years before the current SFU curriculum initiative. In collaboration with bright and imaginative colleagues, Canadian Wildlife Service chair Ron Ydenberg and graphic artist Elizabeth Carefoot, I revised BISC 102 by substantially rewriting the laboratory manual for the course, "General biology BISC 102," and this remains my proudest achievement in twenty-five years of teaching. The re-developed course allowed students to apply the concepts they learned to interpret experimental findings and new information. They planned experiments on incipient species of stickleback fishes in British Columbia's lakes; they investigated how coot parents decide which chicks to feed; they measured cardboard dinosaur footprints to determine the speed of a running tyrannosaurus rex; they were expected to understand the interconnections between concepts; they considered the relations between Mendelian genetics and heritable variation; they discussed whether evolutionary principles can offer insights into the demographic transition. Although the course has always had a high enrolment (250–300 students per semester), another feature of the BISC

102 course was that students are required to write an ecology essay based on reading from scholarly articles. Some preparatory assignments and the opportunity to revise drafts had long been part of this assignment, because in fifteen years of teaching, I had seen first-hand that writing is an excellent tool to motivate students and that students write to learn and, with careful feedback and the opportunity for revision, they learn to write.

Modifying the essay

I had been calling this assignment an "ecology essay" since the subject matter was to deal with a feature of ecology. When I decided to pilot 102 as a W-course, I met with Wendy Strachan, the director of CWIL, to begin our collaboration to plan the modifications needed to meet the W-criteria. Wendy began by asking me what I hoped to achieve with this ecology essay assignment and why I thought it was important to introduce first-year general biology students to primary literature. Those questions established us in a relationship where we were both learning and inquiring as we worked through the various constituents of the course. I explained that, in a very real sense, science is its primary literature. Scientists communicate with one another and share their findings with the world through peer-reviewed articles in printed or online journals. Science is not the body of facts and ideas summarized in a general biology textbook. It is the constantly changing, heavily qualified understanding of the natural world recounted in scholarly articles in peer-reviewed journals. I wanted students to understand and be able to distinguish between the simplified versions of scientific findings that journalists write for newspapers and popular magazines and scientists' own reports in primary, scholarly articles. Students in a general biology course may be taking a single laboratory course required by an education or arts major; they may be planning for a career as a doctor or a biologist. Whatever their intended path, students need to be educated and critical consumers of scientific information.

First-year students find it easier to understand scholarly articles on ecology than such articles on cell or molecular biology. Thus, it seems reasonable to me to require students to read primary sources in order to gain an understanding of an aspect of ecology. The ecology essay assignment required them to locate one article in popular science literature and five scholarly articles that bore some relation to the same topic. They were to use these articles as background material to write a 1500-word essay that clearly and simply explained an ecological topic of current interest in the field. Students had several problems with this assignment. Many asked me to clarify the intent of the essay. I advised them that their goal should be to

summarize their topic in an essay that could be read without further explanation by a fellow student in the class. Some students were unsatisfied with
this response. Plagiarism was a continuing problem in BISC 102. Students
charged with plagiarizing their source articles pleaded that they could not
clearly explain the material in the primary articles in their own words.
They felt they had no choice but to use the wording of the original article.
Some students did not understand how to paraphrase and cite from source
material. In any academic subject, students must learn to explain ideas in
their own words and to credit the source of those ideas appropriately. In
their essays, they needed to paraphrase and cite sources appropriately and
to provide an accurate list of the literature cited in the essay.

Wendy suggested that part of the reason for students' difficulty was that
they did not have a good sense of what the finished product should look
and sound like. She queried me about the professional genres in the discipline that would draw on several sources to summarize a topic. One of the
biology journals that would be quite accessible to students and did indeed
include pieces with that purpose was the journal *BioScience*. This journal
is intended for a general science audience. Articles are peer- reviewed,
secondary reviews of current topics in biology. They serve as "overviews"
of topics. Sources are cited and a list of literature cited is included in
each article. This would be a genre that could achieve the objectives of
the assignment, would enable students to imagine an audience, and since
there were many examples in the journals they would be reading, they
would better understand its purpose as well as what their own version
might look and sound like. Since we had decided on a target genre, the
"overview article," we next began to plan how to scaffold students' work
toward the finished product.

We developed a set of preliminary assignments: the *annotated bibliography*, due early in the semester, would include full citations and summaries
for both the popular article and the primary, scholarly articles selected by
the student. This assignment ensured that students started on the major
assignment in a timely manner. It gave TAs the opportunity to assess
whether students understood the difference between popular articles
and primary, scholarly articles, and also to determine whether they had
located articles relevant to their chosen topic. The annotated bibliography
also gave students an opportunity to cite their articles correctly. An *abstract
analysis* would be due two weeks later. The purpose of this step was to help
students read research articles with an understanding of how they are
structured. They selected one of their own articles and used the abstract
as a cue to the overall structure by linking each sentence in the abstract

to content in the body of the article. The assignment gave students the opportunity to analyze the organization of a primary source by identifying the kinds of information provided in the introduction, methods, results, discussion and conclusion sections. The *paraphrasing assignment* would be due two weeks before the draft overview article was due. Students selected one paragraph from each of three of their own primary articles, each of the source paragraphs dealing with the same aspect of their topic. They then wrote a 200-word summary drawing on the information from all three paragraphs. The likelihood of some redundancy in the originals or of different perspectives, as well as the limit on length, made it fairly easy for students to avoid copying exact phrasing and to grasp the purpose and meaning of paraphrasing. The source articles had to be cited correctly and a full reference list provided along with the paraphrase. This "anti-plagiarism" assignment provided students with an opportunity to organize and write a paragraph that clearly and simply explained their understanding of their topic, to paraphrase and cite sources appropriately, and to provide an accurate list of the literature cited in the essay. TAs could readily identify and assist students who might need help. Students had the opportunity to learn this crucial skill in a relatively low-stakes assignment.

These changes were greatly beneficial to students, providing them with the necessary tools to meet the objectives of what I recognized was a challenging assignment. They had a much clearer understanding of the intent of the ecology assignment when provided with a model from the literature. The preliminary assignments described above were also diagnostic, allowing TAs to identify students requiring extra help. They were formative, providing TAs with an opportunity to teach and students with an opportunity to practice the skills necessary in the final high-stakes ecology overview article. Once they had done a draft, students met one-on-one with TAs in 30-minute meetings. The one-on-one meeting gave students the opportunity to see how a skilled reader responded to their writing. TAs were instructed not to pre-read the drafts, which had been submitted in advance. Instead, the TA read the drafts with the student, often aloud. This gave the TA an opportunity to reflect and comment on how they understood what the student had written, and to point out misunderstandings of the content, the appearance of technical terms that were not defined, and flaws in grammar or sentence structure. At the same time, students could ask the TA questions about the biological content or about the structure of the article. Students could clarify where improvement was needed and try out possible improvements.

Writing to learn: adding lab questions

Students in BISC 102 were evaluated at mid-term and at the end of the semester in timed exams. Both exams required one or more short essay-type answers to questions. As we reviewed the course and its requirements, Wendy raised the question of how we might prepare students to write answers on the exam. Their lab books required them to complete information about their processes and observations, but not to link ideas and information around the concepts they were learning. Since this was one of my goals, that they understand the relationships among facts, it made sense that we should create an opportunity for them to practice forming those relationships and making connections in their own words before they were asked to do that on the exam. We added writing assignments to the weekly laboratory sessions in the form of questions about the biological concepts the lab work had illustrated. Half of these would be treated as low stakes and students would hand them in for completion marks. The other half were graded. The low-stakes answers would be useful to the TAs to assess student understanding of challenging topics, to the instructor to develop subsequent laboratory questions, and to the students to demonstrate that they had completed assigned laboratory readings. High-stakes questions would address the most challenging and subtle of the topics encountered in the laboratory each week, requiring students to master high-order cognitive tasks in order to do well. TAs would mark the laboratory questions for students in their tutorial sections, providing feedback to individuals and reviewing answers for the group.

In developing the laboratory questions, I called on Wendy to give me some feedback on the wording. I was eager to challenge the students, but also wanted to be clear and consistent in my messages to them about the purpose and use of these questions. They were not intended to be tests. They were to provide practice in writing about the biological concepts and to help students think through what they had learned and noticed from their lab work. It was useful to me to have an outside reader, particularly someone who would not make assumptions about the meaning and was not familiar with the biology. Wendy was able to read for the logic and think about the reader's perspective, which helped me be more aware of the assumptions and expectations embedded in each question, what each question assumed the students knew and what it expected them to do.

For example, on a question based on "The Nature of Inheritance," Wendy's e-mailed reply invited me to think about my use of the word "accounts" in the following question posted to students: "State Mendel's

Law of Independent Inheritance. Explain how the behavior of chromo-somes during meiosis *accounts* for this law." Wendy's response: "*Probably my ignorance here—but does 'accounts for the law' identify the relationship you intend? Is the behavior evidence of the law? Was it observation of the behavior that led to the law?*"

And on the same topic, I asked students to "Explain how a diploid and a haploid cell differ from each other." Wendy's response drew my attention to my assumptions and led me to consider whether they were actually tacit or had been made explicit to the students: "*I assume here that there are obvi-ous aspects/dimensions of the differences that you are asking them to identify—that they could not give you differences that are not significant and would be differences but not count?*"

She raised several questions about the following assignment about human evolution:

1. What caused the extinction of the woolly mammoth? Suggest one or more hypotheses, and summarize the evidence for (and against) each hypothesis that you mention.

Joan, when you ask them to "suggest one or more hypotheses," what will be the basis on which they would propose them? Is the assignment a matter of reading the articles and picking out the correct information and then summarizing it? Are they to deal with some conflicting evidence or arguments? It sounds as if they are select-ing material and reporting back so you know they have understood the readings and can accurately summarize it. If that's the case, I'm not sure why you say "suggest." Will they be choosing?

2. Describe how Neanderthals and anatomically modern humans dif-fered from each other.

Are there certain differences that they should attend to and not others? Do they describe first and then answer the questions in a and b?

3. What happened to the Neanderthals? Did they go extinct, and if so, why? Are they our ancestors (i.e., did they interbreed with modern humans)?

Suggest one or more hypotheses, and summarize the evidence for (and against) each hypothesis that you mention.

Again I wonder about "suggest." Might you say "present one or two?" And then, I wonder if there are competing hypotheses that they need to examine and explain the "for" and "against." Sorry, but it's not clear to me exactly what's happening and partly of course that's because I don't know the sources. . . .

Writing answers to the lab questions had been meant in part as practice for answering an essay question on the exams. In both, I wanted to see that students could go beyond simply reporting what they had found in carrying out directions in the lab. I wanted to see some sophistication in their analysis and hoped to prompt them to notice subtleties. Wendy's responses helped me to word these questions in ways that made my purposes and expectations clearer, but she could not know whether these purposes and expectations were realistic for first-year students. Each question emphasized a difficult and subtle aspect of a key concept from that week's material, and students became somewhat frustrated by the graded questions. As one of the TAs pointed out later, they were so challenging that the feedback on one did not apply to the next, so improvement became impossible for some of the students, even though they worked hard and took the assignment very seriously. The TAs helped me understand that, despite my intentions, the questions had not fulfilled the formative purpose and did not provide students with the opportunity to practice skills necessary to do well on the final laboratory examination.

Teaching assistants for BISC 102

As course instructor taking on a pilot W-course with 14 TAs, I also took on the task of marking student assignments for two of the tutorials so that I could understand what was involved in the W-course experience for the TAs and also be able to assess the TA training provided by CWIL. I wanted to feel confident that the TAs would be able to provide effective instruction, feedback, and marking of student writing. Thanks in part to the training and in part to our regular weekly meetings, the TAs proved very successful as instructors and markers for writing assignments. In working with them to develop effective rubrics, I gained considerable insight into the flaws and strengths of writing assignments that I had developed and modified over the course of a decade, as well as into the problems TAs were noticing with the new lab questions assignment. The rubrics played a dual role. They proved to be excellent tools for instructing students as they approached writing assignments, and they also guided marking and feedback on completed assignments. The CWIL training sessions addressed a number of important topics that we were able to draw on in our course planning meetings: incorporating low-stakes writing in the course, clarifying the objectives of assignments for students, providing instruction on reading scholarly articles, developing effective rubrics, and providing meaningful feedback on student writing. I found all these TA training sessions enormously useful for myself as well. They helped me to develop and deliver effective instruction on writing in lectures and to provide meaningful feedback to students when responding to drafts or final assignments.

Future directions

Although I was very pleased with the outcomes for student learning in the course and with the writing, which had again confirmed me in insisting on its importance in science, it was clear that both students and TAs were on overload. I needed to make some adjustments if this course was to be acceptable to the department and be certified as a W-course on an ongoing basis. The pilot had served its purpose. We had figured out what to do and what to change. When I next teach BISC 102, I plan to develop a new set of questions that address the objectives of each week's laboratory session. The questions will be similar to those found on the final lab examination. They will show whether students are able to integrate concepts encountered in different laboratories, interpret novel information based on concepts learned in laboratory, interpret data from experiments, or plan experiments to test hypotheses. I will administer a brief test in lecture after students have completed two laboratories. This 20-minute marked test will include two laboratory questions from Weeks 1 and 2. Class performance on this test will be used as baseline data to allow for comparison of marks on the final laboratory examination in the two semesters, since I want to see whether we are accomplishing our purposes in assigning the questions and the writing. Eventually, I propose to have some of the questions submitted to the TAs for completion marks and used to plan lab discussions and tutorials as before. But I also want to introduce a method of peer review and have peers respond to other questions. This was something we did not have time to prepare adequately in the first iteration of the W-version of the course. For the peer-review process, we will try working with an Internet-based tool developed by UCLA, Calibrated Peer Review™ (CPR). This system helps students learn how to use a rubric through a "calibration" process, so that they can effectively mark their own writing and the writing of their classmates.

Instructors use the CPR to develop writing assignments, which students complete online. Students then fill in detailed rubrics (developed by the instructor) and mark three sample "calibration" assignments. They then compare their own completed rubrics and assigned marks to those provided by the instructor. When students have mastered the calibration exercise, they use the rubric to mark three anonymous peer assignments and, finally, to mark their own assignments. This seems like an effective method for enabling students to read for particular features in a piece of text and to learn how to assess them in relation to each other. I am eager to try it.

THE TA'S PERSPECTIVE: W-CRITERIA AND TUTORIALS (ERIN BARLEY)

When I applied to be a TA for BISC 102 as a W-course, it was the right opportunity at the right time. I had just completed a Master of science in biology and was happy for part-time work while I began to search for a job. I had really enjoyed TA-ing this course in past semesters and was at least tentatively hoping to pursue a career in teaching. I was especially interested to learn that BISC 102 was being offered as a W-course as I felt from experience that there was a real need to develop and support writing skills in science students. As an added bonus, I hoped that involvement with the W-initiative would help me professionally.

Pre-W TA experience in 102

Right from my first semester as a TA, I really enjoyed BISC 102 for both its content and format. It is very much an ideas-based course and covers many topics related to the broad fields of evolution and ecology—for example, natural selection, genetics, animal behavior, and human evolution. The broad scope of the course was at first challenging as it required a lot of review and even self-teaching to keep on top of the material. At the same time, I found it very rewarding to return to some of the topics I had ploughed through as an undergraduate, and to be able to appreciate and integrate the material on a whole new level.

In each lab section (up to 40 students), the lab instructor, Joan Sharp, was supported by two or three TAs. Typically, we assisted the students with microscopes and instructions and answered questions about the lab content. However, the generous ratio of TAs to students also allowed us to circulate and engage students in discussions that went beyond the basics—how does this exercise relate to the lab's theme? What is the evolutionary reason for this observation? Why did not this experiment produce the expected results? Additionally, it gave us the opportunity to talk with interested students about research, in general, and our own research projects, in particular.

As a new graduate student, I was very impressed with the level of responsibility we TAs were given. Each semester I was assigned one or two tutorial groups (12–20 students each) and given both the freedom and responsibility of coming up with an original 50-minute lesson plan each week to support material already covered in lectures and labs. In my first semester, I was both excited and nervous about the prospect of planning and running a whole 50-minute tutorial. I attended several workshops offered by the university on topics such as preparing for the first tutorial, leading group discussions, and dissipating student fears. These were quite helpful. However, I still found myself guessing which topics students needed help with most, as I experimented with different approaches to teaching. From experience, I learned to balance mini-review lectures, question and answer sessions, and interactive games or activities, all in a 50-minute block.

As a new TA, I found it very informative to mark my first batch of exams. I was surprised at first to find that students had not done as well as I had hoped. It was a disappointment to see students perform poorly on some of the topics that I thought I had explained so clearly in tutorials, and that the students had said they understood. It emphasized to me the importance of tests not just as a means of evaluating student performance, but also as a means of assessing student comprehension in order to guide our teaching efforts. While weak content in some of the answers surprised me, what shocked me more was the weak writing of many students. Some of the answers were so poorly written or awkwardly worded that they really made little if any sense at all. Many semesters of marking confirm this as a too common problem: answers that contain key words but that lack the basic grammar and vocabulary necessary to demonstrate that the student understands the key words and the relationships among them. One student approached me with her marked exam and asked that I re-read her answer for more possible part marks. I re-read her answer. It was an answer that, to my reading, contained a couple of key words buried in a completely meaningless mess of words that showed no comprehension or clarity of thought. I was floored—not only had she written a nonsensical answer, but she seemed unable to judge for herself the poor quality of her answer.

Learning to write in a scientific style

With the introduction of a writing-intensive approach to the course, our group of 14 TAs (up from the usual eight to ten) was given a weekly training session. We used these to discuss how to teach and evaluate writing, the relationship between writing and learning, and characteristics of scientific writing. The most important realization that I came away with from our first meeting was that like the other TAs (who completed their undergraduate degrees at various universities across Canada), I was never provided with any formal instruction on how to write in a scientific style. Furthermore, although I was never *taught* how to write in a scientific style,

I was often *expected* to write undergraduate papers in a scientific style. For example, I remember a second-year course where we were asked to assemble a proposal (never having read a proposal myself) and to include an abstract (having no idea what an abstract was or how it was different from an introduction).

I also remember comments made by professors and TAs on assignments or to the class as a whole on "what we were expecting and didn't get," and thinking that if only they had presented "what we expect" more clearly before we did the assignments, they might have gotten it! Without exception, my instructors were much better at critiquing writing than at teaching it. My experiences were fairly typical of those of my fellow TAs. If anything, I was fortunate to have completed my undergraduate work at a university where papers and reports were an important component of most courses. By the end of four years, I had worked through enough trial and error to have developed some scientific writing skills.

Also surprising to me was the realization during our first CWIL training meeting that there was a skill to reading scientific material and that without knowing it, we (the TAs) had learned this too from experience. For example, one does not need to begin with the Introduction and then proceed through the Materials, Results, and so on, grasping one section fully before moving on to the next. It is perfectly acceptable and often even advisable to jump forward and back, and to skip entire sections. Reading to learn is not necessarily linear reading (as a novel might be) but requires frequent re-reading, cross-referencing, and summarizing.

TA-ing the ecology assignment: A teaching and learning situation for me as the TA

One of the objectives of the W-initiative was to provide some instruction on how to write in a scientific style. Joan has already detailed the process that we used to scaffold students as they worked toward a finished essay. From my point of view, as the TA giving the instruction for these steps in the tutorial, I found it very helpful to be able to focus on one specific aspect of writing at a time. For example, one week I discussed some of the differences between paraphrasing and plagiarism. Another week, I put up a sample of scientific writing and discussed the placement of references in the text. Following each assignment, I reviewed common errors in tutorials. This allowed me to provide more detailed feedback to supplement the brief comments on individual assignments. Students often had more questions after an assignment than they did before. Following the paraphrasing exercise, they had many excellent questions on the use of references and the correct format for in-text citation. Although the paraphrasing assignment was done, these questions were still relevant as the students were able to incorporate this information into their essay. The assignments also raised other interesting points. For example, students who selected review papers had trouble with the abstract analysis as it was better suited to data papers. I used this as a starting point for discussing different types of scholarly papers, such as data and review papers.

Reading and providing constructive comments on the assignments also proved to be very useful to me as it taught me a lot about how to write well myself. Although I had written several abstracts before, I had never been taught how to do so. It was enlightening to learn that there is a precise structure to a well-written abstract: each sentence should link to a specific section of the text, in the same order as it appears in the text, and all major sections (Introduction, Methods, Results and so on) should be covered. Delightfully simple! Reading 40 abstract analyses clarified the value and qualities of a well-written abstract. This was reinforced when several students had trouble with the assignment, and it turned out to be because the articles they had selected had poorly written abstracts. By the end of the three assignments, the students had improved their writing skills and were familiar with their topic in general as well as with how it was detailed in their selected articles. They then prepared a first draft of their essay. To get them started, I put up an example of the genre of review paper in tutorial and briefly discussed the characteristics and content of a Title, Abstract, Introduction, Main body, and Conclusion. I used the sample review paper to show them what style of writing they were aiming for and to illustrate the importance of subtitles. The assignments proved to have warmed the students up well: compared with other semesters, the students showed *much* more interest and initiative in asking questions about how to write about their topic and how to use citation in their essays.

Each student submitted a first draft of their essay for comments from their TA. We were budgeted a generous 30-minute meeting with each student to discuss their paper in person. We were instructed in our weekly writing-intensive training not to pre-read the papers, but rather to read the essay aloud to the student, and to comment as we went. I admit to being rather skeptical about this approach, but was quickly won over. This was an extremely effective way of providing personal constructive criticism. I began each meeting by asking the student first if there was anything in particular that they had found difficult or wanted help with. By allowing students to identify their own weaknesses, I hoped to make it clear to the student that I was not just there to find and expose their errors, but rather to provide support and instruction. For the first time, I read each essay aloud in the presence of the student. This allowed the student to see my honest response to their writing as I read. I thought aloud too. I commented on catchy titles, well-chosen vocabulary, and the strengths of each section. I also commented on awkward writing, missing links between ideas, and poorly structured sections. If I was confused, I asked questions to show exactly why I was confused and allowed the student to explain his/her thoughts. I corrected minor errors. For bigger grammatical or structural errors, I refrained from making the changes myself and instead tried to provide the students with the advice and tools necessary for them to make the changes themselves. Through the whole process, it was the student's responsibility to record corrections and suggestions on a second copy of the essay. It became clear to me as I worked through these meetings, that my role as a TA was not at all that of an editor, but really that of a teacher or a mentor.

Judging by the students' comments, I think they found this exercise helpful. I expect too, that as first-year students many of them probably benefited from these meetings far more than they realized. The stronger writers got positive feedback on *why* their writing was strong, and were given advice on how to transform their writing from good to excellent and even sophisticated. The weaker writers benefited from individual advice and discussions on how to improve structure and content. In the end, I was quite impressed with (and even proud of!) the final essays. Many of the papers showed definite improvements, and some even showed touches of sophistication that I would not normally have expected in a first-year essay.

The effects of weekly writing assignments on tutorials

When I began the writing-intensive pilot project, I assumed that the main goal was to provide some much needed instruction and feedback to students on how to write clearly and concisely. However, what quickly became apparent to me in our training sessions was that the writing initiative was not just about developing writing skills, but also very much about using writing as a tool for learning. Listening to lectures, taking notes, and reading can be passive, but writing as a composing process always engages the mind. In our training sessions, we explored ways to incorporate low-stakes (non-graded) writing in tutorials as a tool for brainstorming, reflection, and communicating with students.

As part of the writing initiative, students were expected to hand in answers to a weekly question set related to lab material. We read over the assignments and provided comments every week, and grades every second week. I used these assignments to find and address common writing errors with students. In tutorials, I gave mini lessons on simple grammatical items such as *its* versus *it's* and *effect* versus *affect*. Students responded well to these, and in one case a student was actually quite excited to learn for the first time that there was a reason for the use of *fewer* versus *less*. With a number of grammatical points, the students appeared simply never to have been taught the rules before or certainly had not remembered them.

Additionally, the assignments provided an opportunity to address the topic of how to read and interpret questions. On an exam, students often feel stressed and rushed and will sometimes fail to fully answer the question that was asked. On an assignment, failure to fully answer the question suggests sloppy reading or interpretation. As an example, when asked to "describe two differences between objects A and B," a number of students will list *two* states of *a single* difference, for example, "object A is red, and object B is blue." Or, when students were asked to consider the costs and benefits of two aphid responses to stress (staying or walking), some discussed the costs of one response (staying) versus the benefits of the second response (walking), rather than the costs versus benefits of each individual response. The assignments provided an opportunity for me to bring these types of errors to the students' attention.

Sometimes students will get stuck or even give up on a question that is long and has lots of terminology. I suggested the students de-code a question by working from the last word back to the first. I use, for instance, the question: "Does a large selection differential for a particular trait guarantee that natural selection will favor directional selection for that trait?" First, we consider the word *trait*, and propose a trait like the size of frogs. Then, we can consider *directional selection for that trait*. Directional selection simply means that a trait will change in a specific direction. For example, the size of frogs will increase. *Natural selection* should bring to mind three necessary conditions: a trait (frog size) must vary in the population, it must be heritable, and frogs of different size must be more/less fit relative to each other. We can now consider whether frog size meets the conditions of natural selection. Finally, we note that there is *a large selection differential for a particular trait*. This simply means that a trait has changed in a population over time. In other words, the size of frogs now is different (larger) than it used to be. Put it all together, and we get "Does the difference between past and present frog size guarantee that natural selection will favor larger frogs?" Or, because the question was generalized to include any trait, "Does a difference in a trait between past and present generations guarantee that natural selection will favor a change in that trait?"

This question is certainly challenging because of the amount of (excessive) terminology it contains. However, it is all terminology that the students have encountered in lectures and the text, and so it should be decipherable by a reasonably determined student. Working through it backwards is a good test of students' comprehension of the terms.

From the perspective of learning content, the assignments were very useful to both the students and me. They forced students to review and think about each week's material on an ongoing basis. This made them better prepared to discuss the week's material in tutorials, and to bring up their own questions. The assignments also provided me with insights into student understanding and misunderstanding, and helped me to figure out where exactly the misunderstandings lay. In earlier semesters, I had guessed at problem topics when planning lessons and had been surprised at misunderstandings in exam answers. With the writing assignments, I was better able to identify problem topics and to gear my lessons around these.

In fact, the assignments were so effective at highlighting important topics that I sometimes had more topics than could be covered in a weekly hour of tutorial. For example, we can seek two types of causes for an animal's behavior: a proximate *how* cause and an ultimate *why* cause. In earlier semesters, I had gone over causation with each tutorial group and thought that I had done a good job of explaining the two question types. The assignments taught me for the first time that students were quick to memorize which was the *how* and which the *why* question, but few of them knew how to apply these words to causation. As a result of the assignments, I changed my approach and downplayed the one-word questions in favor of longer more meaningful questions such as "how is this behavior *triggered?*" and "why has *natural selection favored* this behavior?"

The assignments also helped me to identify topics that I did not need to cover. Meiosis is a terminology- and detail-heavy biological process, and I had to spend a lot of time on it in tutorials. I was quite surprised to find that one of my tutorial groups did very well on the meiosis question of their assignment. Rather than boring them with a long lesson, I was able to hit on a couple of small points in tutorial, then move on to other topics.

Better understanding and knowing students

Another consequence of the writing assignments was that I got to know my students better. My Friday tutorial group was an interesting but challenging mix of students: as a group they were very reluctant to either ask questions or offer answers. They were generally shy, but there was more to it than that. From their writing, I was able to figure out that there were several students who were very bright, did not have questions about the material, and were not challenged by my general questions. At the same time, there were a number of students who found the material and my questions very challenging, perhaps to the point of being intimidated. The dichotomy seemed to be stronger in this tutorial group than in others I had worked with, and I suspect the split made many of the students feel awkward in tutorial. While this group remained a challenge, the assignments did help me to assess the abilities of individual students (despite their reluctance to participate) and to direct more appropriate questions to individual students.

In contrast, my Wednesday tutorial was a very cohesive group, and made my job easy by asking and answering a lot of questions. I think much of this had to do with the personalities of individual students in the tutorial group. However, this group had an additional advantage that came about entirely by accident. For logistical reasons, this tutorial group (the Wednesday group) turned assignments in to my office door, whereas the Friday tutorial group handed them to me during lecture. By the end of the second week of classes, every student in my Wednesday tutorial group knew exactly where my office was. Once they were already at my door, students were much more likely to stop in with a "quick" or "not very important" question. I think I had more students from that Wednesday tutorial group show up for office hours than all four of my other tutorial groups, past and present combined. The more I saw of them, the better I was able to assess their understanding and plan lessons accordingly. The more they saw of me, the more comfortable they became asking questions of me both in and out of tutorials.

The assignments provided an additional means of evaluating the students throughout the semester. There were both positives and negatives to this. I had expected that receiving grades on the assignments would provide the feedback necessary for students to improve their answers through the semester. This, in turn, would better prepare them for writing the lab exam, which they must pass to pass the course. In reality, there was a downside to the graded assignments. The assignments tested students simultaneously on their abilities to interpret a question and their comprehension of some challenging topics and subtle points. As a result, students did more poorly than they expected. With the first couple of assignments, the students were not too upset. They resolved to correct their mistakes and work harder on the next assignment. However, because the students were expected to grasp challenging and subtle concepts each week, the marks did not necessarily improve, and students got quite frustrated. I had the sense that students took low-assignment marks to heart much more than they did low exam marks. I think this is in part because many students really did work hard at the assignments, they thought they had done well on them, and the assignments had been marked by me, not put into the whole pool to be marked by more anonymous TAs. These feelings were reflected in my poor ranking with them on the "grades fairly" section of my TA evaluation!

In the end it was clear that the weekly assignments were most valuable as a learning/teaching tool rather than an assessment tool. The greatest benefits of the assignments were that students became more engaged with the lab material, they developed reading and writing skills, and they helped us assess student understanding on an ongoing basis and adjust our tutorial lessons accordingly. In future, I think the students would benefit more if the assignments focused on testing general concepts and developing writing skills, rather than testing for subtle details. Marks would likely be higher, and student frustration would decrease. Higher marks could be compensated for by decreasing the value of the assignments in the grading scheme so as not to end up with inflated marks. Another benefit of the assignments was that they stimulated discussions of lab material between the instructor, Joan Sharp, and the TAs. With a couple of assignments, it became clear that even we, TAs, had missed out on some of the more subtle details of the lab concepts!

What difference does it make to writing-intensive a course or not? Outcomes of the pilot experience

A year after working as a writing-intensive TA, I was hired as a sessional instructor to teach the lab component of BISC 102 while one of the other biology professors taught the lecture component. With the writing-intensive pilot project over (Joan Sharp was on sabbatical), the 102 course returned to its old format. Lecture material was presented on PowerPoint and with most other course material available online, students wrote very little. The absence of the writing assignments and the lost benefits to students' writing skills reinforced my appreciation for the importance of teaching writing in biology.

Following in the traditional format for the lab part of the course, students' marks were based on their performance on an end-of-semester lab exam, which they are required to pass in order to pass the course. This exam is an open-book and uses short answers for questions to test the ability to explain and apply the concepts they have learned. Students are thus simultaneously being tested on their comprehension of the material, and their ability to explain it clearly. Without the weekly writing assignments, the students had very little practice expressing their ideas in writing. Many of them told me that they had a hard time judging the level of detail and amount of information expected of them on an exam. In fact, some students actually suggested to me that it would be useful to have regular assignments that accompany the labs. As the instructor for the labs, and as result of my work in the W-pilot project and such student comments, I am currently re-designing the lab component of the course to include regular writing assignments.

The professor for the traditional format BISC 102 course still included an ecology assignment (without instructional components leading up to it) which the TAs and I administered. Here, I found myself guilty of the same failings I criticized earlier in others: I expected scientific writing from the students, but did not spend much time instructing students on how to write and cite the references in a scientific style. This was because there was already a heavy workload in the labs, and I felt that too much time talking about writing without accompanying practice exercises (which I did not have the time or resources to administer) would be of limited help. While I did not have time to teach the students *how to write,* I did at least try to provide them with clear information on *what was expected of them.* I developed a marking rubric (listing expectations with respect to format, content, referencing and style) for the assignment, and made it available to the marking TA and to students at the start of the semester. The responsibility then fell on the students to meet the criteria outlined in the rubric and to seek help when needed.

The difference between their writing in the ecology essay and that of the students in Joan's W-pilot was striking. A surprising number of papers showed borderline and in some cases blatant and extensive plagiarism. This was despite warnings that I made in lab and online that students must "rephrase the information or ideas into *[their] own words,* and *cite [their] sources* appropriately. *Failure to do so may constitute plagiarism.*" While ignorance is not an excuse, I did find that this type of assignment was so unfamiliar to some students that they really had no sense of the seriousness of what they had done. When I discussed the problem with them, it was clear that some had absolutely no experience at assimilating information from different sources, writing in their own words, and citing their sources. In fact, a few stated outright that they did not know how to write in their own words. This only reinforced for me the value from the writing-intensive pilot project of the skill development exercises leading up to the final essay. I was also quite impressed to find that several students recognized the need for instruction and came to me with their already graded ecology essays to seek advice on how to improve their writing on future assignments. Most of their questions related to paraphrasing and citing sources properly. A couple of students even asked for a course on scientific writing.

The W-course as professional development

Working through the W-course and then contrasting that experience in the same course without a W-framework, made me deeply aware of the benefits to me professionally of the W-pilot. The experience stimulated me as an instructor to think about how students learn, what they need from us and what tools are available (such as low-stakes writing) to engage them in thinking through complex ideas? What do we take for granted? What skills do we not teach but expect them to learn: how to study, how to interpret a question, how to ask questions?

My involvement in the initiative stimulated me to think about the relationship between understanding and writing. I expect I will continue to dwell for a while on the question of whether poor answers result from whether they write poorly or think poorly or both? Or is it a chicken and egg situation—they do not write well because their ideas are unclear to them, and they are unclear because they lack the ability to describe nuances in writing. I also found that students were unable to judge their own abilities, so the Ecology essay and components that led up to it did a great job of breaking down the task of writing an essay (overwhelming to some) into manageable components and skill sets. Tutorial questions were very useful, as I felt better able to assess student comprehension (as a class and as individuals) on material. I got to know my students better. I think with the increased interaction they got to know me better too.

THE WRITING CONSULTANT'S PERSPECTIVE: ON THE BISC 102 COLLABORATION AND THE OUTCOMES IN STUDENT WRITING (WENDY STRACHAN)

Although large, first-year, lecture–tutorial courses had been offered as pilot W-courses in the History and Humanities departments with several TAs, Joan's course was the first to be offered in the sciences and with an increased number of TAs to accommodate the additional workload. The big difference from courses in the Humanities was that TAs' assignment in the sciences includes not only lecture and tutorial time but also hours in the lab. With the adjustment in workload for a W-course, more TAs needed to be attached to a course in science than in the Humanities, even though the total number of students might be similar. Thus, Joan's wish to make BISC 102 a W-course met with some resistance from the biology department. Despite the reduction in number of tutorials and thus students for whom each TA was responsible in a W-course, there was still concern that the workload would detract from the graduate students' commitment and time for their own research and coursework. There was also widespread concern that many of the science graduate students lacked the writing or English language skills needed for effective instruction and response to student writing. Although Joan was given permission to go ahead and redesign the course as a pilot W-course, the department made no commitment to regularize it and have it certified as a W-course. They reasoned that Joan was not the only faculty member who would always be teaching the course, others could not be obliged to do so—which has already been the case as Erin notes in her account above—and that a supply of competent graduate students could not be guaranteed. Given the department's reluctance about modifying 102 as a W-course, the large number of inexperienced TAs, and the adjustments of time and workload that would be required, one of our goals, as noted at the beginning of this chapter, was to inquire into the feasibility of such a project. We chose to do that by documenting and reflecting on our process, interviewing TAs, surveying students, and analyzing samples of student writing. In this final section, I analyze these sources to tease out implications from our experience for the implementation of the writing initiative overall and to identify what seemed to be meaningful outcomes for student learning and writing.

First year W-courses in biology: TAs' observations on feasibility

Joan was advised that TAs who were assigned to her must have a choice about participating in the writing instruction and marking components of the course as additions to their usual responsibility for lab supervision. This caveat could have made it logistically impossible to offer BISC 102 as a W-course. Some instructors might have been deterred by this response which was not simply indifference but quite active opposition. Joan, however, persevered and found all but one of the TAs willing and even enthusiastic about participating in her pilot. It seems likely that this willingness could be attributed partly to Joan's reputation of being a "super approachable" person to work with and to her enthusiasm. She showed her commitment concretely in taking on the extra tutorial herself and in assuring all the TAs that she would do any marking they were unable to complete within their contracted hours.

Joan's presentation of participation in the W-course convinced the TAs that although their responsibilities would be somewhat different, there would be advantages for them in the experience. In post-course interviews with eight of the twelve TAs who joined the course (the remaining TAs not being available for the interview process), individuals confirmed Joan's description. They reported that the experience had met their expectations that "we would get to know the students better, we'd have a chance to work with a small group as opposed to being responsible for a lot of students" and that "it would be a good experience to learn more about marking essays and that sort of thing which we don't usually have a chance to do." All agreed that the success of the course overall depended very largely on the instructor: her energy and commitment inspired them and, among themselves, as one person noted, "it was really valuable in the beginning of the semester to be in a room with a group of people who were all actually interested in teaching." That agreement notwithstanding, as well as agreement that they were impressed by the effects of their instruction on student writing and the kinds of improvement they were able to see, their reports on the experience pointed to issues that needed to be taken into account, but that did not necessarily challenge the feasibility of offering such a large first-year course as a W-course. Among these issues were workloads for students, the struggles of English as a Second Language (ESL) students with comprehension and expression, and assignment scheduling.

As Joan and Erin noted above, the lab questions required a level of sophisticated understanding that undermined the informal learning purpose of the questions and created a heavier workload for students than was intended. The TAs comments on the lab questions supported the practice of doing these short and regular pieces of writing that would assist understanding, but they recommended a different format, less strictly marked, that would be less overwhelming. Joan has already decided how to respond to that problem in future iterations of the course. In addition to the lab questions, students had the major review assignment intended to teach them how to read scientific articles and write in an appropriate scientific style. All the TAs reported on the value of the staged process attached to this review assignment. One of the TAs summarized his thoughts on what students had gained in terms of "now these students know how to reference material properly and write in a reasonable way and that will benefit them in all the courses they take now in biology as well as other areas." Another spoke in favor of the staged process based on his own experience as a student in the course some years ago when no such process was involved. Others pointed out the value for the TAs as writers themselves: "I think it's very valuable for your own writing and editing, especially if the TA wants to go on and do research or be a prof or go into education . . . I didn't know how a scientific paper was written till I was in grad school . . . my learning as an undergrad was by trial and error."

The struggles of ESL students were a major concern for all the TAs. Of the 244 students in the course, 105 reported that they did not speak English in the parental home, which implied these students would fall somewhere on a continuum of English language ability. The TAs felt that the university's accepting ESL students in the W-courses was "setting them up to fail . . . in a course like this where, to a certain extent, their mark becomes more contingent on their ability to express themselves in writing, it puts them at a huge disadvantage . . . I would say that none of them would have been able to achieve an A in the course, regardless of how good their understanding might be of the course material." (While one might query the claim that understanding is distinct from ability to express it, the ESL students' habit of relying on translation for comprehension certainly makes it possible for them to substitute rote memorization of wordings for understanding. It calls into question, however, the goals of education in an English-speaking institution and is not a problem to be taken up here.) The TAs urged the creation of resources outside the course structure since they were unable to spend the additional time the ESL students needed. While these needs will not go away, we did not see them as affecting the feasibility of making BISC 102 a W-course. The university has specified new entrance requirements intended to channel students into a new Foundations in Academic Literacy (FAL) program to prepare them for W-courses if they meet other standards but have difficulty writing in English. The university is also establishing a new Student Learning Commons with a writing centre, where students will be able to access one-on-one tutorial help with writing. These resources did not exist when Joan was offering her W-course.

Assignment scheduling was a logistical problem because of the number of tutorials which were scattered at various times across the week and did not coincide with TA training sessions in ways that would allow all TAs to gain from instruction about topics like giving feedback or helping students understand how to read and write abstracts before the tutorial session in which such instruction needed to be given. The scheduling further complicated the application of teaching ideas since the TAs who attended might find that they were getting guidance after the fact. Because the amount of training was necessarily so limited and because they felt pressed to do all that was being expected of them, they became impatient with anything for which they did not see an immediate application to their work with students.

Of these various issues that arose in reflection about the W-course, it was clear that feasibility was less related to the course itself than to the larger structures within which the W-implementation had to operate. Either at the faculty or university level, some means of preparing TAs for W-courses needed to be established. Given the existing resources, however, the department seemed appropriately justified in its concern about TA workload and qualifications even though this particular group of TAs appeared to be effective, not only by their own account but also by that of their students.

Student response to the W-course and writing-instruction

We used pre- and post-course surveys as one of the sources of information from students that would help us assess the impact of the course on student learning and writing. Writing instruction in the course emphasized researching material for the paper, paraphrasing, summarizing, and quoting others' ideas, drafting and revising, and arguing a thesis. Students' responses to questions about these features of their writing on the pre- and post-course surveys showed noticeable changes. The percentage of students who thought they were performing below what they considered to be satisfactory on all these features dropped in all cases. At the beginning, for example, 16% ranked themselves as "struggling or needing lots of help" with organization compared to 10% at the end; 23% ranked themselves low on researching skills at the beginning compared to 9% at the end. The single most dramatic difference was how students rated themselves on paraphrasing, a topic which was given particular attention with both examples and practice in class and in an assignment. On this skill, 66% of the students at the end of the course said they now feel 'fairly or very confident' compared to 35% at the beginning of the course. Clear differences were also striking in students' confidence in being able to summarize: 64% felt confident compared to 36% at the beginning. In ability to quote effectively, 61% expressed confidence at the end of the course compared to 41% at the beginning. Their self-reports correspond to what the TAs also observed as improvements.

The survey also included statements with which students could agree or disagree, choosing from "mostly yes" or "mostly no" or N/A (not applicable). The direction for this set of statements read as follows: "There are anticipated advantages for taking a course that pays attention to writing as

well as content. Please indicate whether you generally agree or disagree with the following." Since instruction in the course had emphasized some uses of writing more than others, we were particularly interested in students' response to those uses.

1. Rewriting and revising helped me figure out what I was saying. *Mostly Yes—85.1%.*

2. By writing, I got to explain complex ideas clearly and make them my own. *Mostly Yes—68.9%.*

3. Writing gets me engaged in the subject more than just listening to the lecture. *Mostly Yes—70.2%.*

4. The writing-intensive process gave me skills that I can apply to other courses. *Mostly Yes—63.8%.*

In contrast, peer review was not something that was widely or consistently used as a means of giving feedback in this course, and student responses to the statement "I found it useful to get feedback from my peers" revealed that limited use with the following percentages:
Mostly Yes—33.8%, Mostly No—31.9%, and N/A—34.4%.

Analysis of writing samples

In response to the university's call for hard evidence of improvement in writing and learning in students taking W-courses, we undertook a small research project to compare student writing to the same assignment with and without a W-course experience. Two groups of students (in 2002 and 2004) answered an identical question on an open-book final exam. Although, of course, it was a different group of students, the conditions for the writing were similar: Joan had taught the course both years, the demographic distribution of the student population was comparable, students had completed the same readings on the topic addressed by the question and had had the same lab experience, the exam was open-book both years, and the question was identical. The major differences were in the amounts of guidance and practice students had in writing about course concepts and in linking ideas and information around those concepts. The other difference was in the criteria that Joan used to assign marks for the students' answers: all the answers needed to be marked according to the same criteria since we wanted to use marks as one of the variables for comparison. In preparation for the analysis, all answers were typed as written, with all original punctuation and spelling retained. Each response

was given a randomly assigned number to ensure there was no evidence of the year of writing. Joan herself, as the instructor, then marked all 87 answers out of a possible 10 marks, re-marking those from the 2002 exam, and thus ensuring that the same criteria for a successful exam answer were being applied to all samples.

While marks would be one way to compare students' performance, we also wanted tools that would be useful both for describing the students' writing on the biology exam and for possible future use with other samples of writing. We hoped that the results would demonstrate outcomes of the W-version of BISC 102 that could provide useful information about a W-approach for presentation to the biology department. Guided by one of our colleagues, Susan O'Neill, we used an adaptation of Bloom's taxonomy to identify levels of thinking and an adaptation of Biggs' Structure of Observed Learning Outcomes (SOLO) to rate learning. We also developed one scale of four generic indicators of writing development (W1 organization, W2 style, W3 mechanics, and W4 authorship—see below) and another scale of key genre and disciplinary indicators related to subject matter knowledge (e.g., information in correct context, factual accuracy, relevance, technical vocabulary, and so on. See Appendix 6). We chose to use answers written by the 87 students from the two classes (2002 and 2004) who were in their first semester at university and in their first biology course. In hindsight, that decision meant a greatly reduced sample size available for statistical analysis. We had reasoned that more senior students would bring a more advanced level of experience with academic reading and writing, as well as background knowledge. Including them in our sample would add yet another variable to consider, as we sought links between the new pedagogy and changes in writing performance. In hindsight also, we could have confined ourselves to using Biggs' SOLO rather than both Biggs' and Bloom's taxonomies. We were most interested in whether we could identify a relationship between writing and learning and, as we proceeded with the coding, we found the descriptors for the two instruments overlapped more than we initially realized and to such a degree that the high correlations could have been anticipated.

Each answer was then coded across the four dimensions: thinking, learning, writing, and genre and content knowledge. Each was coded independently by two raters, with a third available to resolve discrepancies of more than one interval on the scale. We handed the data from our scoring over to our statistics expert, Ian Bercovitz, who ran a series of tests in a search for statistically significant correlations and relationships across the dimensions.

What we learned from the analyses was that comparison between the two years produced significant differences in only two dimensions: word count/length and marks. There was a statistically significant difference in mean word counts between the years 2002 and 2004. A *t*-test showed a difference in mean length of 180.8 and 211.9 words for the 2002 non-W-year and the 2004 W-year ($P = 0.025$). Increased length is associated with increased fluency and confidence in writing. While these features do reflect on writer characteristics, neither is indicative of the substantive or stylistic qualities of the text. The fact that students wrote more on average after the W-course was a promising sign of difference if there was evidence of a relation to text quality. Quality of content and style in the texts were elements reflected in the marks out of 10 that were significantly higher for the W-students. A non-parametric Kruskal–Wallis test was used to test for the differences in marks between years. These results showed a statistically significant difference (Chi-square, 1 df = 4.49, $P = 0.034$) with an average in 2002 of 4.94 and in 2004 of 6.03 out of the maximum of 10 marks. The evidence suggested that students in 2004 outperformed those in 2002 both in length and quality of writing as determined by the marks.

The conclusion about quality was borne out by further analyses that, while not showing any statistically significant differences across years, mainly because of the small sample, did show that marks overall correlated with levels of thinking and learning. To examine the relationship between the five levels of learning (L1, L2, L3, L4, and L5) and four levels of thinking (T1, T2, T3, and T4), a Fisher's exact test was used. The test showed a highly significant association ($P < 0.01$) between learning and thinking. That is, students who had a higher thinking score tended to have a higher learning score, an outcome that, as noted earlier, was probably predictable given the similarities in some aspects of the scales. An analysis of variance method was used to study the relations among marks, learning, and year. There was a significant effect of learning on marks ($P < 0.01$) and a similar relationship between marks and thinking ($P < 0.01$).

Thinking also correlated significantly with one of the dimensions of writing: authorship (W4). We identified "authorship" by such features as use of metaphors, similes and analogies, by hierarchical structure, by topical elaboration, by the use of metadiscourse elements to accommodate reader needs, and by apt vocabulary choices. We scaled these across three levels from no such features, to one feature and to three or more to indicate the level of control and investment in the topic and the writing. A Fisher's exact test was used to test for associations between W4 and thinking. The results showed a highly significant ($P < 0.01$) association between these two variables. Students who scored higher levels of thinking also showed higher levels of W4. Similarly, students who scored low on thinking also showed a lower score for the variable W4. Marks were significantly affected by quality of structure and organization in writing (W1). An analysis of variance showed a significant effect of W1 on marks ($P < 0.0023$). Finally, the other dimensions of writing, style and mechanics, showed a strong correlation with the higher scores on authorship (W4). We looked at the relationships between W1 (organization) and W4 (authorship), W2 (style) and W4, and W3 (mechanics) and W4. The results showed a highly statistically significant association ($P < 0.01$) for all three variables with W4. That is, students with higher scores on authorship also had higher scores for organization, style, and mechanics.

Students who wrote well and got high marks were also the students who scored at the higher levels of thinking and learning. They demonstrated that they could establish a relationship between elements and make a case for their position. For Joan, the results indicated that in marking the writing, she had attended to all the elements she had identified in the exam question as being given weight: accuracy of information, the ability to relate concepts, and the quality of written expression. The scoring using the scales in our instruments thus confirmed that Joan's marking was consistent with what she had been teaching and what she told students she would be looking for in their examination answers. While there were only the two significant cross-year differences, the other correlations thereby confirmed her as a reliable marker. Even though the marking was reliable, however, the coding process led us to speculate that using this particular exam answer sample was unlikely to provide us with a valid comparison between the W- and non-W-courses. The coding drew our attention to the wording of the exam question, a factor we had overlooked. As we read through all the sample answers and rated them using the learning and thinking taxonomies, we noticed that students who got lower marks and lower scores on these scales seemed to be interpreting the question differently from those whose marks and scores were higher. While we did not know, without consulting the students directly, what they had attended to in the exam question, the writing itself was revealing.

In the W-course, we had taken particular care in naming the genre of the pieces of writing students were asked to do, had worded assignments to make expectations as clear as possible, and had encouraged students to focus on conceptual links, and show they understood the ideas behind factual details. The wording of the exam question, however, lacked that degree of clarity and, despite our intentions that it replicate the demands of in-class work, in fact proved somewhat misleading.

The exam question opened with a series of statements about the frog, *Physalaemus pustulosus,* reminding students of a particular case they had encountered in lab work and which exemplified important concepts:

> In the lab on natural selection, you heard about the frog Physalaemus pustulosus. Male frogs of this species advertise for females by calling. Males produce calls of varying complexity, consisting of one whine and zero to six chucks. These calls are very costly to males. Calling in general and chucking in particular uses a lot of energy. In addition, predatory fringe-lipped bats are attracted to chucking males. However, female Physalaemus pustulosus strongly prefer to mate with males who produce a lot of chucks.

The directions then specified what they have to write using this information, and whatever else they remembered that would be relevant: Write a brief essay speculating about the evolution of male calling in *Physalaemus pustulosus.*

The use of the term *essay* could be read as a generic requirement for a paragraphed text written in sentences, as distinct from bullets or lists. It could, however, be misleading since the necessary brevity of the responses would not justify their being identified as essays, a genre that commonly indicates an elaborate discussion of a topic. In this context, it would not have and was not intended to have, genre implications unless students were alert enough to link the term "essay" with *speculating.* The verb *speculate* should have led them to put forward ideas and possibilities to explain how natural selection might have favored specific features of male calling in *Physalaemus pustulosus.* The exam question at that point was consistent with the principle emphasized throughout the course: that biological knowledge was itself incomplete and changing.

To assist the students in constructing their explanation, the question then provided a list of the concepts that needed to be addressed in the answer:

> Include the following concepts in your essay:
>
> - Conditions for natural selection
> - Trade-offs
> - Sexual selection
> - Handicap theory.

The addition of this list seemed to impose a control on the order of presentation of information and ideas that diverted some students' attention from the purpose of the assignment. Instead of considering these concepts in their speculation about the evolution of male calling, weak students typically used them as a structure to report facts about the male frog and lost sight of the overall idea. Since the exam was open-book, some of these students looked up information on each concept in the lecture notes or textbook, including peripherally related or unrelated information that did not address the assignment. The list may also have prevented students from speculating because it implied that each concept listed had equal significance and required discussion, whereas in a brief essay, it might make more practical sense to focus on a particular concept and consider its impact. A 2004 writer who attempted to speculate in his brief essay named only two of the four required concepts but scored at high levels on thinking and learning and on writing and content because he wrote about the concepts with genuine understanding. His piece opens with a general statement relating evolution to the topic of male mating calls and goes on to raise questions about the effects of the calls on the male's chance of survival. His questions led him to show his reasoning process with such wordings as "in fact . . . but instead," and "though . . . without and despite . . . he is still . . . He also made accurate and con-textually appropriate connections among the concepts using dramatic and engaging phrases, such as "plays the role of the hero" and "mateless; alive without purpose."

> The complexity of evolution and life itself is again proven when examining the male mating call in the frog, *Physalaemus pustulosus.* By performing a series of complex mating calls, the male frog plays the role of the hero, gravely putting himself in danger to ensure the female and her (and his) genetic continuity. Why do females favor these male frogs putting themselves in what can only be described as a dangerous and desperate attempt for attention? It is in fact not because females favor stupid males, but instead fit males. Sexual selection occurs as the female chooses to mate with the male she in fact finds most fit demonstrated by the male's display of actions. Though the male frog reveals himself to predatory bats by performing these calls, without making them he will find himself mateless; alive without purpose. By performing this simple trade-off, the male manages to attract a mate and also impress her by showing that despite the danger he has put himself in, he is still alive and well.

Another 2004 writer seems to be dependent on the introductory statement and list of concepts provided in the question. The first three sentences are more sophisticated than those that follow. These sentences present peripherally related information and are likely taken from the textbook available to him in the open-book exam. The fourth sentence is taken directly from the question. Although the answer does not include incorrect information, it is a laundry list of statements that fails to apply the concepts to the case of the calling frog. The writer fails to draw meaningful connections between the concepts and does not make reasoned claims about the case. The usage suggests a non-native speaker of English, which might partly explain the approach he took.

> Natural selection occurs through the interaction of environmental factors and the heritable variation present in a population. Environmental factors set the criteria for success, determining which characteristics increase an organism's fitness. Natural selection favors organisms with inherited traits that lead to increased reproductive success. For Physalaemus pustulosus (frog), it is advantage for males to chuck more because female select to mate with males who produces a lot of chucks. However, calling in general and chucking in particular uses a lot of energy. As a result, males who produces more chucks more mate and reproduce more successfully and natural selection will eliminate those which do not produce chucks less and favors those with more chucks.

We could not, of course, change the wording of the exam question if we were to compare responses in the sets of exam answers from the non-W-course and the W-course. The process of analysis, however, drew our attention to the ways in which the question itself directs responses, and in this case may have prevented students from writing in ways that could reveal their understanding of the course concepts. As was the case in the economics course described in the previous chapter, this collaboration was a first attempt to implement new approaches to teaching writing in the context of the discipline. In this course, we moved toward engaging the students in the kinds of thinking needed to be biologists and in the genres of writing typical of the discipline. While we could not go back as we can in writing, to make changes in the product of those efforts, each of us recognized that the whole experience of planning, teaching, reflecting on, and assessing the course and our collaboration served as preparation for the next iteration. As her comments suggested, Erin saw that making shifts in practice transformed her perceptions of what was going on in her teaching, encouraged a different level of self- and student-awareness, and established her in a new relation to the course content and her pedagogy. In the next chapter, the focus on such shifts moves to dwell on how we, as consultants to faculty and TAs, conceptualized and used our consulting role to mediate the application of principles from genre theory.

5

TAKING A GENRE APPROACH TO TEACHING WRITING
The Consulting, Collaborative Process

Our roles as CWIL consultants to faculty and our pedagogies grounded in new rhetorical genre theory were at once both visible and invisible. We engaged with faculty to help open up their thinking about writing, about teaching, and about pedagogy, to reveal new understandings. We used genre theory, broadly defined, as our text. From that text and the principles it embodied, we created scripts that would serve to interpret genre to faculty with whom we worked and whose performance in the classroom we wanted to affect. Theatre director Jerzy Grotowski speaks of an author's text as being "for both actor and producer. . . a sort of scalpel, enabling us to open ourselves, to transcend ourselves" (Grumet 1988, 148). It is a dramatic image. Dramatic too were the awarenesses that engaging with genre could reveal to faculty and to their students. We used the genre text as scalpel, as a means of opening ourselves and the faculty, of finding the unconscious and tacit hidden in our understanding, and of transcending surface appearances and unexamined assumptions. Grotowski talked about what he as director does to "give life to the inanimate words of the text." He serves as an interpreter, mediating between the script he has chosen and the people who will be its visible representation. In our work with faculty also, we mediated between our scripts and the faculty members, not requiring them to engage with our "text," the genre theory itself, but focusing rather on the performance. Grotowski acknowledges that he fulfils a key and highly visible role but neither he nor the text is foregrounded in the performance. For good or ill, the action always belongs to the performers and not, in our case, to the consultants who became invisible along with our theoretical text.

This analogy to scripts and theatre as way of thinking about pedagogical change may seem somewhat strained. Our stance, however, had a significant influence on the relationships we developed with faculty and on their willingness and confidence in performance. In obvious, explicit, and perhaps somewhat mundane ways, our consulting influenced such processes as the construction of syllabi, the choice of genres and sequencing of assignments, and the marking of student writing. At the same time, we had a limited part in the delivery of the course to students; faculty needed to assume ownership as well as responsibility for any changes they made in their pedagogy. While the processes and strategies we advocated and assisted in developing for writing were obviously visible to faculty, they sprang out of our interpretation of genre which was itself largely invisible and largely of little interest as theory to those faculty. One of the lessons I learned almost immediately (as I mentioned in the discussion of criteria) was that using terms like rhetoric, genre, and discourse could freeze people's faces and stop up their ears. We were not going to make faculty open to our text or our direction with the academic equivalent of telemarketing or by foisting on them our scholarship and disciplinarity. At the same time, efficient communication required some shared vocabulary. We found we could avoid stopped up ears as long as rhetorical terms emerged informally and even unobtrusively in a context that made meanings readily apparent, as was the case during discussions of assignments.

In earlier chapters exemplifying engagement with faculty in economics and biology, I referred to proposing and developing writing assignments that reflected genres common to the disciplines: in economics, students wrote letters to the editor and a memo to a government official; in biology, students wrote an overview article similar to those that appear in biology journals for non-specialist readers. In the context of those chapters, I identified the choice of genres for the assignments as a response to issues the faculty members raised. In this chapter, I explain how applying principles from genre theory effected a transformation in discourse about writing and also in faculty understanding of the role of situation and exigence in writing. That understanding included seeing the complex and subtle relationships between the features of text and rhetorical situation that give rise to their disciplinary genres; it made clear the importance of relating genre and situations of use in planning and implementing successful writing assignments. Through three examples from faculty with whom we consulted, I demonstrate how the genre approach we adopted influenced faculty to re-examine their assumptions and expectations for student writing, to reconsider the sequences they planned for writing assignments, to revise the ways they conceptualize writing and the teaching of writing, and consequently, their performance as writing teachers. Each example is framed by Coe's (2002) three basic principles for teaching with genre theory:

1. Genres embody socially established strategies for achieving purposes in rhetorical situations.

2. Genres are not just text types; they imply/invoke/create/(re)con-
   struct situations (and contexts), communities, writers, and readers
   (i.e. subject positions).

3. Understanding genre will help students become versatile writers,
   able to adapt to the wide variety of types of writing tasks they are
   likely to encounter in their lives (Coe 2002, 198–200).

Since our practice was to begin with the existing course material and
faculty goals and objectives, the examples described here explain the ways
in which we assumed the role of interpreters and mediators between our
genre 'text' and the faculty's own texts to enable changes in the ways faculty used existing materials to achieve their goals for student writing. This
account begins with a detailed descriptive analysis of one particular course
as illustration of the process and principles which directed our practice.
The two examples that follow are briefer echoes of this approach with
genre. In them, I point out particular aspects that differentiated the applications of genre from one course to another. In these examples, I focus on
those aspects rather than setting them fully in the context within which they
occur. Like the first, more detailed example, the brief ones reflect the shifting of our roles and our theory from positions of visibility to invisibility.

RE-SEEING THROUGH GENRE IN ARNE MOOERS' FOURTH-YEAR
BIODIVERSITY COURSE

Assumptions and expectations

When he heard that the university was supporting pilot W-courses, Arne
e-mailed to ask me what he would need to adjust to make his course qualify
for that support. He explained that students write:

> a term paper (worth 50% of their mark) that they hand in 2X. Their final mark
> is the mean of those received on the separate versions. We treat the first version
> as we would a manuscript from colleagues—i.e., it is torn apart (by both me and
> my TA, who has been a senior PhD student). As half of the comments concern
> grammar and style/clarity, it seems we are doing much of what a W-course is
> supposed to do. The students also hand in a one page précis each week for the
> first third of the course, so that we can gauge at what stage they are in their
> writing and so that they can see what we expect from them. Would I have to do
> more to make this a W-course?

My reply the next day acknowledged that he assigns a substantial amount of graded writing and gives feedback intended both to

communicate his expectations and to lead to revision and improvement. I also commented that:

> In order to help advise you on what else might make it fully meet the W-criteria, I would need to know more about the purpose and nature of the major assignment and its relation to the course content, the relation between the précis and the term paper and the course content, and the way in which students come to know the criteria for producing the form of the paper and for marking it.

My response here made assumptions about the purpose and the overall coherence of his written course assignments. At the same time, I shifted attention away from the grammar and style issues that he seemed to be attending to in student writing. My response implied that writing was integral to the course's disciplinary content, and that the longer paper subsumed aspects of the shorter précis.

When we met, I had already positioned myself as needing to understand Arne's goals for students and his rationale for the structuring and sequencing of assignments. I did need and want to understand these aspects of the course. But I also wanted to direct our viewing of them to take into account the context for writing and the purposes the writing would serve in the discipline. If we could agree on this vantage point, we could then move to defining the genre he was using and work on how to make its patterns of style, structure, content, and audience visible to students.

As it turned out, Arne was quick to confirm that his belief, and thus goal for students, was that being able to write well was essential to successful participation in the work of the discipline. In one of his notes to students he had advised them to "Keep in mind that after you are dead, the only way people have of knowing what you meant is by reading what you wrote. Badly written papers just don't get read. You are in training for a career in research." He thought students should be able to distinguish between and produce different styles of scientific writing. He was also committed to having students write in the form most typical in the field of biodiversity: the research report. The problem in assigning this form, however, was that the students in his course did not do independent research on which they could report. He had decided to compromise and instead assign them to write a critical analysis of biodiversity claims in a scholarly research article. Although critical analyses typically only appear as a constituent of a scientific research paper, he believed that understanding how and what to critique in others' work was fundamental to developing knowledge in his field and thus to disciplinary participation. He felt he had been unsuccessful, however, in enabling students to succeed in critiquing. Looking at this goal from the point of view of genre, it appeared we needed to identify and define a suitable genre for this situation.

As it happened, the readings Arne was using to initiate students into the controversies around species definition also lent themselves to achieving parts of both his goals: first, that students be able to distinguish different styles of scientific writing, and secondly, that they learn to critique. These readings included a scholarly article (Xu and Arnason 1996) a critical commentary on some of the claims in that article (Muir, Galdikas, and Beckenbach 1998) and a lengthy response to the critique by one author of the claims (Arnason 1998). The students had previously read these mainly for their content, not form since it was, as Arne said, "easy primary literature about naming species. We discussed all three papers in one 3-hour session, spending about 10 minutes discussing how bad Arnason's response to the critique was (i.e., how it WASN'T scientific writing). They wrote a précis of the session just to record it."

Three or four weeks after this discussion of content, students would select a scholarly article to critique, and Arne gave them a three-page handout of guidelines. In this handout, he named the assignment an "essay" and said the purpose for writing was "to assess your understanding of biodiversity science by your ability to: understand and assess the quality of a current research article, evaluate its importance in the field, and suggest a program of research that might reasonably follow."

In notes to guide students in writing to this assignment, he identified specific elements to include and aspects of the research that might be critiqued, indicated what could constitute significance of a study, and outlined the key points to include in their own research proposal. He also advised them to "use a clear and lively style and avoid use of passive voice" and to be concise. In marking, he would look for "thoughtfulness, originality, and understanding both of the field and the particular article." Despite these and other explanations of his expectations, he said "I could talk until I was blue in the face, but they still don't get it."

The assignment was ambitious. It assumed that students would understand the overall purpose of the assignment in the larger picture of the course or field, that they knew how to take a critical position, summarize key information, and represent analysis in ways conventional in science writing and that it was clear to them what meeting the evaluation criteria would look like. In our discussion, Arne had made it clear that what he wanted was critical analysis of biodiversity claims. I suggested we concentrate on this goal. We needed a shift in purpose away from the limits expressed in "assess your understanding" (though assessing was clearly not Arne's only purpose, it was the one he articulated) toward the function of the genre in the rhetorical situation it would serve in the discipline, with consequent shifts in the expectations of what students would write, in the use of exemplars of the genre, and in the sequence planned for the writing.

The Muir *et al.*'s (1998) critique was not an example of the research reports typical in the sub-field of Biodiversity. It was a sample, however, of what Swales (Swales 1990, 58) defines as "comparable rhetorical action" to achieve a community's communicative purposes. The sample illustrated the rhetorical strategies used in the social situation of a critique of a study in Biodiversity, the purpose of which was to challenge selected claims and conclusions of a colleague in the field and to invite consideration of significances apparently overlooked by the study's authors. The genre positioned both writers and readers as participants in the discipline's research community. While Muir *et al.*'s critique was not embedded in a report of their own research, in all these other respects, the sample was comparable in purpose and in its use of rhetorical strategies to sections of the more typical research report.

In order to make these features explicit and thereby help validate its use as an exemplar that Arne argued was 'non-intuitive', we discussed its social/disciplinary purpose and examined its rhetorical strategies. I annotated the sample, indicating structural moves and the writer's purpose in making those moves, wordings for claims and challenges, the use of citation, and so on, and invited Arne's comments, additions, and amendments. The experience was enlightening for him. He later commented "I've always prided myself on being a good writer but I didn't know why, and so Wendy made things explicit that I didn't know." We agreed that the sample would serve as exemplar for the critique. Arne, however, did not feel ready at that point to do the analysis with the class himself. I offered to step in and do it with him and the class in a three hour tutorial session. We would invite them to position themselves like Muir *et al.*, as knowledgeable readers and potential researchers on the topic of their choice. They would respond to a scholarly article on their topic in the genre of the "Point Counter Point" (PCP) that appears occasionally in *The Journal of Molecular Evolution*. Their own counterpoints would exhibit the formal features they derived as we read the sample together. I worked inductively, beginning by modeling the process of discourse and rhetorical analysis with the opening paragraphs and then asking them questions about moves, purposes, wording, choice of data, and claims to critique and so on in the rest of the piece. By demonstrating this process, I aimed at assisting them, as well as Arne, in becoming "more observant readers of the discoursal conventions of their fields and thereby deepen their rhetorical perspectives on their own disciplines" (Swales and Lindemann 2002, 118).

To become knowledgeable readers, capable of making a critique, they also had to fully understand the claims and evidence being made on the basis of data presented in their article and understand the scope of their critique: What might it include and exclude? On what grounds are choices made? In examining the Muir *et al.*'s piece, we were looking at the outcome of much groundwork, a critique that arose from extensive background knowledge. To avoid participation in the genre simply at the level of formal features, we needed to ensure that students had the means of acquiring sufficient background knowledge and knew how to go about developing a critique based on their reading. Arne knew from experience that it was a mistake to assume that simply reading was an adequate strategy to achieve understanding of complex material or recognition of points to critique. We needed to develop a plan for that preparatory work.

Reconsidering sequence

One of Arne's two main goals for student writing was that they be able "to recognize and produce different styles of science writing." With our new strategy, they had been exposed to different styles, and we had examined one style rhetorically. As mentioned above, Arne had previously discussed the content of the three early readings with brief reference to their styles. Some weeks later, he had given students a list of scholarly articles from which to choose as the basis for their essay or term paper. We had now shifted the pedagogy around the use of these three articles and redefined the writing assignment, as I interpreted it, in terms of genre.

Since Arne was well aware of students' struggles with reading scholarly journal articles, it seemed that a first step in reconsidering the sequence for the counterpoint assignment would be to add space for reporting on the substance of their chosen article and for determining a secure level of comprehension. Since we had not yet provided for his other goal of producing different styles of writing, we decided to structure the first report on the substance of their article in the non-academic form of a journalistic report in a magazine like *The Economist*. As part of the course work on diversity and species definition, Arne would use examples from the popular press, in part to illustrate how information about such topics as extinction of species was taken from scientific reports and how dramatic findings were highlighted out of context. While he had not treated these readings from the perspective of genre, he believed students should recognize a responsibility to educate the public about scientific matters. *The Economist* article became another tool through which to think in terms of genre, and we undertook a process similar to the one we used with the counterpoint piece, establishing a context, communicative purpose, reader and writer roles, and genre features. In reflecting on this stepping stone toward the critical counterpoint piece, Arne commented that for students, it seemed

> they realized how little they knew about writing and were exposed to . . . how much is involved in one piece of writing. It was for them a realization that wow, there is a lot of—even if it's subconscious when they're writing it—structure that's there, that they hadn't noticed before. I think it was the realization you really have to think about not only what you are going to say but how you are going to say it. For a lot of them, it didn't seem like they'd ever really come to grips with that fact, just the fact that you have to do that. They're used to just writing stuff down. (Mooers 2006)

He thought that writing *The Economist* piece, in contrast to an academic one, highlighted context, purpose, and audience for the students, and it was exciting for them to experiment with by taking on different roles for different situations and communicative purposes. "I would say there was jubilant understanding of the difference between the rhetoric in *The Economist* article and that in the PCP: we talked about it informally quite a bit (i.e., what you *could* say in one but not in the other). Also, it was fun to see who was more at ease with the journalistic writing (not always the 'best' students)" (Mooers, 2006).

The genre, and examination of it, served a heuristic function. As Jolliffe and Brier point out "The methods writers are able to use to develop their subjects are sharply constrained by the form that their texts must take. Knowledge of organization, arrangement, form, and genre, therefore, has a heuristic function: writers are systematically led to know their subject matters by systematically considering textual form" (Jolliffe and Brier 1988, 46–47). The examination of genre helped students to read and interpret the subject matter of their scholarly articles from the point of view of explaining its significance to a non-expert and also helped them to generate ideas to include. They were puzzled at first and quite challenged to adopt a different position and discourse, but in grasping the differences from the academic, successfully wrote for this different context. Arne's judgment was that the students "kind of made that connection that 'this is not only a skill, but it's also a kind of process and a practice' and they developed a more professional approach to thinking about their writing, as science majors. I think converting the scientific article to *The Economist* article really settled that process in the end . . . they were getting into the idea of finding the different types of rhetoric that were in that editorial. They were seeing opinion to argument or critique in this perspective and back to the original science and the differences. . .. My intuition is that seeing different sorts of rhetoric (the PCP, then *The Economist* article) would make the students more self-aware when they write their own PCP, and I'm guessing you think/know that is the case. I think it has helped me in my own writing."

Arne also noted that the sequence of assignments meant that students had a firmer grasp of the core content of their individual scholarly articles before attempting the critique. He felt that writing for a non-expert audience and also explaining the substance of their articles when they worked in pairs in class meant they "couldn't hide when explaining in the pairs what the article really was about. I saw them squirm." He saw evidence of this deeper understanding in the students' writing on the critique paper: "They did a better job—the paper was more focused this year and shorter. They had more context." He also found that he was responding differently as a result: "I marked the paper harder, of course, because they had the examples and had written *The Economist* article, so I knew they understood the content, so I feel like I'm marking them at a higher level. . . I can *read* them as if I'm reading my grad students' papers." In part, this was because he had a clearer sense of his own expectations for the writing, embodied in the form it was to take. "The problem before was that I hadn't really had a form for it, so they were all very different."

REVISED CONCEPTUALIZATION OF WRITING
AND THE TEACHING OF WRITING

Perhaps the most striking outcomes of this experience are summed up quite succinctly in Arne's comment that students discovered "how much is involved in one piece of writing" and in his recognition that the discussion of context and purpose and the processes of analysis uncovered his own tacit and unconscious knowledge of writing. Exploring the material instantiation of genre in the specific articles served as a vehicle for a new understanding of the rhetorical ends that particular genres serve in particular situations. In its previous formulation, the assignment to critique a scholarly article was described as an essay and characterized cognitively as a piece that would show evidence of critical analysis. With a shift to a genre approach, the piece was now named "point counter point" and characterized in social terms as a genre, which functioned in a particular disciplinary context to achieve social ends of contributing to debate and discussion in the field. While the previous formulation was certainly intended to achieve those same purposes, the context was not explicitly demonstrated, nor were the textual features that would cue a reader to the role and situation being invoked. Without this information, student writers would have, in fact did have, difficulty assuming the role they were intended to take. Arguably, without a genre to work within, "essay" being so general in scope that it does not serve, there was no role to assume that would be recognizable in this discourse community, and perhaps no real sense that taking a role was part of the task, other than the role of student who is to be assessed on the basis of what is written.

Biodiversity 440 was not a writing class, and we did not attempt to teach a vocabulary of rhetoric, or to foreground genre theory. Theory was visible only as application. We worked inductively to arrive at insights upon which everyone could reflect and verbalize. Students acted upon and used what they learned in performance of the genre. I noticed that the novelty of examining a text from the point of view of how it was written, and the excitement of gaining insights from the rhetorical and discourse analysis, tended to attract more commentary from Arne and the students than the context in which the genre functions. But that context was made visible through discussion of the different genres, even at the earliest stages of the course when students read an extract from Darwin's Origin of the Species, and we noted there, for instance, how he positions himself in relation to his peers.

The role of context and rhetorical situation as embodying purpose and relation to audience were woven into examination of the course readings throughout. Indeed, following Carolyn Miller, it can be argued that writers come to understand their ends from their means: "What we learn when we learn a genre is not just a pattern of forms or even a method of achieving our own ends. We learn, more importantly, what ends we may have" (Miller 1984, 165). Developing an understanding of the particular genres by means of which they would represent their subject matter would, according to Miller, include learning the purposes available to them in those genres. It may be that a more didactic approach to the rhetoric of the genre would help students be better able to know what they know or say what they know about writing in the chosen genres. Arne did not ask, however, for that kind of reporting. I felt a certain hesitance in imposing my vocabulary, cautious about associations with "English" teaching and preferring instead to induce the *ways of thinking and seeing* deeply embedded in the disciplinary texts, using my genre text as scalpel. While Arne felt students were more self-aware when they wrote, we had no way of knowing what the level of awareness would mean for their eventual versatility as writers. The attention to genre, however, had clearly equipped them to think more complexly about writing and afforded them strategies to apply in new situations.

I had played a fairly active role in this course, joining the class for genre analysis tutorials several times during the semester and attending lectures relevant to the topics we would take up in the tutorial. I also read a wide variety of texts that Arne proposed for our use and did detailed analyses of the ones we planned to take up in class with students. I was, however, only one of a number of guests Arne had invited to his class. He brought in four other speakers on topics of current and course-related interest, so from the point of view of students, I had a clear and visible role, but came and went and had no contact with them outside of the class. Although Arne always participated as learner along with the students when we looked at the texts, that positioning reinforced rather than in any way diminished his authority. He was the disciplinary arbiter on the accuracy of my reading and interpretation and spoke from a depth of knowledge of the field and its discourse to which I was obviously an outsider. I offered tools. He and the students appropriated them for purposes they took on as their own. Once this was the case, both I and the genre text with which we had together opened ourselves to insights and awarenesses receded off-stage. Arne taught the course again as a W-course, and will continue to do so.

ELEMENTS OF A GENRE APPROACH

Environmental economics 260 is an "applied topics" course that builds on economic models from introductory courses and extends them to relations between the economy and the natural environment. It focuses on the reasons environmental problems develop and what can be done, in part by economic policies designed to improve environmental quality, as well as by society and governmental organizations. Typically, the course enrolled about 100 students, and was run with 2-hour of lecture and a 1-hour tutorial with two TAs assisting the professor, Nancy Olewiler. Readings were mainly from a course text, written by the professor and a colleague, and assignments, which counted for 25% of the grade (the remaining 75% was based on three test marks) and included short policy briefs, quizzes, and analytical work involving model solving, graphical and algebraic analysis.

In order to qualify as a W-course, that distribution of grade allocation would have had to change, but our work with Nancy was ahead of the formal criteria development and two years ahead of the certification process. In fact, Nancy Olewiler's was our first pilot W-course in the Fall 2002, so very much experimental for both of us. The focus of our attention in this environmental economics course was simply on shaping the assignments and instruction to include more writing. This meant adjusting the balance of marks in the 25% allocated to assignments but, more importantly, figuring out how to differentiate writing in economics from writing in other disciplines and what genres would most effectively help students express themselves like economists. To uncover some of the features that Nancy responded to as an economist when reading novice student writing and to help me understand what we might need to point out to students when they wrote and the TAs when they marked, Nancy did think-aloud readings on three student papers, articulating her responses to what was said and how it was expressed. She had already included short policy briefs as one of the assignments since, for many economists, writing such briefs is their daily work. They prepare them as advisory documents for politicians and civil service workers in the government and as research documents in private industry and consulting companies so we began an inquiry into these as a potential genre. We agreed to make the policy brief a formal assignment and structure a process which would help students understand its function and purpose as well as its features.

Nancy found samples of the kind of brief that would make use of data that she intended students to analyze using graphical and algebraic analysis that could then be put into the realistic reporting context of a policy brief. A key part of the process was in presenting the annotated samples to the TAs and the students who were neither accustomed to writing in their economics courses nor accustomed to thinking about writing rhetorically. The assignment was being transformed from a question asking for fairly brief policy recommendation on an issue to a conventional and formal document that required constructing a context and making a persuasive case for recommendations based on evidence. Students were given one-half of a benefit–cost study of the Greater Vancouver Regional District's AirCare program of vehicle testing for air emissions. The study provided data on the benefits and costs of the program. Students had to complete the study by computing the present value of the net benefits of the program under different assumptions about the costs and benefits. They then were to examine their results to recommend to the provincial government that the policy be continued as is, scrapped, or modified. They had to justify their conclusions using the data and their analysis. Previously, the assignment would have required them to do all the computation, but not write up their results in a way that communicated them to a policy-maker. In this new version of the assignment, they had to understand their results rather than simply derive them. They also had to write in a form that would serve the needs of the intended readers, most of whom would be non-experts. Such readers would not be receptive to accumulations of un-interpreted figures and tables that might communicate understanding of economic models in a classroom setting in answer to a question but were inappropriate and ineffective in a real-world context.

It was by grasping the significance of the purpose and structure as rep-resented in the annotated sample that students could orient themselves to the roles the brief assigned to both readers and writers. The assignment description named the genre, specified the audience and format, to be followed as presented in tutorials, and indicated the content that would need to be included:

Policy Brief—Air Care for British Columbia?

Your task is to prepare a policy brief of approximately five pages (~1250 words), using the AirCare benefit–cost study. You will complete the study by computing the present value of the net benefits of AirCare from the data provided in the study. You might also want to compare your result to the present value of net benefits from no policy, or operating AirCare differently (e.g., less frequent test-ing). If there is no AirCare, it is still possible to have improvements in air quality from the normal turnover of vehicles (people replacing their old vehicles with new ones that produce less pollution per kilometer traveled).

The policy brief should be addressed to the Minister of the Environment for British Columbia and indicate whether or not the Air Care program should be continued for Greater Vancouver.

Your policy brief should be clear and concise following the guidelines cov-ered in tutorials this week. Data and analysis should be incorporated wherever appropriate.

Your brief should be typed, double spaced.

A draft of your policy brief is due by the end of Wednesday's class on October 23rd.

We will review and comment on your draft and hand it back to you at the end of Monday's class, October 28th.

This description was, however, despite its details, quite inadequate on its own to communicate the shift the students needed to make in position-ing themselves in relation to their set of data. Indeed, even specifying audience and situation would be almost meaningless without the evidence of the genre features to which they gave rise, and those features them-selves would be almost invisible or lack significance if not made function-ally explicit. It was by working with the sample with Nancy and her TAs and discussing what we were seeing that we were able to transform this assignment into an example illustrating the complexity of writing and the purposefulness of writing in the discipline.

The sample we used was produced by the Environment & Economy Program for Southeast Asia Policy Briefs and was identified as "A Summary of EEPSEA Research Report 2001-RR7, An Economic Analysis of Coral Reefs in the Andaman Sea of Thailand," by Udomsak Seenprachawong. Since students would also be summarizing a report and providing an economic analysis, the sample served as an appropriate indicator of the genre. By isolating and naming the structural parts, we articulated features students needed to notice. As well as walking students through the sample, section by section on overheads, I prepared a handout articulating function:

> What does a policy brief do and what does it look like? For instance, the title identifies the issue to be addressed and name the site of the research: e.g. Putting a Price on Paradise: Economic Policies to Preserve Thailand's Coral Reefs
>
> "*Putting a price on paradise*" is the issue being addressed
>
> "*Economic policies to preserve Thailand's coral reefs*" tells us the site, which paradise is referred to and the purpose of the proposal to preserve.

On this brief, the next section was in a text box and elaborated on the title:

> Millions of people have read about "The Beach" and/or have seen it in the Leonardo de Caprio film, while many others have visited it, or similar ones, in Thailand's Andaman Sea. And there lies the rub: The famous 'paradise' islands of Phi Phi are so popular that they are in danger of being loved to death. Tourists from all over the world are putting increasing pressure on this fragile ecosystem. In response to this problem, a new study has found justification to introduce a system of charges to reduce the pressure on the islands' coral reefs and provide money for their conservation.

I annotated with a comment that "This section explains the issue named in the title in a little more detail and makes claims that show the writer's belief that this is a problem and let us know the view of the writer." In presenting this to the class, we invited them to identify which phrases indicate the writer's view. I then annotated the remainder of the brief, indicating purpose with questions that each of the sections answered, as well as pointing out what the writer was doing that would help make his case to the reader and how he used graphs and tables. For the TAs, the annotation afforded them a way to explain and discuss the genre features with students in their tutorials as well as to consider the purpose and situation to which this genre responded and in which it functioned. In the process, the concept of genre from a new rhetorical point of view became part of our shared understanding about what we were attempting to accomplish in the class.

One of the TAs reflected on the experience after the course and was candid about his initial skepticism about the emphasis on writing and the students' willingness to engage with it: "I felt that maybe they were not going to be able to absorb the economics as well as they should, if they were so concerned about writing and expressing their knowledge. However, my feelings have changed," he said.

> My skepticism continued up until the final copy of the policy briefs were marked and I had a chance to see some feedback from students regarding their feelings about what was going on. The first draft of the policy briefs was discouraging. It seemed that they did not care and were ignoring all the advice and instruction I was giving them in tutorials. With the incentive of a grade increase for improvement, it was then they realized that 'hey, this just might be useful.' We all know that what we are trying to teach is very valuable to them. I do think they began to see this near the conclusion of the course. I no longer felt like I was beating my head against the wall and wasting my time with this . . . . It was also interesting for me as it made me really think about the way I write reports and papers, and try to explain it to students and use it as a template for their own writing.

CONTEMPLATING GENRE IN PHILOSOPHY

Phil Hanson teaches a second-year metaphysics course that is required for students planning to major in philosophy. Although about one-third of the class usually does not plan to be majors, the course attracts students with a serious interest in philosophy, and he felt a commitment to help them "bump up their writing" before they went any further. Exams, he pointed out, may test comprehension but do not encourage students to learn how to show their thinking and make connections between issues "in the imaginative ways" made possible through language, either written or spoken. Being able to express one's understanding discursively is essential in philosophy, and consequently, Phil had based grades in his course on four equally weighted papers 1400–1800 words in length.

When he decided to experiment with a pilot W-course, Phil made a number of changes in the requirements. Instead of four papers, students would write three papers and ten short commentaries in class.

He distinguished these as low-stakes and high-stakes assignments. The draft of the first paper and the short commentaries would be low-stakes, worth 30% of the total grade. The revision of the first, based on detailed feedback, and the second and third papers would be graded, high-stakes assignments, together worth the balance of 70%. Although there would, of course, be new topics for the second and final papers, the genre would be the same as for the first revised paper.

In philosophy, participation in the discipline is constituted largely in written work. Successful philosophers address certain kinds of problems in recognizable and distinctive ways. Credibility is achieved by choosing issues considered philosophically significant and by writing about them clearly and critically. For students at the second-year level, the process of being initiated into the discipline would not require that they recognize or select significant issues but that they learn to write philosophy. That is to say, the writing *is doing* the philosophy. They must set out ideas and arguments, appraise and critique, and establish principles which move them along a line of reasoning to a conclusion. This is a quite difficult concept to grasp for students accustomed to *write about a topic*. Much of the same language might be used to name what they are to do if they are to write an essay or produce a research paper: construct an argument, provide examples as evidence, establish a thesis, and so on. The challenge in Phil's course was to assist students in grasping the characteristic processes of philosophical reasoning that would prepare them to write in the genre that would be philosophical writing.

To begin, Phil proposed that we work with a non-example that had been submitted as a philosophy paper but exhibited non-philosophical features. In the paper, the writer took a position on an exhibition of photos in a public art gallery, making a case against such an exhibit in such a space. Having learned what Phil was looking for in student writing, partly through his think-aloud responses to student papers and partly through discussion of this non-example, I stepped in to talk about the structure with the class. I used the sample inductively, inviting students to look for evidence of a thesis, for analysis and explanation of this thesis, arguments for and objections to the thesis, and finally, for response to the objections. In other words, we began to inculcate understanding and recognition of the genre by looking at a sample for evidence of discursive moves rather than for accuracy of content or for particular positions toward the topic. This approach established at the outset that what counts in writing philosophy is the quality of reasoning and thinking, the ability to countenance and fully explore and explicate ideas.

The short in-class commentaries reinforced the emphasis on how to write philosophy because of the way Phil responded to them. Although only 10–12 min was allocated, students had a chance to reflect on an aspect of the lecture topic and get feedback. The point of these pieces, in common with current assumptions about the value of informal writing, was to give students practice in representing their thinking in writing in a non-graded context. Phil might insert clarifying phrases that refined the student's claim and prompted further thinking:

> I do not see how the realist is able to escape the notion that everything [even exemplification] is an exemplification of something of higher order.

He pointed out extensions or implications of what students wrote:

> This looks like yet a further argument against exemplification being a relation: if it were, it would have to have its own properties. Interesting.

He challenged student claims, inviting further elaboration:

> Since the realists maintain that universals are in the objects, we no longer need concern ourselves with the nature of the exemplification of particulars with forms. Why not? Don't we want to understand how universal exemplified by objects make our predications true or false?

Sometimes he would simply affirm: "Your suspicions are well placed."

I cite these examples since they represent one of the ways in which Phil was now able to construct a rhetorical situation in which students were positioned to engage individually in philosophical dialogue with him through their writing. In addition, he also set aside time on a few occasions for students to engage with each other's commentaries in small groups. Since this was mainly a lecture situation, small group discussion represented a noticeable departure from the usual practice, but had the effect of reinforcing the social situation that philosophical writing ostensibly replicates: the presentation of arguments, statements of objections, and response to objections. Students responded enthusiastically to these opportunities and later requested in feedback that they be a more regular part of the course.

The formal papers that students wrote for the course also needed to conform to discursive expectations. The initial non-example served as an introduction and its principles were partly exemplified in Phil's responses to the short commentaries. To assist in making what we hoped was a growing confidence in writing philosophy, we added a component to the first formal paper that would encourage articulation of genre knowledge. Students were to submit the draft of this paper along with the feedback, the revised version, and a detailed statement of the changes they had made and why the changes represented improvements. In introducing the plan to include a revision of the first paper, Phil positioned the students' writing in comparison with scholars in the discipline for whom rejection on the first submission is a common occurrence. Scholars revise in response to commentary and resubmit. It is this process that Phil suggested he was following with them in this course. The addition of a statement about the revisions would correspond to the kind of thinking required to make the revisions in the first place, and also positioned the students as apprentices in the discipline.

Predictably, students responded very positively to both the low-stakes commentaries and the opportunities to revise based on feedback. Critical to the success of both was the nature of Phil's response that students saw as helping them "examine my writing more," "differentiate the philosophy papers from papers in other subjects," understand "what was expected," and experience the feeling of "some personal attention in being able to submit a work-in-progress."

OBSERVATIONS AND REFLECTIONS

In each of these three courses, the collaboration engaged all of us actively in the process of interpreting genre and in performing in response to what we understood to be its implications for student learning and writing in three distinctive cultural contexts. For students in Nancy Olewiler's economics class, doing economics meant mainly applying theoretical models to economic problems and producing graphs and tables to illustrate possible solutions. Introducing writing in her course meant transforming student assumptions of what it means to do economics. The concentration on the technical and cognitive was re-contextualized by a new discourse of social participation in the genres appropriate to economics such as the policy brief. In Arne Mooers' Biodiversity class, writing to report on and interpret data was a conventional social practice. Introducing a genre perspective meant being explicit about purpose, situation, and audience, and illustrating the ways in which, in this case, scientists critique the work of colleagues or explain scientific findings to a lay audience. In Phil Hanson's philosophy class, the instantiation of genre mainly meant creating spaces and occasions for students to exhibit and practice the dialogic activity that characterizes writing in philosophy and that is modeled in the texts and lectures.

It was my role, as outsider, to mediate concepts of genre and offer ways of seeing through this theoretical lens that could be grafted onto practices that neither the culture nor the professor and students would reject. In the particular context of a course, the professor is the representative of the culture. In these pilot W-courses, we saw a high level of acceptance from faculty. We saw students repositioned by new theory and pedagogy. Successful transformation of expectations and concepts about the discipline and the genres through which it is represented depends on many factors; not least for students will be sufficient exposure to similarly imagined and constructed disciplinary contexts. I take up the challenge that sufficient exposure poses for the W-initiative in the final chapter.

6

VOICES OF EXPERIENCE
Reflections from the W-Faculty

In my role as director of CWIL, I knew my own motives and biases; I was ambitious. When I thought about the place of writing in the university, I envisioned a transformation of the university culture of teaching and learning. I envisioned a writing environment that apprenticed all students as writers, an environment where writing and teaching writing were so fully integrated into learning that the fact of teaching writing would no longer attract bewildered critique or opposition. In embarking on the W-strand of the curriculum initiative, I knew that as consultants, we in CWIL needed a certain passion and conviction about its purposes as well as credible expertise that could help propel the initiative forward. Yet, it would be unwise for us to make assumptions about faculty's convictions or views on the uses of writing or about their first-hand experiences of the W-initiative. The story of the W-implementation would be as much a story about the experience of those faculty members who piloted the first courses (in the three years leading up to the start of the new requirements) as it would be about CWIL's contribution to their practice.

Initially, therefore, I considered asking two or three people to write accounts of their experiences, but this would not have given the broader perspective that I wanted. I wanted to know what the initiative meant at both the local and institutional levels from the point of view of the faculty who had taken part. I had learned not to take either enthusiasm or denigration at face value. I also knew that my CWIL colleagues and I had been constantly learning from and with the faculty. An in-depth interview process seemed to be one way to enrich that learning and to refine an understanding of what factors or elements appeared to affect the experience for faculty in this process and for the university culture, if indeed anything was affecting the culture. In order to include their experience in this account, I approached faculty who were both willing and available to meet with me. Each of them was an "early adopter" who had been willing to take a chance on doing something new and different, and whose experience was either recent or had been ongoing. Ten people volunteered to participate: five men and five women, each with different academic positions and from across the disciplines: Arne Mooers, assistant professor in biology;

Lee Hanlan, senior lecturer in chemistry; Richard Smith and Catherine Murray, both associate professors in communications; Robbie Dunlop, senior lecturer in earth science; Nancy Olewiler, professor in economics; Sean Zwagerman, assistant professor in English; Karen Ferguson, associate professor in history; Phil Hanson, associate professor in philosophy; and Andy Hira, associate professor in political science.

CONCERNS AND ISSUES: CUES FROM THE INTERVIEW PROCESS

As might be expected, deciding what I wanted to know and what questions to ask would be at the heart of the process. I was in the position of having been an advocate of the W-initiative and a visible person in its direction and development. At the time of the interviews, however, I was also a retired director, at a remove from the actual work. I situated myself, therefore, as a listener and learner, much as I had tried to do in consulting with the faculty about writing in their courses. I was not disinterested but I refrained from foregrounding or seeking endorsement of CWIL participation in the process of pedagogical change. More important it seemed to me at the time was to be able to characterize some of the qualities and conditions that the faculty seemed to have in common when they were able to embrace change as well as when they felt impeded.

Each of the participants would have been talking about their experiences to others at departmental meetings and perhaps elsewhere in informal conversations. What were the elements uppermost in their minds when they reported on what they were doing? Whatever these elements were, it seemed likely they were ones that warranted further thought and reflection. I opened the interviews by asking: "What would you tell a colleague about offering a W-course? What are some of the reasons for taking it on, and what aspects should someone be cautious about or aware of?" From the range of everyone's responses, I hoped to identify some common themes to pursue in a longer interview. The first interviews, set as half-hour sessions (though most stretched close to an hour), highlighted such aspects of the experience as the variety of relationships each person had with writing as scholar and teacher; evolving awareness about self as teacher; perceptions of the effects of writing instruction on students; concerns about workload and the trade-off between content and writing instruction; roles and relationships inside and outside the department; and perceptions of the institution's commitment and responsibilities to support the new curriculum. What became apparent from the first interview was that each person's experience of developing and teaching a W-course seemed to be influenced by a spectrum of variables and dimensions ranging from the intimate to the more distant. On the one hand, there were the knowledge and beliefs about their own writing and about themselves as teachers that each person brought to her practice. On the other hand, there were the contexts and situations that framed their practices and work at the classroom, department, and university levels. The question of influences on the practical matters of using and teaching writing in different classes and disciplines invited deeper and more complex questions of philosophy, ideology, and the politics of the institution. These more complex questions (see Appendix 7) became the springboard to prompt discussion during the second (two-hour) interviews.

In looking at the transcripts from both the first and second interviews, it was clear that there were many stories to tell. It was important to me in choosing what to include (and the form the stories would take) that I convey as best as I could the reflections and insights that clustered around the teaching experience, the more intimate dimension, as well as the spectrum of issues that sprang from the broader university context, the more distant contextual dimension. I have chosen to separate these two dimensions and deal with each of them in its own chapter. In this chapter, I use faculty comments and observations to weave a detailed representation and analysis of, first, how the faculty interviewees saw writing and themselves as writers in their own field, and secondly, how they saw themselves in their classrooms and their interactions with students as teachers of writing. Their reflections on these two aspects of their experience in the W-course reveal very different personalities and styles that nonetheless come together in deeply engaging teaching ventures marked by ambiguities, tensions, and considerable intellectual pleasure.

RELATIONSHIPS TO WRITING

Writing is what university professors do. What they write plays an important part in constructing their identities as scholars and determining their careers as researchers. Despite the significance of writing in their working lives, however, faculty are often, if not typically, unaware of how they acquired the rhetorical skills of their disciplinary practice or indeed, that disciplinary writing was a matter of acquiring those skills. As Catherine Murray observed during our interview, "some [faculty] are very much appreciative of the craft . . . others ignore it or take it for granted." Focused on "what" they are writing about, academics are seldom called on and seldom motivated to reflect on what is entailed in the writing that they do. Successful writers quite reasonably might say with Arne Mooers, "I thought of myself as a naturally good writer," or they could be as likely to look back as Lee Hanlan to recall that, "I don't think I was ever taught to write in chemistry, it just happened along the way." Andy Hira was drawn to writing early on because, as he said, "I think I had a natural talent for story-telling at a young age." For some of the faculty, writing seemed to come easily. Robbie Dunlop, for instance, told of her experience of writing: "I don't have any problems with the process of writing and never have. . . things just kind of fall out of my head. I don't think I've ever had writer's block. I know that's not the same for a lot of students. I'm teaching and I don't know why that is." As an historian, Karen Ferguson commented on her writing process and the psychological demands of writing. Like Lee, Karen did not recall being taught to write: "I never did take rhetoric or composition, although I could have, but I never had to do it, so I didn't do it. . . . I am somebody who understands history and it feels as though it came to me through osmosis or something, but that is the problem with people who are good at something and for whom it comes instinctively."

For all of the faculty interviewed, it seemed that the process of the acquisition of their particular disciplinary discourse was so embedded in their apprenticeship in the discipline that it was invisible to them. Being able to think and write like a chemist or political scientist was what happened as part of the experience of being a student in the discipline. In each case, of course, these were people whose interest in their subject went well beyond taking a few courses; it became their life's work. The sense of having simply acquired the discourse through immersion seemed to be common among successful academics and thus academic writers, and this tendency is supported by studies of the acquisition of academic discourse (Berkenkotter and Huckin 1995; Dias 1999) among others. In the case of these particular W-faculty, however, taking on the teaching of a W-course helped to engage them in a dialogue with their own teaching and uses of writing. It gave them access to recognition and reflection on their own experiences, which encouraged them to be reflexive about their process and become more aware of the conditions that influenced their own writing. Their shared awareness of what was entailed in the production of writing, if not in the acquisition of writing skills, and what assists the process of writing, made them receptive to the value of teaching as well as assigning writing.

WRITING AS PRODUCTION

Getting ideas down, using writing to think and to learn, and working through multiple drafts all figured as part of the process for these faculty interviewees. As a graduate student, Arne learned the value of "starting right from the beginning and getting all of your ideas down on paper, instead of every third or fourth idea down on paper. It's not as easy as it sounds and that's what I try to tell my students all the time." Sean affirmed the need for what he referred to as "time to futz around and brainstorm and let things ferment." Lee said that she learned how to write in chemistry by "using writing in the process of learning, so when I was studying, I was constantly writing; I could organize my ideas better or things I wanted to remember by writing things down." Nancy also used writing this way, noting that, "I may have to re-write, three, four, or five times because writing helps me think." Depending on what they were writing, drafting was a common practice. Phil talked about writing "multiple drafts, using pencil and paper in a few drafts before I get to an electronic version because my ideas are just not formulated enough to put them on the screen. There would be too much reworking."

While each person had his or her own way of getting something down on paper, everyone agreed on the need for time, frequency, regularity, and freedom from being evaluated during the figuring-out, early drafting stages. As Phil commented, "these sorts of things tend to take time; it's as though your brain needs time to sift through, make connections. You can't hurry it." No one underestimated or minimized those conditions for enabling their writing, nor did they underestimate the absence of such conditions as potentially disabling. Perhaps, most importantly, for students in their classes, and for their planning and scheduling of writing assignments, all stressed the roles of feedback, revision, and audience as key influences on their own production.

It was getting feedback that distinguished Arne's "best undergraduate course" and as a graduate student, it was the feedback from his peers that helped him as a science writer and gave him an understanding of the important role that writing would play in his professional life as a scientist. Karen also remembered the importance of feedback on her work in progress. She noted, in particular, her participation in a writing group of Americanists at The University of British Columbia [UBC], which stimulated a new long-term writing project: "That face to face feedback is really important to me." While feedback from others was clearly important to these W-faculty, as expert writers in their own fields, they tended to seek feedback in situations where the genre was particularly challenging or unfamiliar or the audience was new. Karen noted, for instance, that she struggled with and sought feedback on her research-driven writing, but other things "come fairly effortlessly, like book reviews that I have to write professionally. I know the genre." For everyone interviewed, others'

feedback seemed to serve mainly as a kind of scaffolding that led to independence as writers, to self-review of their own writing, and to ability to
read their own texts dialogically. When Sean observed, for instance, "I can
barely see something after I have written it. I have to distance myself from
it for a while," he indicates knowledge of what and how he wants to write
and confidence that he can, with that distance, revise without referral to
someone else. Phil, as a philosopher, was acutely aware that his writing was
a "trial and error" process to which he himself could respond as if he were
the intended reader. He described his experience as "a process of writing
and then stepping back to see what you've got. . . . You suddenly notice
this pattern of connections you've never seen before and then you can
take it to the next level, ask what the consequences are, what hangs on it,
why is it important?"

The interplay of feedback and revision seems almost taken for granted
in these faculty observations, whether the feedback is from themselves as
they re-read or from an external reader. Also implied or perhaps assumed,
is their audience awareness, a crucial element in the writing production
process. Andy put it most succinctly: "Everything is going to vary depending on the audience." He identifies himself as a "breadth scholar" whose
area of specialization is Latin American studies, and whose audiences are
both economists and political scientists. He spoke about becoming adapt-
able since "pieces are different across the discipline," and although he can
speak the languages of different disciplines, "none of them is completely
comfortable" for him and he constantly adjusts his modes of reasoning
and uses of evidence as he determines who the "someone" in his audience
might be. Catherine, as a communications professor and trained political
economist, writes professionally to critique public policy. She noted that,
"You have to write to someone *for* something. And the 'for something' is
the 'so what' of it." As an economist, Nancy also focuses on her purpose
of trying to influence environmental policy, and she thinks in terms of
writing to "fit the audience to make sure the writing vehicle fits what you
are trying to do." Since her writing about such topics as "deep time" is
almost always connected to teaching, Robbie thinks about how to "explain
difficult concepts to people in basic levels of language so that I am not
lecturing them but telling a story." Richard, a communications professor,
corresponds electronically with most of his audiences. He finds himself
adopting a hypertext mode, his writing becoming "highly parenthetical"
and extending his scholarly reach into such public venues as the "massively distributed collaboration" (Kapor 2005) that is Wikipedia and its
online readers.

WRITING AS ENGAGEMENT IN SOCIAL SITUATIONS

For these faculty, writing in their discipline is deeply embedded in, and reflective of, the main issues and topics in their fields, and for each of them, what they write is driven by individual purposes for audiences they have identified. They know, from their own experience, what is likely to assist a writer's development. Supported by the demands of the criteria for W-courses, they had a context within which to apply what they knew for themselves to their work with students. They did this in such ways as inviting informal writing as a means of learning, allowing time for drafts, giving feedback, and expecting substantial revision. But important as it is to provide for such processes and interaction with texts, it is insufficient by itself. It becomes merely procedural unless grounded in the purposes for the intellectual work of the class: in the concepts and modes of reasoning of the course that are expressed through its characteristic genres. Even if students encounter a subject and discipline only as a matter of taking courses, and not a means to a life-work as it became for their professors, they still need to gain some grasp of its discourse and the contexts of use if they are to succeed in the course, and, more importantly from an educational standpoint, to understand the discipline's particular way of seeing the world.

Discussing their disciplinary discourse proved to be an intellectually engaging process for most of the faculty. As noted earlier, they seemed to have acquired their discourse knowledge almost unconsciously, so making its characteristic features and purposes explicit was not only interesting to them, but also valuable for communicating to their students. They needed to articulate features of the genres they were teaching as part of the W-course instruction, and began to do so during the planning processes for teaching those courses. Later, during the interview conversations, they elaborated on what seemed to them to be distinguishing genre characteristics. These characteristics were not identifiable simply as technical aspects of structure and form. More importantly, they were ways of being in the discipline, ways of thinking, and representing disciplinary knowledge that they believe have implications for student learning beyond immediate course applications. Arne describes his field, evolutionary biology, for instance, "as an historical science: as for all sciences, the nature of it is what is written down." But, as Arne points out, the distinction from sciences such as physics or chemistry is that evolutionary biology, while based on empirical evidence, has an interpretive aspect. Students learning to participate in this discipline have to evaluate multiple interpretations of the same phenomena and look for and recognize assumptions on which the case for a particular interpretation is being made, and these are skills they can use in other contexts. Phil knows that few students will become philosophers but he sees writing in philosophy as excellent training for thinking through arguments and laying out a case.

The distinctive ways of thinking also have implications for handling structures and considering audience. Nancy's students will probably not become graduate economists, but probably will need to produce written explanations of numerical or technical information. She explained that, "The translation of the symbolic content into the explanation requires writing. If they have to produce policy statements, they need to know they are not writing mystery stories, and the message needs to go upfront." She favors writing in forms that will give students flexibility as writers and help them understand the need to address an audience and tell that audience what it wants to know. Similarly, Lee has become interested in the question of audience for her chemistry students. She wants to "get across to students the difference between what they write in their lab notebooks, which is for themselves or a peer who will be re-doing their experiment, and the research perspective which needs to be presented in the lab report. The lab report isn't for yourself primarily, it's for other people in the discipline. That is the audience when you are writing something formally."

Audience and purpose influence the way Andy and Sean conceptualize writing in their disciplines, political science and rhetoric, respectively. Both believe strongly in helping students discover the social uses and usefulness of writing. "I want them to be in a place to make a difference," Andy suggests. He wants to see students "generate problems and questions and apply them to real life with due regard for actual contexts." Sean hopes his students will "use writing to negotiate conflict and disagreements and to discover opinions" and that in critically examining the rhetoric of all kinds of texts, they will see that "it's about getting your hands dirty in the real world. They'll write about things that have some significance so writing in English is not just about, 'What's beautiful in this poem?' " Karen discusses the challenges of teaching students that writing history is not about reporting facts but about making a case for interpreting facts in a particular way. It is about ways of seeing the past: "I focus on why it happened and how it happened. . . and help them see you are deep in dialogue with these other historians over these great questions of history. Students can get an intellectual confidence from understanding what they are doing." Richard rejects the traditional "term paper" as a genre in his communication classes. He encourages writing in more professional forms like news stories and reviews of new software and technology. Similarly, Catherine sees the professional need to persuade and argue in her discipline and teaches students to both read and write critically.

For these faculty, their experience as writers and the level of self-awareness that emerged or developed through the W-teaching process had become key to a transformation in their understanding of students' needs as writers and in their pedagogy. Embracing the criteria for the W-course meant that they could take aspects of their own practices into their classes. Incidentally, it also affirmed the rationale behind the university's decision to situate the teaching of writing in the discipline. But the criteria do bind the instructor to certain elements of a pedagogy for teaching writing. For some, the implications appeared to challenge and even threaten their academic freedom. For others, the criteria challenged their perceptions of themselves and their role, not as writers but as teachers. They found they had to make accommodations and adjustments as they adopted a new pedagogy.

The next section of this chapter shifts to the other "intimate" dimension that reflections on their experience brought into focus for the interviewees: their teaching. The section opens with some observations about being a teacher in a post-secondary institution, and is followed by a series of snapshots, each of which seeks to capture an aspect of the challenges that emerged from the process of teaching a W-course. The insights from these snapshots cross disciplinary contexts and boundaries, and, as a collection, they testify to the valuable learning that occurs when faculty from across the disciplines exchange ideas and experience about teaching. Individually, these professors describe attitudes, practices, and quite different personal recollections of experience of writing and beliefs about themselves as writers, from seeing writing as Robbie does, as almost as natural as talk, to Phil's meticulous and painstaking process. We see how awareness of those individual characteristics plays out in their teaching. Becoming conscious that her students do not find it natural to write, Robbie conscientiously demonstrates and illustrates what she expects from them in their writing and gives them opportunities for practice. Phil, as a writer, is aware of coming to realizations during his composing process; in his teaching, he is reluctant to define expectations too precisely for fear of leaving his students no room for such realizations and unanticipated new insights.

Others' teaching is also shaped by their own experience, beliefs, and attitudes: several are very sensitive to audience and the ways they themselves adjust what they say and how they say it in order to communicate effectively. Nancy teaches economics students to write policy briefs as well as news items; Arne teaches students the difference between writing about a scientific topic for academic and lay readers; Lee helps students distinguish peer from scholarly readers; Richard selects a variety of professional genres in communication to encourage sense of audience. Feedback has played a significant role in Karen's development as writer, and in her teaching she reserves time for individual consultations with her students on their drafts. The purposefulness and social implications and consequences of writing are particularly important to Sean, Andy, and Catherine in their own writing. They take that belief to their classes, emphasizing in Sean's case how to recognize that writing affects thinking and action, in Andy's case, the consequent need for passion and scholarly integrity, and in Catherine's, the power of critical perspective and argument.

Each of the W-faculty, in his or her own context, moves toward enacting Coe's principles for teaching from a genre perspective: assigning genres that embody socially established strategies for achieving purposes in rhetorical situations and that imply/invoke/create subject positions for the student writer in those situations.

ON TEACHING: AM I A TEACHER?

Catherine laughed when I asked the question. "No, I don't think I'm a teacher, no. I'm from a generation of academics who did not actually think about teaching. They presented the field. They presented their perspective." But, she says, she does her best to interest her students. Like Catherine, Andy does not see himself as a teacher. He believes that he has neither "the training, natural ability or inclination to be a teacher." But he, too, works hard to engage students' interest. Karen sees herself as a "tortured teacher" who lives in a love–hate relationship with teaching and who feels, like Catherine, that it is not her role to bail out students who do not seem to want to learn. Arne says he is "paid to be a teacher so I have to see myself as a teacher . . . but how I define myself given that, I don't know . . . I really feel a strong responsibility to the students I mentor and I take that quite seriously."

For Phil, Nancy, and Richard, however, teaching and research seem to be compatible and mutually complementary roles. For Phil, teaching is a "lifelong avocation" that enriches his thinking about the topics that fascinate him. Nancy links her role as researcher and writer to her teaching through her textbooks, the writing she sees as "a natural extension of my work as an educator." She says the textbooks are actually more important to her, since they affect a lot more people, than her articles in professional journals. Richard's sense of himself as teacher is bound up with his own scholarly attitudes toward learning and reflection, which he seeks to model to students. Newer in his professorial role than the other tenure-track faculty, Sean seems to feel that teaching is at the heart of how he sees himself at this stage in his career. He feels "very responsible for students' learning. I definitely feel responsible if on a particular day they are unresponsive or apathetic." For both Robbie and Lee, as lecturers whose roles are defined as teaching, rather than research and publication, the question about teaching is more straightforward: teaching represents who they are, as well as what they do. Yet, as Lee pointed out, "unfortunately in this position, they don't hire someone who is trained as a teacher." The academic qualifications take precedence over the professional, even in what are identified as the teaching positions.

These are all faculty whose first passion, nonetheless, is their field of study. None of them, including the lecturers, is a teacher first. They teach because it is part of their job; they put energy into teaching because they care to do it well, and they care about student learning. Taking on the W-course made demands on them as teachers by asking for enhanced attention to how they teach. Too often at the university, teaching seems to be treated like the symbol of a black box that appears, according to cyberneticians, "whenever a piece of machinery or a set of commands is too complex. In its place, they draw a little box about which they need to know nothing but its input and output" (Latour 1987, 2). In like fashion, professors may carefully plan their courses to ensure that the content of their input is interesting and reasonable in quantity, and that their presentation of it will also be engaging and appropriate. They or their TAs attend to student output in the form of papers and reports and exam results. What is in between—the pedagogy, the teaching—is all too seldom subject to the scrutiny and reflection it deserves. Opening the black box, however, immediately renders the processes of teaching and learning as both complex and problematic, subject to a multiplicity of factors, many of which can otherwise easily escape notice.

IN THE CLASSROOM(S): TALES TOLD ACROSS THE DISCIPLINES

Adopting new and unfamiliar strategies embodying new genre perspectives on the nature of writing tended to bring those multiple factors into the foreground for the faculty engaged in W-courses. They become available to be examined; they become objects of inquiry and suddenly, often unexpectedly, intellectually engaging. The brief snapshots that follow provide an opening of the black box: they invite observation and reflection on some particulars of the individual tensions and struggles faculty experienced as they worked to accommodate and make sense of alternative practices that could be more effective in bringing students into their disciplines and the genres of those disciplines.

"GIVING UP STAGE TIME"

Nancy was attuned to the uncertainties inherent in estimating the degree to which her teaching affected her students' learning in economics. No matter how lively her presentation, too many of the students, she thought, seemed "disengaged; they are like cabbage heads because that is about all the sentience I could see while I was up there burning up 400 calories a minute. My TAs were being answer machines; the students were not engaged. I can give a lecture, the students can take impeccable notes, but five minutes later, if you ask them what they learned, they don't have a clue. I pride myself on being able to explain things clearly and always thought of myself as a good teacher. But it dawned on me that this is not the true test. The test is, are they learning it? I finally, after many years, came to the realization that it's not what I say, it's how I get them to think about it. Learning has to be synthesized by the learner, not the teacher. So doing the writing with them really pushed me over the edge, pushed me to slow down because they have to express it themselves and I realized that simply going through analytical assignments is not going to do it." Students needed to be positioned differently in the learning process.

Since Nancy's first experiment with a W-course was with a large class of more than 100 students, she recalls the challenge in having to interrupt her own talk, and in trusting students' willingness and ability to respond, for example, to a short writing assignment that would summarize what she had been saying, or make connections with an idea they had read. "But," she says, "I am really glad I tried a lot of the things I kind of struggled with when we did the course, things I fought you on. I don't think I could ever go back to the regurgitating, even in an organized way, because you just feed them the material and they give it back unchanged. Even colleagues in my program are caving in. One of my students in the fourth year class claimed that this was the first time she had felt confident about her knowledge of economics in her writing. In that class, she picked her topic and focus and did a draft that needed a lot of correcting, but she didn't get penalized for the analytical problems in it. As she said to me, 'I built up my confidence and I understood it.' In the end, I think they are a lot less terrified; they have confidence in the economic material and their ability to work with it as economists would. The way I am teaching now lets them know what they don't understand. They know that if they don't get it at first, they'll get feedback until they do get it. So it does put responsibility on them and those who take the opportunity get a huge amount out of it, and those who don't, are missing out. People say if you let them hand in a draft then they won't work hard, but that isn't true. The more you work on the draft, the more feedback you get. The payoff is in mastery of the work. It isn't shadowed by, 'What does the professor want me to say?'"

Nancy positioned herself as an expert initiating students into the ways of thinking in economics. With her responses, she positioned them to engage in a dialogue that enabled them to understand the processes of economic analysis. Since she has taken a W-approach in all of her classes for the past three years, Nancy reported that she did not waver when teaching a course at a Chinese university to mature Chinese students who already had their MAs in economics, and who were accustomed to being read lecture notes by their professors. Unwilling to follow that model, Nancy planned a much more interactive class. She had them doing a lot of short writing, small group discussions, and presentations. "When I saw them looking a bit vacant, I stopped and got them to write about what they thought I was saying, or gave them an economic problem to work out. All this was quite alien to them, so I was quite eager to get their evaluations. They were very enthusiastic, and said that the way they had written and talked was linked for them to better learning. They wanted more of that. Teaching this way is also linked to giving up some control, of course. I've been fortunate in having small classes in recent years, and I think that's a good way to begin, but I'm ready now to do this work with large lecture groups. And, luckily I'm at a stage in my career when I don't have to worry about proving anything to anyone."

CHANGING THE CLASSROOM DYNAMICS

Phil Hanson was also in the position of no longer needing to prove himself and like Nancy, willing to give up "stage time." As a tenured associate professor with more than twenty-five years of teaching experience, he felt comfortable about experimenting with his teaching in the interest of improving its effectiveness as well as enabling students to improve their writing in philosophy. Also as department chair, Phil felt a responsibility to participate in an innovative initiative, which he strongly supported and that he wanted his colleagues in philosophy to support. He needed to be able to talk from personal experience. The decision was not difficult. As he put it, "I was always grabbed by the slogan 'writing to learn' and this idea that there was a kind of integration of course content with a focus on writing skills. I think that normally there is this obvious close connection between clarity of thought and language skills.

You can't really separate them. Clarity of thought about difficult issues is supposedly paradigmatic of what we are supposed to be doing in philosophy. So the idea of writing to learn, with a self-conscious focus on writing skills, is just the idea of focusing on thinking skills at one remove, externalized, in a certain way: focusing on the writing is an externalized way of focusing on thought."

In the 200-level metaphysics W-course that he planned, Phil tried out some new strategies to encourage the structures and patterns of reasoning and the dialectical habits of exchange between students that he associates with philosophical thought. "There were a few really interesting features: besides the four equally weighted papers, the first of which involved rewriting after initial feedback on both philosophical content and structure, there were 'low stakes' writing assignments. These latter were pieces written in class in response to a prompt of some kind. We also divided the class into smaller discussion groups sometimes, and asked them to develop some sort of précis or commentary, and then present to the class. First of all, I discovered that the low-stakes assignments were useful for an instructor, to give you quick feedback on where students are at, how well they're understanding, as well as about their writing, and it comes cheaply, because you don't have to give them detailed feedback. Another thing that surprised me was how successful the pedagogic tool of breaking the class up into groups could be. I never had that experience as an undergrad, and I had always thought of it as kind of hokey; but these were good students and they really seemed to profit from it."

Phil sees "teaching as a dialectic, and learning as a kind of puzzle solving. It is the student who must solve the puzzle, but can learn things that help through interactions with the teacher. The teacher is not passively simply waiting for the student to 'get it' but rather, tries to nudge the student in the right direction through dialectic. But there does have to be uptake on the student's part, and that uptake is bound to be to some degree individualistic and idiosyncratic." One of the outcomes of experimenting with group work is that Phil acquired "more respect for more informal interactions in the classroom" and became more willing to have students nudge each other through dialectic. The classroom became more of a social situation inviting rhetorical action for social purposes than it had been when Phil took all the class time to lecture. While his lectures demonstrated philosophical reasoning, students previously had limited opportunities for participation. "For instance, I now have a lot more classroom presentations, where people are paired up or in groups of three or four. It was just a matter, I guess, of being confronted with the idea that there was pedagogical value in this kind of thing. Part of the joy of being a teacher is seeing some uptake on philosophical reasoning take place and part of the frustration is seeing in particular instances that it isn't." Through discussion but also through their writing, students were being re-positioned and, in Phil's view, were acquiring new understandings.

> We are not talking here about rote learning, but about the student acquiring rather general analytical skills, and a critical perspective that can be applied in various contexts. From my experience, a good student who has managed to write a couple of good papers and has got appropriate feedback can generally be expected to write more good papers on diverse philosophical topics . . . . Students who are struggling with their writing require patience and attention and encouragement . . . so you go over the paper with them and identify problems with their thinking and they usually find that exercise very helpful. It's not necessarily advice that is going to map directly onto their next assignment, but it doesn't mean they haven't learned something that will benefit them later.

This is not to say that Phil considers revision and rewriting unnecessary. Rather, it is a matter of what is achievable given the size of the class. At the 400 level, writing-intensive classes will be capped at fifteen, which will both enable and encourage detailed feedback and opportunities for rewriting but, he points out, with larger groups of thirty-five, the size of classes at the third-year level, "That's a lot of rewrites to grade."

KNOWING "WHY" PREVENTS GIVING UP TOO EASILY

Richard has taught "Introduction to Information Technology: The New Media" for more than ten years, each time making adjustments to the content, his modes of delivery, and his interactions with students. He was willing to make more adjustments when he decided to make it a pilot W-course, but introducing more writing, more systematically, and in different forms proved more problematic than he had anticipated. Since the course included an inquiry into social software, he required students to use the genre of the blog. The blog offered a rhetorical situation that could serve to represent a familiar and genuine community; it would also be a means of encouraging the students to write about what they were observing and reading as the course developed and to reflect on course concepts. Writing in the blog was meant as a low-stakes assignment, worth few marks overall. Richard planned to read and respond to blog entries, but would not grade them. At first, he was not pleased with what he saw: "It was just ghastly, absolutely ghastly stuff that they were writing, with only a few exceptions, so that really put my expectations at a low level." At that point, he might easily have abandoned this low-stakes strategy as a failure, but instead, he decided, he says,

> to show them I was reading the blogs, I would post one or two from the day and make a pretty substantial comment about it. Then I started making compendium postings, trying to draw them to read each other's. Things began to improve. Eventually, I was able to say genuinely, "Oh look at this interesting posting." They began to read and comment on each other. What that showed me was the value in informal, ungraded writing, and the value of nudging them toward the social situation that blogs represent in the real world. In those circumstances, when people can see each other's writing, it raises the level of engagement. I guess they're in competition with each other, and even though the stakes in terms of the grade don't change (the mark for each posting was really inconsequential), they really started to write better stuff.

As a communications scholar, Richard is fully aware that "you have to write about something to someone," as Catherine said, and here there was the testimony. When there is no response and what they write seems like a monologue that has no apparent impact on anyone and—in a case like this—does not count for much in the grade, there is little motivation for thoughtful expression of ideas. Once Richard created a dialogue, and activated the rhetorical situation, the context changed dramatically, inviting and engaging students' individual intentions in a purposeful exchange of ideas. His modeling gave them a meaningful reason to participate.

In his own teaching, his own writing practices and strategies were foregrounded in the process of planning for the W-course. What he noticed from our planning sessions was that, "being asked to justify something resurrects the rationale that I'd forgotten, and that means that I am 'revived' myself in teaching it. If I've forgotten the reason for what I'm doing, or am simply taking it for granted, the thing is being only half done. I remember in a class recently, I started to say something that I remembered having said before, but now I knew why I was saying it and what it meant. So the whole process has put me onto a track of being explicit about why I'm doing things, which I have found is just better teaching in general." It meant that his planning entailed constructing and articulating the social context and purpose for the writing he would ask of students.

Richard translated this insight into what he would tell students:

> I've started to realize, I can tell students why they're doing something and be explicit about it—university students are perfectly ready to understand

rationale—because they don't want to be run through something that is a mystery to them. The explaining of the why is very empowering to people. . . for example one of our assignments gets them to write in the genre of the discipline. So you could just kind of construct that assignment without any back story at all. Just say, "Okay, we want you to do this." And they would do it. But by explaining, "This is the genre of the discipline which you will be entering," and so on, treating them as future colleagues, essentially, it builds rapport and confidence. So I've told the *why* of what I'm doing and that also gives them a *why* for learning it. Because you know, most people think, "Okay, we have to learn this because it's on the exam." And that is the flimsiest of structures to build your pedagogy upon. They learn the bare essentials and then forget it; but if they know that, "Oh, I need to know this to get a job in some kind of communications area someday," it's part of what it means to be in this field. Then, not only do they learn it for the exam, but they retain it and they have fun when they're doing it.

READING/WRITING: THE JANUS FACES OF COMMUNICATION

Explicitness was also a feature of Catherine's teaching in the W-course, and she found that it had some unanticipated consequences. She wanted to focus students' attention on making arguments in her first-year communications class. To use as their first example, she chose an article by a notable scholar, Noam Chomsky, someone whose name students would recognize. The piece, she acknowledges, "was impenetrable in writing style in some respects, but I wanted them to understand the argument and see it as a model. . . . We worked through the flow of academic argument, and reasoning, and elements of proof, mapping the reasoning." Her purpose was to assist students with their writing by making the elements of the argument explicit. The working-through in the tutorial groups was supported by a detailed, online guide that included cues of wordings for students to locate. But, she says,

I believe both the TAs and myself identified a problem, and that is, that my design was focused on writing, but what we saw was that we needed to work on reading. I cannot emphasize enough that these students are not used to reading, do not read easily, do not read purposively, and if they don't read, I suspect they don't understand why they should be writing or why they should be polishing their writing . . . . One day, I was in total frustration because there were a few students who were really struggling and couldn't concentrate and couldn't string two paragraphs together and couldn't seem to read two paragraphs together. I kept thinking it would be interesting if we could just turn

off whatever it is, the music, whatever, and just simulate some sort of medita-
tive state, so they understand where they need to go. Reading takes a mental
discipline. I don't think they understand that, when so many write and read in
constantly interrupted sensory environments.

As someone deeply interested in the broad, social, and cultural environments that influence individual communication, Catherine tries to
be aware of, and respond to, the conditions under which students learn
and work. Developing the writing assignments in her course had resulted
in sets of explicit instructions, examples, and expectations. But teaching
always involves following a map of planned processes in new terrain, which
itself throws up the unexpected, such as the importance of reading to writing, to a watchful eye. Catherine had structured the assignments through
the course to move students toward taking critical positions on what they
were reading and learning. The final piece of writing, worth 15% of the
grade, invited them to write a 300-word critical piece, a creative commentary typical in her field. It was to be about a topic they "cared about
intensely in the media." Despite urging them to choose something of
personal significance, an issue that aroused their passion, Catherine found
students struggling with the need to start with their own view and move
from that view to identifying and using strategies that could persuade
others. Reflecting on what seemed to be impeding them, she proposed a
journalistic structuring of questions.

I found that the simplest way was to have them return to authorial questions:
'What is it that you want to say? Why and how does that make sense?' And really,
the journalistic craft helps them to sort out their situation a bit more. It helps
them to be conscious of speaking to someone, and have to keep their audience
in mind. Once they identify that perspective, then you show them how others
may go about the same sort of issues, but in a different way. That, I think, is
important. Situating the authorial voice—the self—first, to have them feel sort
of somewhat empowered is important to me because clearly most of them have
not had that sense of themselves. We tried this on and I think it worked. It is
very much the model that you become somewhat self-aware, and then learn to
begin the inter-cultural and inter-disciplinary dialogue with other thinkers.

She had planned the assignment in two parts, one written and one oral,
the intention being that the written would precede and constitute the
substance of the oral. Instead, however, after "talking about using audio
methods" many students "absolutely loved the idea of going into it orally.
They prepared their talk first, and then the writing to go with it . . . it is

very much, I suppose, a creature of the time." It also, as Catherine imme-diately appreciated, made the "speaking to someone" a concrete experi-ence that assisted the students in understanding and thinking about how to persuade that person.

The experience suggested the importance of the social situation in help-ing students understand and meet the demands of the genre and also the implications and consequences that new media has had in repositioning stu-dents in relation to their learning. Catherine observed that, "We talk about media imperatives; we cue to those who have an audio bias or a visual bias, or a textual bias in learning. But I think we are seeing more and more stu-dents able to talk well and able to actually design media presentations using a kind of PowerPoint bullet style. They can represent the bits, but not actu-ally work with the writing flow, which establishes the relationships between and among those bits. I found that if they tried to talk, to have a conversa-tion with someone, and verbally play out their ideas, they cued into the idea of a script, a sequence, and then could edit on paper more easily. It was a way to get around the 'rip and read' or 'copy and compile' approach to expression." It meant that students were assuming roles in a social situation they recognized and engaging in critical commentary became meaningful.

YOU MEAN WE SHOULD HAVE AN OPINION, TAKE A POSITION?

Andy Hira also sought a way to "get around the copy and compile" approach that students often take when assigned to write a research paper when they lack a sense of the paper as a genre that functions in a par-ticular social situation. Reflection on his own struggles with research as a student confirmed his resolve to treat his fourth-year Latin-American stud-ies seminar, "Globalization, Integration, and the Free-Trade Agreement of the Americas (FTAA)" as an initiation into professional participation in the field. He planned a step-by-step process that would culminate in conference-style presentations open to the broader university community. In an e-mail in the first week of class, he made his purposes and direction clear: "This is both a writing and labor-intensive course designed to help you to begin to learn how to write a good policy analysis." He emphasized that students' projects would imitate the work of an analyst in the field and would be at the centre of their work; course material used to support those projects would provide background. He explained that he would not be doing a lot of lecturing but would spend "significant portions of the class in writing exercises and instruction. So, let's be clear about the neces-sary commitment and orientation of the course. I am willing to give it my all, but the course will only work if you also have a firm commitment."

Andy's commitment to "give it my all" was no cliché. He felt passionately that students were typically not given adequate support to do the kind of independent research and thinking that would serve them well in their future lives and work, and that low expectations deprived them of opportunities for intellectual growth and development. Despite the 90% grading emphasis on the constituents of the independent research project, however, the formal course outline (as distinct from the email in the first week) also identified topical sequences of the subject matter and advised students about preparation of weekly readings, both of which rhetorically oriented students to professor-led presentation of information. At the outset, this may have been a source of some conflict in expectations. Students could interpret the course description as conforming more or less to a typical *listen, read, discuss and then write* model, enhanced by more class instruction and individual coaching in writing. The research project, however, required a parallel pattern of reading and writing that needed to run concurrently if students were to work through the processes to arrive successfully at a well-substantiated, independent view of their topic. Managing this parallel pattern proved more challenging than Andy anticipated. In practice, about 30% of class time was spent on background information through lecture and discussion, 45% on a variety of writing exercises, and 25% on troubleshooting problems students had with their projects.

I think they expected to come to the lecture, take notes and then memorize that," said Andy. "But the lectures were not a substitute for their independent reading, so if someone said they did not know enough about *x* to proceed with their project, I sent them sources to consult. I was doing that all along. Plus they had outlines for each part of the project that I explained and walked through with them in class. I modeled asking and answering the kind of questions that structure analysis, and made myself available almost daily both in person and on e-mail to respond to queries and to drafts. But it seems they did not know how to answer the questions, even with that modeling. And I am trying to tell them that they don't need to have a clear answer, and that they are only going to be able to see some part of the horizon. I am trying to get them to see nuances. In the end, that's what makes academics exciting, trying to tackle these bigger, unanswerable questions. They are very impatient with unknowns.

Some students' sense of insecurity was reflected in the amount of feedback and assistance they sought and by an incapacitating level of procrastination. Despite the carefully staged process, some students were weeks late on the earliest elements, and consequently, could not benefit in the research training as Andy intended. "I think oral consultation is important, and the best use of time may be to explain verbally where they are in the process, and sometimes that got left out. What I will do next time is require them to write a short summary paper that summarizes the background they need as the basis for their analysis. That way they will answer the 'what' questions before tackling the 'why' and 'how' questions."

He recalls when he started teaching,

> I ended up overwhelming them with facts and now it is more about me setting up questions, and they have to try to answer those questions. There is no canned response. This is what I learned by teaching the writing course, by setting these clear examples that they have to sort out for themselves, I can lead them along a path, they start to become more confident and then the goal is to answer questions that haven't been addressed. Early on, it seems that they have no thoughts of their own because they haven't really acquired enough knowledge. Because they haven't let the material sink in, they had no horizon. By becoming comfortable with being uncomfortable, they could proceed from there.

HOW DO I GET THEM TO TAKE ME SERIOUSLY?

Karen made a particular effort to be explicit about what was required in students' writing in her third-year history course: "The difficulty of historical genres is that students can't see the forest for the trees. It is narrative-based but also analytical and argument-based. I focus them on the importance of not thinking about what happened but why and how. That is how they can become better readers of academic history, by understanding that there is an argument answering a question. They can get lost in the details." One of the ways she uses to support students' grasp of history's requirements is through specific feedback during the drafting process. Individual students met with her, who, she says,

> have decided that this is going to help them. They've come to see me several times through the semester. It has helped clarify their analytical and critical thinking. For example, when I talk to them about the introduction of their papers and how to articulate their argument, it really starts to help them clarify their thoughts, and when I look at their drafts and show them how every section needs to lead to their argument, that also really helps. Even just getting them to do drafts of their introductions helps them, I think, to see the forest. My frustration now is that I think they think these requirements are particular to me, that I am some kind of weirdo! But I am certainly not as frustrated with their writing now, especially the writing of the hard-working B students who are clearly getting something valuable out of this. There have even been a couple of eureka moments for these students who have then gone on to do A-level work.

She noted, however, the difficulty of communicating expectations, even with explicit instruction and support through feedback.

In my 300-level class, my innovation was getting students to map out a historical article; they each had to make some sort of graphic scheme or map of the structure of the article, and then we talked about it together and identified the essential elements collectively. They then wrote their first papers, but they totally ignored what we had done; practically none of them had even made an attempt to articulate an argument, which had been the focus of all of our discussions and my class handouts, pointing out argument as the linchpin for the rest of the paper. It was as though they didn't think I was serious about it. When they saw that I was, by the way I marked their papers, then they were really scared and started to take it seriously, by coming to visit me in office hours about what they might do differently, and talking to each other about "what I wanted" and as a result, the final papers were really good. I think old habits die hard, and I think it also has to do with how much work they have with their jobs and other courses, and that they decided to write their first paper using their tried and true method rather than puzzling through "my" way. I was adding a new burden to their over-committed lives, and they simply were not ready or did not have the additional time to spend on the assignment. There's also the possibility that they just hadn't wrapped their head around the new concepts I was introducing to them, and were afraid of the demands I was making of them. I think their fear is mainly intellectual. This structure demands a kind of intellectual rigour, and independence, and curiosity, and critical thinking. It's what they need to understand as potential historians. They have to come up with a "why" question and they are not used to that and that's what scares them the most.

One of the advantages to being explicit about requirements that Karen saw for herself was that it gave her much more confidence in her grading.

Everything is very clear cut for me and I have a better sense, especially with the bottom range. My grades went down and I feel better about that because I feel that it better reflects what my students are doing. In the past I've felt very insecure in giving students low grades, partly because I felt I needed to justify them, and sometimes I felt I couldn't articulate what exactly was so problematic with them. Now that I've made explicit what once was implicit in terms of my standards and expectations, I feel my grading is much more straightforward and objective. My grade distribution has gone down about half a letter grade, which is where I intuitively knew it should have been before. Becoming more explicit about my expectations has made both me and my students aware of why that is the case.

DISRUPTING ASSUMPTIONS AND TEACHING HABITS

Making changes to how you teach involves some disruptions that may be discomforting and inconvenient. In wanting to initiate his students into the field of evolutionary biology by giving feedback on their writing, Arne had been a conscientious editor. He corrected errors and rewrote sentences as well as commented on lay-person thinking and overlooked evidence. But, he says,

> I was treating my undergraduates as graduate students. I assumed they would know this was what would happen to their papers. I assumed they knew what they wanted to do in their papers, but just couldn't do it, as opposed to what was actually the case: not knowing, in fact, what they wanted to do, not knowing who they are writing for, and all that. The kind of feedback I was giving assumes that they can try to go back to that passage in their text and realize why it was awful. But they're not used to the volume or the extent of the feedback. The first time, they were definitely surprised; they were hurt. I didn't realize they would take it personally. That was a very important lesson, that these aren't attacks, and that it is about the material. So I've become much more explicit about why something is wrong and doesn't work. I am better at modulating the feedback, so they aren't so traumatized. I know better now what to expect from them, and they know more about what they are supposed to be doing.

But structuring his course to provide time for drafts, feedback, and revision has disrupted Arne's teaching habits. He places a high value on currency of information; new ideas and evidence about biodiversity emerge constantly, and he wants his students to stay aware of research at the forefront of the field. That priority creates some tensions for him in planning. He explained that, "this year I wanted to do a whole section on global warming, but I realized that it wasn't going to work because we had set everything up with all these deadlines, so I couldn't just say, 'This week, let's look at this, instead.' I didn't feel that I had the flexibility to do something new. Everything was all lined up and there were only so many weeks. If I had had full flexibility, I could have skipped something, but I didn't feel that I could do that. It feels less flexible, especially when you are critiquing over two or three weeks."

"Before, when looking for material for in-class workshops, I just went through the most recent issue of a few journals for examples, but now, there are so many outcomes tied in together. So, for instance, we have invested a lot in organizing how one analyses a journal article, but as a reference source the article we chose is getting stale. You prepare so much, but the content may no longer be relevant." He does feel able, using the samples developed during the pilot course, to take a fresh source and apply a discourse analysis technique that will be useful for the students. But the tension is between wanting new samples and the work required to prepare them. "It's always more work . . . and this isn't the work that I saw the teaching would be. . . . Maybe when I was learning I was naive, rather than thinking really hard about learning styles and content and structure and evaluation. As a grad student, I took some courses on teaching but they were about delivering information, they weren't really about learning. Now I'm beginning to understand about learning. That's harder."

"CHEMISTRY DOESN'T SUIT WRITING"

Lee found that the idea of writing instruction in chemistry took some of her students by surprise. "The word 'writing' seems to interfere with understanding what this is about," she said. "We need to get across to them that this is about communication. The whole concept of writing means something different to the science student. I think they take the meaning they have learned from writing in English classes, and don't see it applying to the sciences." It seemed that identifying a course as writing-intensive shifted students' expectations about the focus of attention, but as Lee commented, "Of course this is a chemistry course and they will be doing a lot of chemistry, mainly doing chemistry, in fact. I think a lot of them were underestimating their own abilities, worrying and thinking they couldn't write. They may think that writing is an extra chore, but they don't realize how much they are already doing. When I introduce this next time, I would like to present it in terms of why the writing is important to their learning. Or maybe even play down the writing aspect, because some of them worry that all they will be doing is writing. So instead, I'd focus on writing to learn."

Other students' misperceptions of the nature and purposes of writing took a different form. One of the goals of instruction was to teach students how to write for the different audiences who would use and read the lab notebook, as distinct from the formal lab report and to recognize these as different genres. The lab notebook is for themselves, but as Lee points out, "they are also writing for a peer who wants to re-do their experiment; from a research perspective, this is what the lab notebook would be used for. This is different from the laboratory report that isn't for yourself primarily; it is for other people in your discipline. That is your audience when you are writing something formally, you are writing for the scientific community." Lee found that, despite the information we were giving them about how to write the lab report, a certain number tended to ignore it. They just wrote things the way they always would. We saw this as well in the daily notebook. We checked the notebooks every week, and told them what they weren't doing and how to improve, but they just did the exact same thing the following week, either forgetting about it or ignoring the feedback. So we constructed a written checklist of features for them. I think they needed that, because they don't look back and refer to what you've said, and at the end of the next lab, you're telling them the same things over again. I think the reminder helped a bit but after the third or fourth week of checking notebooks, we started assigning a mark to it and they responded to that.

While the written list seemed an effective solution for that purpose, Lee saw potential hazards in supplying students with an excess of direction. She noted that students did not seem to trust their own reading of instructions. The lab manual was very explicit but "they come to you when they've got the result as described in manual and want to know if they got it right. In one of our courses, we have web instruction with detailed step-by-step pictures. The students like it but they still come and ask what to do next. It seems they want reassurance from a real person. I wonder if we are spoon-feeding them so much that they think they can't think. They want to know the answer, rather than thinking it through as novice chemists. It's interesting, it does all tie in, how are we going to teach them how to do this writing so that they don't get too hung up on rules and criteria?"

Since the entire class was held in the lab, another problem for working with writing was the physical space. Lee substituted written explanations for some of the quizzes she had previously used to check on understanding, but found that there was both "no good time to take the writing and talk to the class as a whole to show good examples, or to have them share with the person next to them, not without totally changing the lab structure and process, and really cutting back on the chemistry." Fortunately, this first experience of the W-course has drawn attention to constraints that she will no longer have to deal with in the next iteration of the lab course: a tutorial time will be added. Importantly, for perceptions of the role of writing in the discipline and course, the tutorial will be located in a regular classroom space, making it clear that doing chemistry includes doing the writing.

TEACHING AS PROBLEM-SOLVING: THE NEED FOR CREATIVITY

In Robbie Dunlop's classes, as in Lee Hanlan's, students were initially tipped off balance by the idea of writing in science, but Robbie's "Rise and Fall of the Dinosaurs" represented a required first-year science credit for generalist arts and social sciences students and was a gateway course to Earth Sciences. Robbie felt strongly that this course should offer students an introduction to both Earth Science and to how to be an effective university student. That meant, in part, that they should learn to write to university and science department standards. "My conscience won't allow me to shuttle students through my science courses without learning and understanding the science content. Likewise, I can't allow them to go through my courses without improving weak aspects of their writing and English skills," she explained. A really early adopter, Robbie has been adapting her dinosaur and paleontology W-courses for three years. She has continually revised and reinvented her practice in response to students' performance, TAs' comments, and her own observations about the uses of writing in developing understanding and critical thinking. Her experience has led to adjustments in emphasis from attention to the most visible problems to the more complex.

One particularly visible and also important feature was citation practices. She wanted students to understand that different disciplines have different conventions that are related to the ways the discipline constructs knowledge. Since these were Earth Science students, she assigned them to use the style of the *Canadian Journal of Earth Sciences*. When she found them ignoring the style, she devised small group exercises in highlighting the differences from the APA style with which they were more familiar. She also required a specific format on title pages of papers. The challenge she found was to convince students that she was serious about such details. "I gave them a criteria sheet, and yeah, some people actually kept it, others I'm sure just threw it away, because then they came back later and said 'How come I got marks off for this?' and, it's like, 'Did you have the criteria sheet?' Well, no. But that's something I think I will have to hammer into their little heads right at the beginning. These pieces of paper are important, put them on bright yellow or something that blares at you. Put this somewhere special like on the bathroom wall so you don't lose it!" These correct formats were not trivial matters: they represented clarity and careful attention to detail, observation, and procedures—habits of mind as well as skills of the field of paleontology and for students learning how to learn to do future labs in Earth Sciences.

More complex as a problem and more difficult to address were students' reading and technical writing difficulties. Seeing that admonition and lists of instructions did not produce the kind of writing she sought, Robbie became explicit over other highly valued skills for university students: the ability to think critically, and to be able to express under-standing of concepts in discipline-specific ways. To help students read the scientific articles that they were to cite, for example, she introduced an exercise to analyze the structure of an abstract. She taught the scientific IMRAD (Introduction, Methodology, Results, Analysis, and Discussion) structure as well as the journalistic pentad in titles. Students worked back-wards from the article's abstract to locate keywords that signaled places in the article where each feature of the IMRAD originated. This approach seemed to help students better understand that the structure of the abstract represented the structure and reasoning of the whole article and they were better prepared to read both the abstract and the article itself.

> As someone who used to stand up and lecture and work basically just with the textbook and have students do the writing exercises in the lab manual, designing these courses from scratch to put in all this writing is challenging my creativity. For assignments, I really wasn't doing much more than the manual required, so the W-course was a big challenge. One of the problems I noticed in the lab work was that students were not making connections between the videos, the lectures, and the textbook. I used to have them watch videos and then write notes. Now they keep a field notebook that they can use during the exam. They can bring notes from videos, Internet searches, and textbook. The more that is in that notebook, the more useful it will be in the final exam. They are now writing material down and researching; they are studying actively, and I think it helps them retain the material better. They comment that if they weren't asked to do that notebook throughout, they would just be reading the text the night before the exam. That's what I want to avoid!

Robbie sees teaching as a complex process of constantly trying out, noticing what happens, and revising. "For myself, I am not stagnating any-more, which is what I was feeling—overwhelmed with doing nothing. And I still find it really challenging; I am constantly thinking of how to make assignments that are interesting. I am asking more questions; I like in-class activities, and I like quick-writes. It is a quiet time for students, because they have hectic lives, so I think it is good for them. In the dinosaur class, I call them *dinowrites*." The dinowrites evolved from experiments in get-ting feedback on lecture topics to being a creative way for students to synthesize information they have been acquiring all semester and to assist learning. Recent versions ask them to "invent a new dinosaur and describe its characteristics and environment." Or "You've been given $2 million dollars to do a dig—what equipment would you take, where would you go, what would you look for?" The students love it.

IT'S ABOUT WRITING OR IS IT?

As a rhetorician and writing teacher, Sean Zwagerman's taking on a W-course did not mean making new demands on his understanding of the role of writing in learning or on his thinking about processes that would assist student writers in his class to acquire skills in the genres of the discipline. The new source of complexity in teaching writing came for him in his adjustment to working in the context of a first year "Introduction to Prose Genres" lecture course with almost 200 students and TAs. As he described it, Sean's plan was,

> to integrate writing into this writing-intensive course in a really thorough and systemic fashion. Rather than have a content course with writing added, I wanted to dissolve that false distinction between content and writing by making writing itself the content in as many ways as possible. So my goal was to discuss, for each of the assigned readings: (1) the issue addressed; (2) the position taken; (3) how each writing stands, implicitly or explicitly, as a claim regarding language in society; (4) the effectiveness of the writings themselves as persuasive attempts, given the issue, the position, the context, and the audience; and (5) how particular strategies from each piece could be applicable to student work. In other words, we would consider not only what these essays say, but what they do—as purposeful acts of language—and how well they do it. But I did not get to number five often enough. So although I was lecturing about writing, I was still, well, *lecturing* about writing!

The challenge, he said, was that, "I had to keep reminding myself that I was doing a W-course because of the constraints of a lecture format." Although he felt he had "only limited success" in the integration, this first W-course attempt enabled him to try out approaches in ways he can refine the next time he teaches the course. He used some of the 50-minute lecture time for quick-writes because these

> give frequent feedback on what the students are and are not getting that I don't think the instructor can learn in any other way. That is invaluable. In my own tutorial, I have some sense of what's going on with my fifteen students, but extrapolating that to the entire class of 200 is another matter. In addition, for me to put that feedback to use, I had to be willing to adapt my curriculum and realize that some of the things I think are 'givens' are not, and then respond and restructure. I'm okay with that. I'd rather spend time giving students what they tell me they need than giving them what I think they might need. I don't want to be up there 'professing' about Montaigne's ethos or some such thing if they are still trying to figure out what I mean by a "thesis."

Sean also used the lecture time to explain formal writing assignments.

> I wound up in lecture, shortly after handing out the assignments, spending a fair amount of time taking questions which continued over several lecture periods, as students began actually working on the assignment and thus encountered uncertainties or confusions. I think that fielding these questions was useful for all: I don't want students to feel as if the professor gives them the assignment, and then it's all up to them to figure it out and perform. And, it was very useful to me: when I am writing my writing assignments, I try to imagine what students will find puzzling or unclear, and fine-tune the wording of the assignment accordingly. But I can never be completely successful in anticipating how we will misunderstand or confuse each other through the medium of the writing assignment!

As well as responding to feedback and questions, Sean also set aside time for some writing instruction in both lecture and tutorial. He modeled some heuristic devices in lecture, such as a simple fact/idea list, and Kenneth Burke's pentad, and had students work on their first drafts, including some brainstorming activities, during tutorial. He felt that, "these W-course strategies reduced some of the anonymity and ambiguity about the dialogue between myself and this huge mass of students." Overall, he says,

> You know, this course will work better next time. I feel I have a clear sense of what needs improvement: better integration of lecture and tutorial *via* short writing activities in lecture. Also, the writing-intensive model made me want to work in even closer contact with TAs than I otherwise would, and I certainly struggled to find the time for such contact. The TAs' own busy schedules and strict contract guidelines also worked against giving the care and attention to the professor–TA relationship that it really deserves. We'll need to work that out. But I'm still committed to the plan itself: I think it's a good concept of a writing-intensive English course, and I'm confident about improving with practice!

In many ways, what happened in Sean's classroom and how he and the other faculty explained their beliefs and practice was, for each, a private and individual matter; they followed their own trajectories without direct interference from outside. In the context, however, of a new curriculum initiative that rested on somewhat tenuous acceptance by the broader community, that was as yet untested or validated by quantifiable evidence, and that was at this point a surface overlay on deeply embedded pedagogical practice and institutional priorities, the "outside" context was critically important for the eventual growth and health of the private and individual life of the classroom.

At that stage of the implementation, disciplinary differences aside, the faculty interviewed here suggested that "interference" from the context outside the classroom could be both enabling and obstructive. As individuals committed to supporting the W-initiative, these W-faculty were anxious to see that the enabling be encouraged and the obstructions recognized, and if possible, removed, or at least minimized. I invited them to gather together at two dinner meetings to share ideas about how that might be accomplished. The outcome of those gatherings and discussions is the subject of the next chapter.

7
THE INSTITUTIONAL CONTEXT
How is it Helping or Hindering the Writing Curriculum Initiative? A Faculty Forum

In Spring 2005, when I met to interview the ten faculty members who had early on decided to modify their courses to include more writing and writing instruction, we reviewed the pilot phase together. Their analyses drew attention to elements at the department and university levels that were framing and in some respects constraining their work in the classroom. These elements included the political, economic, historical, intellectual, and simply bureaucratic realities that necessarily constrain individual efforts in a large institution and perhaps become particularly visible when changes are being attempted. Such constraints cannot be overlooked but also need not be obstacles. In his book, "*As if Learning Mattered,*" Richard E. Miller (1998) offers a critical analysis of educational reform at several major American universities from the perspective that "bureaucratic limits are ultimately inescapable" and he urges nonetheless an undiscouraged commitment to intended change, a willingness to engage in "the entirely unglamorous, often utterly anonymous work of figuring out what can be done within a given institutional context" (22). It was quite apparent from the individual interviews that these W-faculty had such an undiscouraged commitment. They were also clearly interested in considering what could be done given the institutional context within which they were working. As a way of representing their views on issues that referred to the more distant, systemic, and institutionalized conditions affecting their teaching, I have chosen a discussion forum format for this chapter.

There was no opportunity to have a large group exchange with all interviewees, which meant that most of our meeting time was one-to-one. But we did manage, after much juggling of dates and a few rearrangings, to assemble for small group dinner discussions. These, like the individual interviews, were taped and transcribed. The forum format of this chapter is not a literal representation of the give and take of the dinner discussions. The dialogue did not take place in the exact form presented here. What is presented here is a dialogue constructed by the juxtaposition of commentary and observations from each of the participant interviewees. All of us were agreed that a constructed forum that maintained the contexts, meanings, and intentions of the discussants would be representative of the conversations that we shared. To ease the links and create a conversational tone, I take the role of moderator, setting the context, summarizing, questioning, and pointing the way as I did during the actual interviews. Also, as was the case in the actual interviews, the voices in the forum discussion vary from one participant to the next: some people stayed on longer and talked more, others had strong opinions about particular issues or generated a lot of ideas, yet others tended to offer quiet but observant comments.

ALL THE WORLD'S A STAGE. . .

In this textual "room" are the ten people we met earlier with the addition of three others with whom I have consulted about the same issue of institutional support. As a reminder of who will be present in this forum, I list a few details of their positions and credentials.

From the Faculty of Science:

Robbie Dunlop, Lecturer, Department of Earth Sciences;

Lee Hanlan, Senior Lecturer, Department of Chemistry; Chair, Chemistry Department Undergraduate Curriculum Committee; and

Arne Mooers, Assistant Professor, Department of Biological Sciences.

From the Faculty of Applied Sciences:

Catherine Murray, Associate Professor, School of Communication; Chair, Graduate Studies Committee (1997–2003); Member, Academic Operations Committee; Member, President's University Planning Committee (1995–1996);

Richard Smith, Associate Professor, School of Communication; Associate Director, School of Communications.

From the Faculty of Arts and Social Sciences:

Karen Ferguson, Associate Professor, Department of History; Chair, Undergraduate Curriculum Committee;

Phil Hanson, Associate Professor, Department of Philosophy; Chair,

Department of Philosophy; Chair, Qualitative/Breadth Support
Group, Undergraduate Curriculum Implementation Task Force;

Anil (Andy) Hira, Associate Professor, Department of Political
Science; Member, Simon Fraser University Senate;

Nancy Olewiler, Professor, Department of Economics; Director, Public
Policy Program, Faculty of Arts and Social Sciences; Former Chair,
Department of Economics; Member, Simon Fraser University
Board of Governors (2002–2005); Senior Policy Advisor to former
SFU President Jack Blaney; and

Sean Zwagerman, Assistant Professor, Department of English
(Rhetoric); Member, Senate Committee on Academic Integrity and
Student Learning and Evaluation.

Also invited to add their thoughts are:

Greg Dow, Professor, Department of Economics and current Chair of
the Department of Economics;

Dana Lepofsky, Associate Professor, Department of Archaeology; and

Len Berggren, Professor, Department of Mathematics, member of the
Ad Hoc Curriculum Committee and former Chair of the Breadth
Support Group.

This is a large group representing a broad spectrum of involvement
in and experience of the workings of the university. As they speak in the
forum discussion, I have tried to identify them not only by name but also
by subject as a way of keeping visible the multi-disciplinary nature of this
conversation and their concerns, some of which are general and some
particular to individuals or departments.

IS TEACHING IMPORTANT AND VALUED AT THIS UNIVERSITY?

Wendy: I'd like to ask you first to talk about teaching and the place of
teaching at SFU. In "Radical Campus," his account of the early development of SFU, Hugh Johnston says that Gordon Shrum, the university's first
President, "had no question in his mind about SFU's primary mission—
undergraduate teaching . . . a notion that was probably shared by most of
the early faculty at SFU" (99). That was forty years ago. Much has changed
not only at SFU but also in the environment in which universities compete
for students and, perhaps more to the point, for research grants, and in

which faculty compete for jobs. Having taken on teaching a W-course, all of you have had to do some rethinking of your teaching. It's meant different and, for most of you, more work to teach this way. What evidence do you see that that time and effort on teaching is being valued? Do you think teaching needs to be better supported, given that the new W-requirements make new pedagogical demands? And how?

Arne: Teaching is what we do. When I say that, I mean it from the broader perspective of the public. That's not the case from my biology department's or the university's perspective. Teaching and how you teach are peripheral really; it's not what people are hired to do. It's the research that matters. Of course, outside the university, people may not even know that you do research—you are there to teach their children but, for the university, your teaching has to be good enough so that you don't get into trouble. That's all.

Dana: Exactly. With the new requirements and our making this change in how we use and teach writing, we've raised the quality of education. But that means taking more time, as a teacher and I'm not sure who in my department is going to care. Will I be getting credit for having spent more time? Will it be recognized as a contribution? We all say teaching is supposed to be one of the two things we value equally but we are not convinced that's typical.

Richard: Well, I disagree somewhat with my colleagues here. I think people in communications do see themselves as teachers and value that highly. I don't think that research dominates in our department; teaching does matter. Our chair is supportive of the new curriculum and I think enough faculty support it. I suspect there's this hidden guilt about teaching that our SFU professors have. We teach four courses a year and my colleagues in the East teach six, so when you know you've got it good and if someone says, let's do a little more teaching, then you are not going to fight it. I think SFU does a great job, but we have it good, so when it is about making it better for the students, people are in favor of that.

Len: Well, I was in favor of making it better for our math students but why did I do it? I think it's a unique challenge for a faculty member. . . to think about teaching a course in a different way, especially when a course has gone basically okay, you know, not a lot of student complaints, generally students are enthusiastic about the course, so why change it, especially when it's more work, right? But I think what made me decide to do it was that the math department said that they would commit to keeping the course going after my retirement if there was someone in the department who wanted to train in on this and be the instructor when I retired. Then

I felt it would not be wasting my time. I can actually mentor somebody and do some interesting teaching myself.

Catherine: Well, I found that figuring out how to teach my communications course in a different way was probably one of my most professionally rewarding experiences at SFU. The reason to take it on individually, from a selfish perspective, is precisely the opportunity to identify with others interested in teaching. But the onus is very, very much on the individual professor to sustain a sense of community and most avenues for professional development are individual and not continuous.

Andy: Yes, it's up to individual professors to be enthusiastic, but if they aren't, then how effective is the W-initiative going to be? Faculty see the W-courses as more labor-intensive but they get no recognition.

Karen: Everyone in my history department knows that there is no real reward for teaching. You do have to be a competent teacher, you need to show up on time and make sure all of your readings are on reserve, and do what you say in your syllabus, but other than that, you know, why spend the time taking on something new?

Nancy: I'd like to make two points. First, I don't think instructors get up in the morning and say, I'm going to do a lousy job of teaching today because my department doesn't value teaching. My experience has been that people differ in their innate abilities as teachers, but all can improve and give a good course with some effort. I agree that in departments where there is little reward for good teaching, instructors may put little effort into their craft. Others however, want to do their best for their students regardless of the department's view of teaching. Engaging students in a way that enhances their experience, as I strongly believe the W-course does, is worth doing, period. Who cares what your department thinks? Secondly, there are departments at SFU that do value teaching contributions. I've been fortunate to be in one where there were many excellent and dedicated teachers (who are also superb researchers) and now have helped start a new department where I can tell you, every faculty member strongly supports teaching as the core of the unit and vital to our students success in their future endeavors.

Wendy: There seem to be two things going on here: the importance of personal motivation to do something for students or for yourself as well, as Catherine suggests, and secondly, your awareness of the relative indifference to quality of teaching that you experience in the department. Is this a cultural shift? It seems to contrast strongly with the original vision of what would distinguish SFU from other universities and also with some of the claims still made about SFU.

Catherine: I would even say there is a counter-trend away from teaching. Everything in the professional venue seems designed to streamline and reduce teaching. If you talk to junior faculty to see which signal is being received, it is the university's strategic research plan and the three million dollar pot of money that the VP Research is handling. It's the focus on research that has really stuck. The idea is to reduce the amount of effort you need to put into teaching. The irony is, of course, that the university is sending out the most contradictory signals to its population. There are the teaching demands of a new curriculum and there's effort in making a transition to a W-course and there is effort as well in offering it. Now, it's very personally rewarding, but it's not rewarding in a professional sense. I mean, in terms of the recognition systems at the university.

Arne: There is this idea that you shouldn't be too interested in teaching because then you are seen as not sufficiently interested in research.

Richard: It's seen as a weakness.

Arne: Absolutely.

IS GOOD TEACHING RECOGNIZED?

Wendy: So although you are all clearly committed to doing the W-teaching and get some personal satisfaction from it, it is the external recognition that is missing and importantly missing?

Andy: Yes, and what we need to get over resistance generally among the faculty is recognition. The bottom line is that the incentive structure rewards research and it is only the university that can do something about recognizing teaching as well. When there is recognition, more people will step up to the plate. I believe that people who end up in academics have a sense of honor. It's easy to opt out after all but if you opt in, there's no honoring system to recognize you. There is not enough recognition of teaching and recognition could actually be a non-costly inducement.

Karen: I'm not certain how you would reward participating in teaching W-courses. It would be related in general to teaching evaluation but is a bit more focused and specific since we have this initiative. I guess, because doing a W-course is just one more thing that people would have to do, they would say, "Yeah, it's interesting, but that is two hours of my time." It's almost easier to let it go.

Arne: If you're thinking in terms of tenure and promotion, being will-ing to do a W-course suggests that you take teaching seriously. And that would come up in your record. I don't know how you could make it explicit what's involved; you can't get points, it is all too amorphous and imprecise. I've only sat on the biology review committee once and I know the teaching and research are supposed to be given equal weight, and teaching is given weight, but how much, I'm not sure. The committee goes through the teaching evaluations and the courses people said they would teach and the ones they actually did teach.

Nancy: I agree that research is the major focus, but not that good teaching is seen as a weakness. There are just too many examples of people who are good teachers and good researchers. Excellent teaching without sufficient research will not get one tenure, but lousy teaching, where the person has refused to improve their skills, has definitely hurt people at tenure time in the departments I've been in.

Greg: Based on what I know of the economics department, I think we do take teaching very seriously and we have a lot of people who are very good at it. In terms of how it is weighted in tenure and promotion, it is weighted equally with research. Research may be more controversial and there may be more heterogeneous views on what makes good research than what makes good teaching, so perhaps more time is taken to evaluate the research component. But they are two different things and we are quite serious in terms of salary reviews weighing the 40% research, 40% teaching, and 20% service. In something like a tenure and promotion case, we would be looking at a whole range of things, from the numerical evaluation of students, to course outlines, exams, written assignments web materials, and a statement of teaching philosophy to explain what they are trying to accomplish and why and also, why it makes sense.

Nancy: So, as Greg is saying, we have at least one example of a place where good teaching is recognized. But I do think the university could reward good teaching in more concrete ways. We give out a few teaching awards each year, based on nominations from students. Why just a few? Why not have a "Dean's List" of those nominated by their department each year for excellent teaching, innovative course design? Departments and the University could do a lot more to recognize outstanding contributions to education.

HOW CAN TEACHING BE EVALUATED?

Wendy: Do you think that the difficulty of evaluating teaching is one of the reasons that teaching is not perceived as being given the weight it warrants or that the university claims that it is given in tenure and promotion processes? Are our methods of evaluating teaching part of the problem?

Andy: I think the way teaching is evaluated is very rudimentary. In political science there is no discussion of syllabi, no discussion of students. I think the whole symbolic way that student evaluations are handed out treats them as customers. But students don't think about how this process or class can be improved and I think that many students who are satisfied with the course don't say much. I would rather invite someone who is known as being a good teacher to come into my class and say, "These are things that need to be done."

Sean: I would think that the overall impression that you get from a number of student evaluations would be telling. . . . There are the snipers and you know you can write that person off, but if there is an accumulation of comments, these things do have some sort of cumulative validity.

Karen: Student feedback is part of it, but do they fully understand what it means, what your objective is? That shouldn't be all that we are evaluated by, though it seems to be the way that we evaluate teaching at this university. I think there should be a lot of consultation with faculty who have taught these W-classes to see what they see as the change. I do think the faculty should be the primary source of teaching evaluation, and there should be more rewards for teaching. This is the other thing. People don't want to do this because they do not believe in the 40/40/20 formula. I was on history's tenure and promotion committee and we looked at the student evaluations and thought, what are we supposed to do with these? No peer comes in except when we are up for tenure and then they say, you know, "Not totally incompetent," but the whole enterprise is so private.

Nancy: Well, there is a literature on how to evaluate teaching. Every department chair and dean should have a précis of this literature. We do what is simple; in-course teaching evaluations are simple, but flawed. Students may not fully appreciate a teacher until after the course is over. One of my colleagues had a student whom she taught a few semesters ago come up to her and thank her profusely for the course. The student said, "I didn't fully appreciate your teaching at the time, but have come to see that it was the best course I had in the program." Students should be surveyed after the course is over as well as during the course. Departments should have senior faculty visit junior faculty courses and provide constructive comments. There is a lot more that could be done if the university really wanted to improve the quality of teaching across the university.

Sean: Well, even then, English had someone who was up for salary review and a peer went in to watch and although everyone knows that the person has a very poor teaching record and the observer did not dispute that record, the observer also claimed that things were all fine for the purposes of the review. I doubt we are the only department where this kind of ignoring of teaching goes on in some instances.

WHAT WOULD COUNT AS REWARDS FOR W-TEACHING?

Wendy: Assuming that teaching a W-course necessarily means extra and/or different work, what would count as rewards for teaching W-courses that you think faculty would value? You've mentioned the need for more public recognition of good teaching. You've mentioned suspicions about application of the 40/40/20 formula for promotion. Is that a major issue, do you think?

Richard: I don't think so really. I think people will make of it what they will. Teaching W-courses is not something that I would exclude from my tenure file in communications, but I don't know that anything more needs to be done. I guess if I were in a department where I felt that I was getting short shrift, I might seek lobbying by the W-Coordinator, if we had one, to say, "This is really important," and talk to the chair and the tenure and promotion people. That kind of move would really have to be backed by the VP Academic and the university committee on tenure and promotion. That's where it would have to come from and it would probably still be more of an ad hoc matter when people sensed that it wasn't being properly valued.

Arne: That's my feeling. Biannual review is material, but you need something immediate and less political. Isn't it far easier to just cap class size, so you get to teach a smaller course if it's a W-course? Don't you need a currency? To me, biannual review is not a currency that people care about.

Catherine: Well, I think the reviews are going to become much more rigorous. They have to change, because if we drop mandatory retirement, there has to be some way to deal with non-performance.

Richard: There is another currency, but it's imprecise and it's in the TA hours. W-courses are assigned with extra TA support.

Catherine: Do you think this is good currency, the TA hours?

Arne: No, I think that capping class size is a better currency than the TA support. Just do a survey of faculty and ask them what's the best currency. I think you have to find a currency that works and I'm not sure it works to claim that offering a W-course has institutional currency for the biannual review. I don't think most people care about biannual reviews, really.

Wendy: Well, if the biennial review isn't really a big issue because you've got tenure, what other means does the university have at its disposal to reward developing and teaching a W-course?

Nancy: There is another place where the university could help out. Speaking as an economist, I think they could provide some remuneration and time. For example, you get a course release every three years or so. The first jump into the W-course is the biggest one in terms of time and commitment. But we should provide incentives. I understand why the university wouldn't want you to have a research release instead of a teaching release because it's hard to have that honored. But with everyone having research grants and not teaching, that causes another problem. So sure, an alternative is to have lower expectations for research for a period of time; you can also provide training courses, but we are all so time constrained that people won't necessarily be able to go. We need to free up people's time and provide positive incentives to teach.

Lee: The only thing I am aware of is that in chemistry there certainly hasn't been anything about compensating faculty, but we do get 50% more TA support with the idea that there is more writing to read. We have three new W-courses that are being mounted and there will be one each semester, but that really zaps our teaching resources. I also haven't heard anything about getting more funds for hiring sessional instructors. I don't think that the full impact has set in at the dean's level, and we are bracing ourselves for how many students we will see when the requirement comes into force in the Fall 2006.

Catherine: Choices would be an incentive. TA support has been capped or fixed at some sort of algorithm. I think there is a problem there, too. In other words, I would like to see an escalator clause and I would like to see choice. I want to see a top up in the TA budget. It's not sufficient with the turnover of the TAs that we currently have. It's not sufficient.

Richard: Another incentive would be making the teaching of W-courses a distinction. I think there is some room for an elite class of W-ness, making it a source of distinction with some sort of certificate or other form of recognition. There's "w" and then there's W. Make a Fraser Institute report: How "W" was your W? You could have a College of W-teachers.

ENHANCING THE VISIBILITY OF W-TEACHING

Wendy: That would be quite an imaginative and dramatic development! So, W-faculty would be honored as having expertise and scholarly knowledge to share?

Catherine: Yes, Burnaby Mountain, absolutely. I would really like to see an endowed chair at the Burnaby Mountain College, number one. Let's do something interesting. Say you have an experiment that you want to develop in your program, but you need an opportunity to develop it.

Arne: In what?

Richard: In W-ness.

Catherine: In whatever, but you take this chair and it gives you research and development (R&D) time to develop it. In other words, at present we get letters from the VP Academic, which is some recognition, although the letters are responded to quite unevenly in our tenure and promotion committee. Our department's biennial salary review structure is currently under review and it would be extremely interesting to see how the guidelines that are developed for biennial review reflect this kind of work and how the system of recognition and incentive fits together in a continuous stream. I'm not sure if I'd get in line for Richard's Grade A and B writing courses, but I do want to see attention to the W-courses be far more prominent.

Arne: Yes, visibility is important. That could be another incentive. Could you identify a dedicated W-person in say, our biology department and in every department so that they are the ones who go to faculty and say, "Hey, you should teach W and I'll come and watch your courses and help out." And these people who do that could get extra training.

Richard: It's a good idea. We have an undergrad coordinator and a grad coordinator so we should have a W-coordinator.

Karen: That would be quite a radical thing to do, but yes. I think someone needs to be and should have been designated in each department to be a W-liaison. And I agree with Nancy and Catherine, I think there needs to be some teaching release for curriculum or support for course development, and that would be great. I don't know about financial incentives. Like a research grant? It's difficult. Maybe not even a teaching release but being rewarded with a smaller class or something like that as Arne is suggesting. And that would be fair, too. That's something we could do in History.

Lee: Hiring is another aspect of this. Paying attention in hiring to ability to teach writing will make the initiative more visible and be an incentive thing as well. We have someone new in chemistry who is coming from the east coast and her job talk presentation was very much around the writing. We picked up on that and can see the interest is out there and not only at SFU.

TEACHING ASSISTANTS AND THE W-COURSES

Wendy: You're all emphasizing the matter of visibility and supporting faculty in W-development. There is also the issue of the TAs. The question of TAs and their role and preparation came up a number of times in interviews. Having more of them seems like one of the "rewards" for doing a W-course, but of course more TAs means more large classes, and with the W-courses, it also means additional supervision of tutorial instruction to ensure consistency across sections. Some departments do not have enough TAs who are competent to teach writing and grade written work. It's a major concern. What are the issues here? What is the university's responsibility to its graduate students and what needs to be done?

Greg: If we're talking about inducements to get faculty to participate, a guaranteed supply of competent TAs is far and away the biggest one for us in economics. Secondly, would be smaller class sizes. Beyond that, I don't know.

Sean: One of the issues in English is availability. The department got an endowment and that money allowed us to give out graduate fellowships, which means that fewer grad students will be teaching. I suspect that we will have to hire outside TAs from outside the department. We are also working hard to get MA grad students in and out more quickly, get them in and out in a year. Since they only have to take six courses, that's quite conceivable.

Lee: For us in chemistry, the problem is English as a second language and so much fluctuation from one semester to the next. You can't get the same TA two semesters in a row or they are not eligible because they have used up the allocation of TA-ships they are allowed to hold under the TSSU union agreement.

Wendy: In your situation then, you may be working with the TAs who have the least experience?

Richard: Well, even when the students are new to SFU, they aren't necessarily those with the least experience. Last year my incoming TAs, admittedly to communications not chemistry, looked at the W-requirements and said, "Oh yeah, I did that when I was a master's student." So other universities are doing it and we are benefiting.

Wendy: So it sounds as if there is a potential out there to find incoming graduate students with W-kinds of experiences?

Catherine: What I think we want to drive home here is that currently we are in an anomalous situation where there is no career path for our graduate students who choose to work in a W-course. There is no currency in the external environment. We seem to be facing a national market that is trying to shorten the time of doctoral and masters study, and at the same time we are also trying to adopt an American model that offers some teaching experience. But we don't have any sort of accredited system.

Arne: The University of New Brunswick has a teaching certificate that you get while you're in your doctoral program. We should have that.

Wendy: There is a small program run out of Learning and Instructional Development centre (LIDC) that offers a teaching certificate to graduate students who volunteer to take it, but nothing that looks like common practice across the university. What do you think of the idea of a graduate teaching program? Is this something the university should look at?

Phil: There are many other places that have these sorts of things. A couple of my colleagues are from Pittsburgh and a teaching program is one of the big ways that doctoral students get support. They enter the program and take the training and get the certificate and then they get support for the rest of their time there as a W-instructor.

Arne: But how much infrastructure is needed for something like that? What would be the incentive for graduate students to take these extra hours?

Richard: It could be as simple as recognizing the preparation they already get because right now our W-TAs have to take the W-training and then if they TA in two W-courses, they could get a certificate.

Wendy: The problem is that the training is fairly limited because of the time allocated to it and the certificate does not ensure continued work. Once they have reached the maximum TA-ships under the present union agreement, they could not make use of the certificate for getting additional TA-ships. Under present conditions, they would need to see the experience as having a value in itself and that's a little difficult given the pressures on their time.

Andy: I try to emphasize to my students in political science that there are skills they need to graduate with. I have students who come in and are just going through the motions of going to classes and they don't seem to have a sense of what they are getting out of this degree. The W-course experience will help them. Why not have some people come in who have graduated and are in the job market and who can say, "This is what you need."

Phil: And there would be indirect benefits too, if we had some system here for earning a W-teaching certificate. Even if people hiring are not looking at whether or not someone has a W-certificate, they are looking at their teaching record and, probably, having gotten a W-certificate has improved that teaching record. I was thinking of a colleague we hired because he had an excellent teaching record.

Arne: biology looks at teaching preparation. Because all of our graduate student applicants are always up against other grad students who have done very little teaching, we pay attention if we see that someone has a certificate in teaching; we know that they obviously care about teaching and we consider that.

Catherine: Picking up on Richard's point about incoming graduate students, I'm thinking SFU needs to offer financial incentives to students to acquire the W-training and experience when they are here or to recognize the equivalent training that they have acquired elsewhere. If the student demonstrates interest in the W-course teaching, the letter of offer should no longer be contingent upon finding the financing. We have a tutorial system, which is a tremendous advantage to students when they come to study or are teaching here. Right now we cannot offer unconditional financing, but we could change that. We should guarantee or make TA-ships contingent upon their willingness to acquire or on their already having acquired the W-expertise and then offer them stable, long-term funding.

Greg: If W-certificates and training could be used as a recruitment tool for getting good graduate students, that would be a plus and I would support that and in fact, I am sure the incoming chair would also support that, because we want to encourage incoming graduate students to arrive earlier in summer, in part due to a concern about language training. If there were some sort of program for the W-courses we could put the graduate students through, and that would be a plus. I would love to see the university put serious resources into a systematic process to have our TAs from outside Canada improve their language skills. But we do not have the resources to do that at the department level.

Sean: I think the value of the experience needs to be emphasized more. There has been a shift since I was a grad student. Students now see the TA-ship mainly as a way to make money, whereas for us, it was a way to get experience teaching and this was what you had to learn. Now it seems to be regarded as more of a right rather than a privilege. I think students need to see the connection to their own professionalism.

ARE WE COMMUNICATING THE W-REQUIREMENTS TO STUDENTS?

Wendy: Catherine's proposal would seem to encourage that, wouldn't it? And it's also the case that the TAs can benefit as writers by doing a W-course. We know from our interviews with them that they gain both as writers and as instructors because most will have fewer students to work with and they develop better and closer relationships with them. It can be a very satisfying experience for them both personally and professionally. This feature of the implementation has not had much attention. Mainly the worry has rightly been about workload for the TAs. Workload is also an issue for students and while we're on the subject of incentives for taking on what would be, in some departments and courses, an extra workload, do we need to do anything to encourage student support of the W-course experience or is this not an issue?

Phil: I'd like to see an emphasis in marketing the W-requirement, on the fact that we have this minimum number of courses you must take, but you're not restricted to just one at either level. I think the university is having some problem marketing these new requirements generally and they haven't done it very effectively to the broader community.

Greg: In response to that, I have to say that in economics, we have not done conscious marketing about this to students. We haven't seen our job as needing to explain to the students directly that they should take W-courses because this or that will be the benefit. We let them know that it is a university requirement and that we are making these courses available in our department. In individual courses, instructors can explain, but at the departmental level there hasn't been a push for marketing . . . we are so overwhelmed with students that we are always filling courses and it would not even cross our minds to go looking for students. Most of our W-courses are at the 400-level and all economics majors have to take one of them to get their degree.

Arne: Is information on the W-requirement on the website?

Catherine: Yes, but it's pretty weak.

Richard: I think we are paddling upriver there. To undergraduates, it's seen as non-existent. My daughter just started her undergraduate and she does not have a clue that there is such thing as W. And last semester, I got this comment from a student, quote unquote: "I don't need a W-course because I already write good." That view exists. I'm quoting verbatim from a student feedback form.

Catherine: I think you'll find that comments like "I already write good" are pretty widespread. But the W-initiative has just never been sold to them. That is the issue. So, how would they know?

Richard: Well, operationally, I think the W-course works. I don't have a single complaint about outcomes, about process, about the training I received. The issue is communicating the value to the students, to the greater community, all that sort of stuff. The very fact that they think its about writing and not about learning is a big part of the problem. I have to start my class with a lecture about what writing-intensive learning *does not* mean. It's about intensive learning, using writing, so that misunderstanding or misperception needs to be addressed. As I see it, it is not about the end or the outcome, because students respond very positively to the W-approaches; it's about the anticipation and the perception.

Arne: That raises an interesting question. What are students' expectations generally? Is W fulfilling a need and how is a W-course relevant to someone who has lived on the web their whole life?

Wendy: So we're identifying two things here: student expectations and working habits, both of which affect students' perceptions of the W-course. Ideas on these?

Richard: We are integrating writing into the regular courses, which is good, but the danger there is that because it is integrated, it becomes the standard and it's really vague, what W is and what it isn't; it may be, in the long term, that it may be better to segment it out. It needs to be seen as something that's very distinctive, completely different. I don't know what it is, but there needs to be something definitive and marked so there is no chance to backslide if you are doing a W-course.

Arne: The alternative is that everybody does W because it's a better way to teach, in which case, it will make SFU a better university.

Richard: True, but until then, somehow it has got to be very clear that you are giving them something extra. Tutorials are smaller so they need to be told, "There are eighteen of you in this section whereas normally there would have been twenty-four" or whatever that is. We request and we get additional resources, but then where does it go? The students do not have a clear idea of what they're getting extra.

Johanne Provençal (Research Assistant and TA): As a listening-in TA here, I just wanted to add that when I have done TA work, and I have six or seven times now, I tell them at the beginning that I am also a student and that before I start every course, I look at the number of students in a tutorial and the assignments and I calculate how much time I can give to each student for each assignment and that usually ranges from about 10 to 20 minutes for each assignment. I tell them that this is less than it would be if the course were a W-course and I encourage them to take a W-course if they want more attention and feedback on their work. I think the feedback on their work is what they value. And there is always someone who pops up and says that they have taken a W-course and that it's true, that they do get more feedback on their work in those courses.

Arne: That's true and the visibility of that would be interesting.

Richard: They get that, but we don't highlight it or segment it out. I'm hoping they recognize that they get lots of feedback from the TA, but the problem is they don't recognize that it's because they are taking a W-course that they get lots of feedback. After week one, it's "whatever" and it's not exceptional or distinctive. So I like Johanne's idea of somehow highlighting it.

W-RELEVANCE FROM THE STUDENTS' POINT OF VIEW

Wendy: Making students more aware of what they are getting would certainly help perceptions about the value of the W-initiative. What about the matter of Internet working habits?

Nancy: Most of my economics students are pretty web proficient. What they lack is good research skills. The internet has greatly expanded one's ability to access information from all over the world, but one still has to be able to tell what is good from unreliable. In my W-course at the 4th year level, we spent a lot of time on how to do research and, just as importantly, how to communicate your results. They wrote mini-research papers, briefing notes, book reviews and more. It took a lot of practice and we had to overcome some bad habits the internet creates (such as giving a superficial view of an issue), but by the end of the course, the students had gained a lot of confidence in their own abilities and some skills in how to access information and use it.

Catherine: Well, in my 100-level course, I have started teaching them how to write a blog.

Arne: Yeah, they are all writing blogs, or they can, or they try. The question I want to ask is, is that a good hook? If it's not blogs, it's Wiki, and Wiki is important but do they connect W to blogs or to Wiki?

Richard: As a gimmick, the "W equals Wiki" could be quite good, because Wiki is really about the social production of knowledge and W, as I see it, really is about the production of knowledge, not about writing in the sense of the mechanics of it, but it's about creating knowledge.

Arne: As an advert, it would be great. SFU 100-WIKI. Take a W-course and contribute to the world, or something like that!

Richard: So in your class it would be, create THE entry on, whatever it is, biodiversity. And in my class it could be, create a new entry on new media.

Catherine: I'm in, totally. My students want an editorial procedure. They want a publication, a purpose and an audience and so this Wiki thing would give that additional opportunity. The second thing is that there is an opportunity for this kind of transitioning, for engagement in intellectual activism. But going back to Arne's question about fulfilling a need, I think we can use the W to make an employability case. Unless we look at the students and potential employers at the undergraduate level, we are going to have trouble here. What can we do here and how can we trace that through the labor market to see if there is a value added? It seems to me that there are some opportunities. We know, for example, that Harbour centre offers technical writing certificates that are very highly in demand within the local community. So, it would make sense to somehow or another connect with employment needs more directly in undergraduate preparation. That approach would be going down the road of what all undergraduates students are asking for: they want the arts education, but they also want to make the employability case later on, so what can we do there?

Wendy: We are raising big questions here that really need to be taken to a wider constituency. We might ask the WSG to take on such questions as part of its mandate in the implementation and ongoing support process, which leads me away from the students and their understanding of this initiative and up to the administration. Three or four of you have been particularly concerned about the W-profile at the university level. Where do you think the energy needs to go at this point?

Phil: Just listening to people and what they are saying about directions, I think we are in a kind of a holding pattern right now. A certain mandate got approved, and we've been busy working on it. Now we are close to the implementation deadline, so we are standing back and taking a wait-and-see attitude: how is it all going to come together, or is it going to come together? There has been some planning for monitoring and evaluation, but what there hasn't been talk of is further development and building on this beginning. What we still need are people pushing ideas and trying to carry them forward. While we are all exhausted from implementation and are anxious about potential chaos come September 2006, we still need to be forward-looking.

Catherine: I think there are three areas we've really got to target. The first is to make sure that the elected faculty representative on the Board of Governors' Academic Operations Committee pays a great deal of attention to these items because we do have metrics now for innovation in interdisciplinary academics for the university as a whole. One third is renewal and we have metrics, rather like the Faculty Association (SFUFA) has guidelines and so on, for the very first time. The second thing I think we really have to work on is extremely basic: the second position of power is the Senate committee on Undergraduate Programs (SCUP). Yet in their last report SCUP, who theoretically would be the committee most concerned because they championed the new curriculum in the first place, said nothing, they were silent in their last report. Senate has used a Task Force delegation mechanism and not assumed core responsibility for monitoring performance and continuing on with this. As far as I know, none of the committees in Senate issued their annual reports talking about the W/Q/B initiative. None, which is puzzling to me. How does the responsibility for the task force feed itself into the normal institutions of academic governance and become renewed? Finally, how do individual departments interpret their own responsibilities in championing curriculum reform?

Is it linked to their own external review, their own process of curriculum planning, or their own tenure and promotion (TPC) procedures? Those are the real questions. Those are the three levels: Board, Senate, and local university-wide decision mechanisms. You have to know how to use the normal channels of the university, and they've got to treat these sorts of things as very, very important and do more long-term planning.

Richard: The University does some long-term planning, like the Woodward's building and Surrey campus, but these are on the facility side, not the program side. Maybe that's because there is a discipline of planning for material assets. There you can be seen as living up to best practice, but when it comes to academic planning, who is to know whether you are doing it as well as anyone else? It is all much less concrete, literally. There are institutions, even in Canada, where the initiative could have merit in and of itself as a teaching initiative, but SFU is not one of those places. It has to have a research foundation to be sustainable here. You have a couple of really solid rationales for research support and the nice thing about WILO at present is that it now has a solid group of staff that it didn't have when it began two years ago. The other thing you have is this cadre of faculty who are committed to this project from across the disciplines. We could develop a proposal for a research agenda and apply to the new Community Trust Enhancement Fund (CTEF). That will raise the profile and help the future development that Phil refers to.

Arne: Yes, we can say to them, "Look, you want to be a research university, let's research *this*." Is this an exciting research area—writing?

Catherine: It is. It's reinventing literacy, how we know it and how we think about it.

Greg: I don't think it is research versus teaching. I do think we want to be a research university, so I would not want to de-emphasize that, but in terms of the kind of student experience we provide, which is related to our courses and teaching, we can differentiate ourselves. In economics, we are trying to become good at certain things that our immediate neighbor and competition, UBC, is not good at and then tell the world. So in the field of economics we say, for example, "If you are interested in public economics or in law and economics, come to SFU." But the question of the macro picture that applies more generally to the university as a whole . . . if we are doing specific, tangible things that are going to improve the quality of an SFU education, then we should be trumpeting that.

Wendy: Are we trying to sell SFU as a university that values teaching because, as Catherine mentioned earlier, we have a tutorial system?

Arne: I didn't even know it was anything special.

Richard: Our tutorial system is not a distinctive evidence of commitment to teaching any longer. The land around us has risen, so we can't really celebrate something that so many people are doing. And we have been faced several times by quite aggressive moves by UBC to identify itself as THE research institution. I think what happened in the late 1970s and early 1980s was that UBC decided to capitalize on that original selling point and say, "Look, those people over there, that's a teaching university, *we* do research." Build on your strengths. There was an explicit play for all the research dollars in British Columbia and the message was that, for the big science initiatives, grants, and laboratories, UBC should be where research was done. We decided to fight that hard, which means really emphasizing research. Personally, I can't have too much of a problem with that since I am part of it. It's the ecology in which we live. So, it's kind of like this is a battle ground. It's not that people here don't care about teaching, but we can't lose sight of the research support for a minute. Maybe there is room to focus on teaching now, if we don't have to be so paranoid about research.

Arne: But isn't there a bit of irony that we can't get a research component as part of this initiative?

Richard: Yes, for sure. But it also means, I think, that doing research is the way to do this W-teaching initiative. You can't do any research unless you are doing the activities, so then the activity flows and the size of the W-faculty group doesn't shrink, it grows. You've got this cadre of people and the Community Trust Enhancement Fund [CTEF] is about building alliances within the university. You have that in this W-faculty. There is a great rationale and a great vehicle, which is really important. It's one thing to have a good story, but this vehicle is real.

Catherine: It disturbs me that the Burnaby Mountain development money, which is to be in trust for the university as a whole, is exclusively going to research, adjudicated by three administrators and Academic Vice Presidents. There is no obligation really to feed into initiatives of this sort or to serve the general welfare of the university as a whole. It's shocking to me. And Senate went for it.

Richard: But don't forget, it seems this is a really bad time for student recruitment at the university. There is a real pinch to fill the university for whatever reason. I think we are driving people away with the excessive fees and people are choosing their way according to job opportunities. It's not demographics that are overshadowing these other things, though I keep hearing demographics given as the reason. I think the university is so unsure of the numbers for the coming fall semester that they are not prepared to do anything new. If the number of students were steady or rising, they would do a marketing campaign. When you are under pressure, you are not going to say, "Hey, we're doing W-courses," for fear it could have a negative impact.

Nancy: Following up on Richard's comment, I think the university is missing an opportunity to market itself as a great institution with world class researchers and teaching, where the W, B, Q courses are trumpeted as contributing to excellent teaching and learning. Given the demographic picture, with declining numbers of young people, SFU will have to be more aggressive at conveying its advantages. This means we actually have to deliver on these promises, and if we don't, the market will respond—students will go elsewhere. To ignore the promotion of good teaching is hence, folly on the part of any university.

Arne: Why is the new curriculum not seen as an advantage to "trumpet," as Greg put it?

Richard: Basically, it's seen as just different.

Catherine: Well, it is also because I believe there was significant resistance from the community, from organizations like SUCCESS and the Lower Mainland community, from people who do not speak English as their first or second language and from immigrant service societies. There's been a lot of noise and actually, Milton Wong, the Chancellor, was very concerned initially and so were a number of the Order in Council members at the Board. It was fumbled initially and despite clarification about the new entrance requirements and the plan to offer remedial assistance in the first year for students struggling with English language skills, I don't think we ever regained the ground we lost then.

Richard: Universities do not have a history of selling themselves. Not in Canada, anyway. The selling we do is so amateurish and the faculty of marketing or the faculty of business does not seem to be giving the administration any help. You know, just little things like our website and the way we treat students coming in, it's absolutely ghastly and amateurish.

Arne: These are all connected problems, but I wonder if these are problems we can speak to. They all have implications at a very high political level in terms of how to proceed. If whoever is not pushing the new curriculum doesn't believe it is a good thing, that it actually enhances educational outcomes for students, then who can do the selling and be convincing and to whom?

Richard: I think the university is distracted by other things and isn't focusing on W. That's my sense. The focus is on money and research.

Catherine: Research.

Phil: Research money.

Catherine: That's the only way they see that there's an expansion income to the university right now or doing things like selling private partnerships, like this international college that they've taken on to develop courses that are prep for the university and match up somehow with what we offer. I'm not sure of all the details.

Arne: Well, if the curriculum we are developing here is not supported by the university at the level of student recruitment, that indifference probably travels throughout. I think that's really important.

Richard: Get to the parents! That's the market. You have to put a button on the website that says, "If you're a parent, click here." Students don't see anything about W but if you're a parent, parents will buy that. They want to see their children able to write and succeed in a life-long skill as well as at university.

Catherine: Then you're talking about WILO offering to go out to the high schools and visit the Parents Advisory Councils. I think you're really talking about them and doing social marketing. And I think they've got to get out there!

Richard: Yes, that's where to drive at!

Wendy: Well, thank you for thinking of something more to keep WILO busy! I do agree this is an important constituency to address, and perhaps WILO can be involved in some way. We always have to be careful we are not over-reaching. But there is room here in all the ideas you have put forward for many people to be involved in the advocacy, training and research, in ways that can significantly affect the outcomes of this ambitious initiative. In identifying barriers and challenges, your observations support what Richard E. Miller (1998) concluded, in his analysis of several major university's reform projects, that change is "uneven and with unpredictable consequences." But he also found that persistent individual and collective efforts do bring about change in spite of that unevenness and the institutional obstacles. We now need to hope we can stay the course! Many thanks for your generous participation in today's forum.

8
THROUGH TRANSITION IN SEARCH OF STABILITY

In the first two chapters of this book, I traced the path by which the Administration, the faculty on broad-based committees, the deans and departments, and CWIL worked both together and alongside each other to develop a plan instituting new undergraduate writing requirements and to define how those requirements would be met in designated W-courses. Those two chapters set out the institutional context. The image of 'tracing the path' through the complexities of competing and contentious priorities mainly at the administrative level is rather tidier than the reality, of course. The reality was at times a bit more like uncoordinated bushwhacking that eventually opened up a track that could be both seen and recognized by most, or enough, people as a way forward toward the generally agreed upon goal: improving student writing and learning. Once codified in Senate approval, the goal and the ways of reaching it awaited interpretation and implementation.

In the subsequent chapters, the institutional frame constituted by the administration receded into the background and the story concentrated on accounts of actual, on-the-ground experience. Any effort at curriculum reform was bound to fail without the support of the faculty, without their commitment to using writing to teach their courses, and without their having a sense of satisfaction that compensates for the inescapable extra work of planning their W-course teaching and engaging with students. These middle chapters exemplified the conditions for and the nature of that faculty commitment during the pilot period. They have suggested the inevitable "stumbling" that accompanies first attempts but also demonstrated that pedagogical change and thoughtful cross-disciplinary conversation about teaching fosters engagement in personal and scholarly reflection and a gradual transformation in the teaching and learning culture of the institution. That work of the faculty, however, occurred within an administrative cultural context which framed and influenced any shifts and whose values sometimes collided with those of the faculty or at least existed in uneasy tension. The final chapter of this book assesses the outcomes of the pilot period as they were affected by the interactions of the administration and faculty and particularly as those interactions affected the work being done by CWIL.

I begin by drawing on quantitative as well as qualitative data to assess the extent to which progress was made toward creating an environment that seemed likely to thrive beyond the pilot period and sustain and develop the writing initiative and its genre-based approach. Successful programs, whether designated Writing-in-the-Disciplines (WID) or Writing Across the Curriculum (WAC), tend toward characteristic features (Townsend 2001) and, also characteristically, appear to move through a series of four stages (Condon and Rutz 2006, see Appendix 12) before becoming suf- ficiently integrated into the curriculum and into the university's sense of its mission to be self-sustaining. Using Condon's continuum of this staged process and Townsend's summary of characteristics as reference points, I try to map out the varied and interdependent markers at the faculty, department, and administrative levels at Simon Fraser University (SFU) that signaled where we had made progress as well as what we had overlooked or that warranted more attention. I conclude with a caution- ary account of structural changes made by the administration in the year before the requirement took effect.

WHERE HAD WE BEEN HEADING?

The period between 2002 and 2004 that has been documented here, as well as the following year, were years of preparation for the time when the writing requirements would take effect. We—i.e. CWIL and the various university committees in collaboration with Deans and departments and faculty—worked during this period to ensure that students entering the university in Fall 2006 could enroll in accredited W-courses and meet their graduation requirements. From the administrative point of view, the key concern was course accessibility. Enough courses needed to be available to meet the demand in all departments and disciplines, without shifting enrolment patterns. From the faculty point of view, the key concern was resources. Faculty needed support for themselves in planning and offering the W-courses and wanted writing support for students outside the class- room. By the Fall of 2006, the concerns of both administration and faculty were met: enough W-courses were available, enough faculty were prepared to teach them and, in addition, classroom practice was to be supported as of Fall 2006 by services established in a new Learning Commons area of the library to assist students with writing.

For CWIL, meeting the deadline of preparing for the Fall 2006 require- ment was only the beginning of what we envisaged as the ongoing pro- cess implied by the goal statement in our mandate that "The Centre for Writing-Intensive Learning aims to make the use of writing constitutive of the teaching and learning culture in the faculty of arts and social sciences (FASS) and to foster students' skills as writers." That mandate, as developed with the dean of the FASS, both preceded and was more ambitious than the new university curriculum requirements that, along with the requirements for breadth and quantitative reasoning courses, included the two W-courses. The adoption of the latter did not, in itself, imply widespread faculty participation and, according to reports from some institutions, might in fact deter that participation.

Eager to avoid such an outcome, we took our lead from the experience of successful programs at what appeared to be similar sized and type institutions. Martha Townsend, in her tenure as writing program director at the University of Missouri, saw their WID program grow over a period of fifteen years to become one of the most respected in the United States. From her own experience and from her survey of eleven other successful programs, she compiled a list of the factors that seemed to make the use of W-courses work best (Townsend 2001). These factors include a complex of quite specific attitudinal, material, political, economic, and pedagogical elements that derive from and have effects at the classroom, department, faculty, and senior administrative and institutional levels. Her list alerted us to the importance of starting out with a broad spectrum outlook on the implementation process and influenced some of CWIL's early decisions about processes of development.

From a retrospective point of view, Bill Condon's continuum of stages of development (Condon 2006), based on his experience both at Washington State University and elsewhere, offered a way of looking at what we had accomplished during the pilot period. He posits four stages leading to a well-established and institutionally valued writing program whose vitality wards off demands for its constant justification as well as threats of its demise. While at the first stage the project tends to be driven mainly by the vision and dedication of a single individual, the project itself eventually becomes a driving force in the fourth stage; when fully established, the project is widely valued as a fully theorized resource for enhancing teaching and learning and attracts the active involvement of departments and programs, with the whole initiative marked by expansion. In the context of our local situation, marked by the impact of the university's W-requirements and CWIL's theoretical and pedagogical approaches, we moved forward ourselves in stages, setting out to assess the climate and plan our way forward in the first semester and thence to the subsequent pilot period designed to ensure the requirements could successfully take effect, but equally importantly, to set the course toward Condon's fourth stage.

Surveying the territory: CWIL's first-year

When I took on the role of director of CWIL in the Fall of 2002, the dean and I discussed our objectives for the first semester. We agreed on a target of six pilot W-courses to run in the Spring of 2003. That meant finding six professors who would be willing to work with us in their courses to modify the way they were using and teaching writing. Metaphorically, we stood at the doorway and looked out on a crowd of over 300 professors in diverse and widely dispersed clusters. How were we to reach them and from among them, find six willing participants? Condon characterizes this first stage work as "missionary" and while it needed a certain missionary passion, we recognized there could be no evangelizing. Working with someone would entail establishing a collegial and respectful relationship that began with and responded to their interests and needs. Before we looked for the willing participants, we felt we needed to be informed about what departments already did in their courses and what information was made available to students about writing in the discipline. While such information would not substitute for intimate knowledge of how a particular person thought about and assigned writing in his or her course, it would help us identify points of reference and strategize how to become visible to faculty and departments, both as individuals with valuable expertise and as a unit with resources to offer. We therefore set out on two fronts concurrently: collecting data that would inform us about the current climate and context for our work as well as serve as a baseline for later third and fourth stage assessments; and also informing people about ourselves and our services. In practice, the process of collecting data had the effect of informing faculty and raising their awareness of our mandate and about writing. The baseline data collection at this early stage took three forms: a faculty questionnaire, an analysis of assigned writing in the faculty of arts, and a survey of resources available to students.

With the help of the associate dean of arts we sent out a questionnaire to all faculty members seeking attitudinal and pedagogical information (see Appendix 8). We asked about practice in using writing and concerns about writing. Coming with the endorsement of the dean's office, the questionnaire had a legitimacy that we, as relative "unknowns," could not command. The first paper versions, however, yielded rather low returns nonetheless. With a little help from a technical person, we entered e-mail addresses for all the faculty members into a database and converted the questionnaire to an electronic document that could be completed online. We were thus able to send out individually addressed questionnaires and that approach provided us with 154 responses, an approximately 45% return rate. Because of the kinds of details it requested, it was also a means of initiating a shared language, starting a conversation, and raising consciousness about the role of writing in learning and teaching. As data on practices and beliefs about writing, this first inquiry gave us a good overview of what to consider as we began our search for volunteers to pilot W-courses. We could see the wide range in practices and types of writing being assigned across disciplines and by individuals as well as the wide range of engagement in teaching writing and some of the conditions which encouraged or discouraged faculty from assigning more writing.

One person, for instance, declared that "SFU students are by far the worst writers I have ever seen—across 4 universities and 10 years." Some people commented on the lack of resources available outside the classroom. "The absence of a writing centre at SFU is nothing short of a disaster. It is impossible to give the kind of writing help or feedback students really need given the current workload. This summer, I will have 90 students. If they each wrote the amount I think they should (25 pages total in the term) and I gave them the comments, help on drafts and opportunities to re-write that I think they ought to have, I'd be one dead philosopher. Consequently, the 100-level students are getting largely non-essay in-class mid-terms and finals and one paper assignment. Adequate? Absolutely not, but you get what you pay for." A few others made suggestions for course changes: "We need writing courses, but they must be discipline-specific. A paper using an English lit course style in criminology would be graded lower on writing than one using the appropriate criminology style. Similarly, the appropriate style varies even by courses within criminology." In response to a question about changes in their use of writing, one person said, "I require more writing because they need the practice so badly" and another "I have given up asking for writing altogether in my class." One of the reasons frequently cited for limiting writing was that "Large class sizes make written work difficult." This factor was stressed by faculty in economics in particular: "In economics, many instructors who would probably like to make more use of written assignments or papers are discouraged by the very large class sizes we have at the 100, 200, and 300 level (even at the 300 level, class sizes in the 100–150 range are common). As a result, the 400-level seminars are often the first time for our students to do serious writing." Comments such as these corresponded to and were confirmed by an analysis of course outlines, which showed that the grade percentages assigned to writing across the faculty of arts were lowest in economics.

At the same time that we sent out the questionnaire, we had been collecting course outlines from all departments for the semester. These single-page outlines have a material influence on student decisions. They are used to inform students about the content and requirements of the courses available for the semester. While SFU's course calendar provides a very brief description of all courses offered within the faculty of arts, the course outlines provide the most detailed information available to students who are selecting courses. Some of the outlines are available online through SFU's homepage; other departments opt to make outlines available on their own websites, while some departments only provide hardcopies of outlines. We reasoned that we could determine how much writing was being expected for that typical period and establish a baseline against which to make periodic comparisons with the amount and types of writing being expected once we had increasing numbers of W-courses. For the purposes of our analysis, we defined "writing" as extended discourse in assignments which had the potential to generate instruction and feedback. We excluded exams since no details were supplied about their format and we thought it fair to assume that any essay questions on exams would serve as tests of content, not as a means of evaluating writing or teaching writing (students would not get feedback). On the course outlines, assignments were typically described as "essay," "term paper," "report," "review," or "written assignment," without further details, although the responses on the faculty questionnaires had identified many more specific genres. In some cases, a word count or page number was included, although this was the exception rather than the rule.

One of our research assistants, Tanya Van der Gaag, collected and entered the data from the outlines (Van der Gaag 2003). She learned that the average percentage of a grade based on writing assignments, independent of exams, for all undergraduate courses in the faculty of arts at SFU in the Fall of 2002 was 37.73%. By course year, from first to fourth year, the averages increased from 24.42% in first-year to 30.74, 39.16, and 54.61% in the second–fourth years, respectively. This did not mean, of course, that the averages applied to all departments. Students pursuing an undergraduate degree in English were required to do the largest amount of writing—in economics, the least. The average over the four years for all courses in English was 59.62% of the grade and 12.06% in economics. No writing was required from students in first-year economics courses; writing assignments accounted for only 5%, on average, of the course grade in first-year Psychology classes and ~10% in both Geography and Linguistics. Even in courses like political science, writing assignments accounted for only 30% of the total course grade in the first year. While length and amount of writing and thus percentage of grade tended to increase by the fourth year of study in all departments, it was still only up to 33.9% in economics, while philosophy increased the proportion of the grade based on writing assignments from 28 to 100% in the fourth year. Overall, it is safe to say that the experiences of a student pursing at BA at SFU would vary substantially depending upon their chosen major because course requirements across departments were so divergent.

We assumed or hoped that an eventual outcome of a new emphasis on writing and teaching writing would lead to changes in the amount of student writing and in the kinds of writing assignments. We thought it likely that there would also be changes in the amount and kinds of material that both individual faculty members and departments made available to students about writing in their courses or disciplines. Jodi Lough, our other research assistant, brought considerable technical expertise to our little team and began to search department websites to determine what was on offer about writing to students in their disciplines (Lough, 2003). This would also be Fall 2002 baseline data to use for later comparison. To collect this information, she looked first to writing resources offered by academic units within the faculty of arts (including departments, programs, and centers) and second to sources outside the faculty of arts, university-wide resources available to all students. This was done on the assumption that a student writing a history paper, for example, would look first to the history department for guidance and then to resources outside the department. Some departments themselves provide writing-related handouts at departmental offices, in the same area where course outlines and related materials are displayed. For online material, Jodi began at the departmental or program home page and followed the appropriate links. Additional sources included the library website and the Health, Counseling, and Career centre. For practical reasons of sheer volume and difficulty of access, we excluded any resources that would be distributed through lectures or tutorials, or course-related websites.

Of the twenty academic units examined, twelve units, or 60% offered some sort of information. All units offered this information in hardcopy format, at least at the time of collection. Six units (30%) also had information available online. Of these six, one unit duplicated the hardcopy resources online, one unit offered online information distinct from that available in hardcopy (no duplication or overlap), and the remaining four units offered similar information online as for hardcopy, in some instances offering part of what was included in hardcopy, in others providing additional guidelines. The topics dealt with in these resources included: plagiarism, referencing, style guidelines, mechanics of writing, and disciplinary features.

Predictably, attention to plagiarism featured frequently, from cautionary notes in some guides to lengthy, explanatory handouts in seven. The quality as well as quantity of information varied widely and in most cases could barely be construed as a resource for students, lacking as it did the kind of exemplification and suggestions for avoidance strategies that could usefully guide students. Information typically provided on referencing essentially constituted a style guide for a particular reference format (APA, MLA, Chicago, and so on) but did not instruct on how and when to reference. Occasionally, resources indicated why referencing is important, explaining beyond the need to give credit to the author of an idea. Very few resources offered help with what could be considered the mechanics of writing such as grammar and sentence construction, punctuation, and paragraph structure, or such essay writing strategies as constructing outlines, finding a thesis, formatting a research paper, or tackling critical analysis. The Centre for Canadian Studies was the only one producing an essay writing handbook that discussed such topics at length. The philosophy department in contrast to almost all others provided almost no information on referencing, plagiarism, style, or mechanics. Its guide to students was discipline-specific, setting out key elements of a philosophy paper, how to go about writing one, techniques to use, and mistakes to avoid. It set out both positive and negative expectations and key qualities of a philosophy paper providing examples where appropriate.

Material resources for students outside the faculty of arts seemed to be limited to two areas: the Bennett Library and the Health, Counseling, and Career centre. At that time, the university had no university writing consultation centre for student tutoring and no writing lab. The only tutoring service was based in the business administration department and was only for their own students. The library website offered research and writing guides for every discipline on campus as well as links to outside resources on writing papers and completing assignments. Liaison librarians for each discipline were also designated to help students with discipline-specific research requirements. The Health, Counseling, and Career centre (HCCC) offered a number of resources for students, including workshops, online handouts, and peer tutors. Each semester, they planned a workshop entitled "Writing Papers for University", a "3-part, step-by-step approach to writing research papers." Related workshops included dealing with procrastination, note taking, and reading for university. The workshops were free, but limited to a small group and offered only once per semester. These workshops were supplemented by a collection of online handouts on various topics including a nine-page manual on writing a research paper. A new but small peer tutor program was started in the Fall of 2002, to help students in learning skills as well as writing papers.

While we were able to get a good sense from these sources of the attitudinal, material, and pedagogical territory within which we were working, we had a political obligation to create an identity that would encourage a good sense of us as a unit. We needed our own logo, stationery, and website. Stationery was easy once we had a logo. Unfortunately, however, we ourselves did not have the necessary expertise to construct a website and, not authorized to commission anyone from outside the institution, had to seek help internally. Since we seemed to be fairly low on the priority list and the technical people were very busy, that process took nearly five months. Eventually, however, we had a website up and running with our logo and links to resources we were developing as well as to sites at other institutions. We wanted to move toward what Condon identifies as a second-stage level of creating archives of materials, policies, and history (Condon 2006). Such archives attest to a level of stability and presence from which to grow and constitute accessible intellectual capital (Phelps 1999, 85) that we could share among ourselves and with both W-faculty and anyone else interested in such material. We arranged our collection by discipline and included sample syllabi, assignments, research reports, and articles that we thought might be helpful and that were representative of the practices of our own SFU faculty. Needless to say, we also scoured the sites of our colleagues around the country, borrowed ideas, and tied ourselves into their networks. With help, we created a searchable library database, based initially on our own substantial collection of hard copies of articles, amassed over many years, on writing-in-the-disciplines, writing-across-the-curriculum, writing-to-learn, teaching writing, and so on, which we could not only recommend but also pop into mailboxes.

In these various ways, we claimed a space for CWIL's work and stitched ourselves into the local and broader disciplinary context. These efforts would have been quite pointless, however, merely an elaborate stage set and wardrobe, unless at the same time we were creating meaningful relationships with faculty members. Over the course of the first semester, we made as many contacts as we could. Since we were on the sixth floor of the building housing FASS and department offices, we felt well located geographically to be associated with and participants in the university's academic work. We encountered individual professors in the hallways and elevators and chatted in coffee lines; more formally, we arranged short informational meetings with department chairs and spoke at department meetings. At first, we encountered a great deal of confusion about our role. Both faculty and students quite logically associated a writing centre with help for students, but that was not our mandate. We got calls almost everyday, as well as visits to our offices, from students asking for help with their papers. They went away bewildered and rejected. Faculty too seemed mystified by the creation of a writing centre that would not assist their students. We had a lot of explaining and communicating to do and while it was not our job to justify the lack of a centre to help students, we needed to let people know what we could do and why. By mid-October, however, we realized we needed to take our efforts a step further, to build what Phelps defines as "social capital" (Phelps 1999, 86). We needed to bring people together from across the disciplines to work together on transforming their practice. We planned a series of workshops with the overall title "Getting Started on Writing Intensive Learning" which we scheduled as three sessions: I, *Linking Writing to Learning Content*; II, *Planning Writing: Making Assignments Work*; and III, *Responding to Writing*.

We were very fortunate in having been allocated a bright and airy room, the former writing centre space that had not been reassigned, in which to hold meetings and workshops. Wanting to attract as many people as possible, we scheduled multiple sessions of each workshop, with options on different days and times. With an online registration system in place, we were able to track participation as well as to reply easily to inquiries. The number of sessions proved excessive and we dropped to four sessions per workshop. Despite the fact that our participants were drawn mainly from among the short-term teaching staff and graduate students, those first series yielded our six volunteer professors who would pilot W-versions of their courses in the Spring semester of 2003. Because the purpose of the initiative was to make writing the responsibility of the regular lecturers or tenure-stream professors in the disciplines, we were advised that our budget could not stretch to individual pre- and in-course support to non-continuing teaching staff, nor would we be able to provide them with additional paid hours and training for their TAs, both activities being essential components of the resources we would make available to regular and tenure faculty. Such economic issues moved increasingly to the forefront once CWIL and its role in the broader university initiative became more visible and will be discussed in the next section of this chapter.

The approach we took with these first W-faculty members was modeled after my team-teaching work with Steven Davis a few years previous (Strachan and Davis 2000). We cast ourselves as bringing a kind of expertise that would respond to the writing needs and purposes of the course, its students, and the interests and priorities of the professor. Such plasticity was appropriate and necessary since we were not accountable for any outcomes in the course. As the examples in the earlier chapters have illustrated, the corollary to our expertise was our need to feel confident that we had some understanding of the course purposes and content, and that we had an appreciation of disciplinary norms and values. In the first semester of working with Nancy Olewiler and her economics course, therefore, I attended lectures, sat in on a few tutorials, met regularly with her and the TAs for planning purposes, helped craft and write directions for assignments, facilitated norming and grading of those assignments and collected samples of the students' writing and responses. Through that trial period and in our preparation for work with the newly subscribing faculty members, we were developing our sensitivity to and understanding of what was entailed in making our relationships work effectively. We were moving toward what Condon identifies as an essential feature to achieve by the second stage of development: building a model of relationships. While these relationships were time-intensive in most cases, they proved, as the previous chapters indicated, immensely important in building a constituency across the disciplines.

In the second semester, we concentrated mainly on building our own skills of cross-disciplinary consultation with the six volunteer professors who came from the history, humanities, economics, and philosophy departments and sought out others to work with in their courses over the summer semester. But we also had two other concerns: we wished to expand our presence and engage the nascent W-community in ways other than course-work, and to add to the data collection that would serve the institution's assessment and accountability demands. Outreach to the secondary schools seemed another logical way to engage faculty in conversation about writing. Two professors in the history department were particularly interested in collaborating with us. With the cooperation of the school board, we planned a half-day (followed by lunch, of course) of concurrent roundtable discussions of writing in history at the high school and university levels. Several professors explained their practice and attitudes toward teaching writing and history; teachers shared information about their own settings and constraints as well as ideas for making history writing meaningful and interesting to their students. CWIL also initiated a poetry workshop session for secondary teachers, led by Roy Miki from the English department. More informally, we brought W-faculty together three times during the second semester for brown bag lunch-time talk and idea sharing. Along with the workshop series that over the first year gave us contact with 265 participants (93 faculty members and 172 TAs) from 23 departments, and our ongoing scheduled appointments with departments, their chairs and individual faculty members, these other kinds of interaction contributed to our growing sense that we were creating a new space for writing and establishing ourselves as what Townsend refers to as "well-informed specialists."

Our second concern was to accumulate data for assessment purposes. As both Condon and Townsend advise, "'multiple measures, over time' is an excellent starting place" (Townsend 2001, 144). From the outset, we wanted to be able to provide some kind of local evidence of the impact of W-course work on student learning and writing both to encourage participation by faculty in taking on W-courses and to help the various levels of administrators to justify the effort and expense of the new curriculum. While the key indicators for both faculty and administration would eventually need to be rigorously developed measures of improvements in student learning and writing, we settled at the beginning for developing a survey of student beliefs and attitudes about their writing and their responses to the W-course. We drafted, in consultation with our first W-faculty, pre- and post-course surveys to be completed at the beginning and end of each W-course (see Appendices 2 and 9). We also prepared an interview protocol to use with faculty after their W-course. The hour-long interviews, recorded and transcribed by our research assistants, were a means of encouraging assessment of the processes and student outcomes in the course and a means of reflection that could help us all plan changes in a second iteration of the course. (Many of these subsequently provided material for some parts of this book as well as a basis for various analyses by CWIL faculty for conference presentations and publications.)

To ground their assessment of their new writing pedagogy, we also encouraged faculty to collect a range of samples of student writing in their courses and, particularly in situations where they had given feedback leading to revision for perhaps the first time, to discuss the quality of revision as well as their overall impression of any improvements they thought they observed. Since a general dissatisfaction led to a willingness to work with writing, satisfaction with the outcomes of W-course writing, however informal, seemed one important step toward commitment to continuing the instructional effort. We further saw such selection of papers and discussion as being yet another way of fostering collegial discourse about writing and bringing writing to the foreground in faculty's responses to student assignments.

By the end of the first year, we had set out a territory that seemed to us to fall within the mandate assigned to us in the FASS, that had a number of the features that Townsend suggests are significant for successful program development, and that Condon identifies with the first and second stages. These included buy-in from faculty and adequate, if not strong, administrative support; a focus on devolving responsibility for writing to all faculty with the emphasis on integrating writing to achieve course content goals; writing as a means of learning as well as communication; workshop planning and development; and the building of a materials archive and data for scholarly analysis and assessment.

For the major part of the first year, we had no administrative assistance. Producing estimates of our workloads per W-course and estimates of additional costs for TAs in W-courses at the request of the dean's office, making projections at the request of the vice president academic for the number of W-courses that would eventually be needed when the writing requirement took effect, and drafting budgets for both, were all tasks which I felt ill-prepared to take on with any confidence but, as director, was charged to produce. In June, however, we were funded to hire an assistant who would manage our budget and take care of many of the logistical tasks associated with workshop registration, publicity, and so on. We were also allocated funds for an additional consultant at the start of our second year. With her help, we were able to develop eight new W-courses in Fall semester 2003, enhance our fledgling program of TA training and mentoring, increase the number and kinds of workshop sessions, and sustain ongoing outreach to departments, data collection and the continual revision, and re-thinking of our practice.

BEYOND THE LAUNCHING PERIOD: THE NEXT THREE YEARS

Although it was named the Centre for Writing-Intensive Learning, CWIL was not an officially designated "centre" governed by university policy, nor was it a department, or a unit within a department. What this meant was that we were somewhat anomalous: there was no established infrastructure within which we could be identified or within which we could locate ourselves, nor within which the director could be assumed to have certain distinctive and commonly recognized responsibilities. My role was always "under construction" with all the ambiguity and vulnerability that status entails. As administrative and institutional frameworks for the writing requirement began to be articulated and more people across the levels of governance got involved in the planning and implementation process, CWIL was swept into the confluence of larger institutional currents: financial and political, logistical and bureaucratic. The next period of development is thus characterized by widely dispersed efforts on many fronts, including encouraging departmental participation, publicizing faculty practice through presentations, establishing processes for course accreditation and so on. CWIL faculty contributed substantially to these processes when consulted, but were often excluded, sometimes inexplicably, sometimes inadvertently, and sometimes because we had no clearly defined position in the institutional hierarchy and were missed out in the lines of communication. Townsend's summary of characteristics typical of effective writing-intensive programs is useful as a way of assessing this next period in terms of progress made (or not made) toward a sustaining environment for the writing initiative.

At the broad institutional level, Townsend identifies the *sine qua non* combination *of strong faculty ownership and administrative support* as two interdependent characteristics of a successful W-program. Five other key characteristics at this broad level include: *symbiosis with other institutional programs/missions* to encourage coherence and collaboration in purpose and effort; *a reward structure that values teaching; a low student-to-W-instructor ratio,* along with TA help if necessary; regular internal assessment procedures combined with periodic external review; and *flexible but sound W-criteria.* At the classroom and teaching level, she identifies *integration of W-assignments with course goals and instructor's pedagogical methods* as distinct from add-on approaches to writing in a W-course. Finally, with respect to faculty support for the W-course program, she identifies two requirements: *knowledgeable, diplomatic W-program personnel* with expertise and strong interpersonal skills; and not least, *patience and vigilance* as the W-program evolves.

In what follows, I use these ten characteristics as a basis of reference to our own context and development on the one hand and to our movement along Condon's continuum on the other. I also make some attempt to estimate where we still needed to go beyond at the end of the pilot period to reach the conditions Condon identifies as the third and fourth stages of a writing program that is not only stable but also a staple component of the institution's educational and scholarly identity. I begin by outlining our development with respect to the institutional level characteristics, followed by those related to the classroom and teaching level and to faculty support.

INSTITUTIONAL LEVEL CHARACTERISTICS

1. Strong faculty ownership of the WI system

At the basic level of structuring, SFU's W-curriculum initiative was set up to meet what Townsend defines as the need for faculty ownership. The processes of implementing that initiative encouraged ownership that was evident in four different arenas: committee participation, W-course development, workshop participation, and boundary negotiation.

Faculty Committee Participation

The new requirements for writing were the result of faculty choice, exercised through the various committee decisions described earlier. Faculty constituted the WSG charged with peer review of W-course proposals and with establishing policies regarding W-criteria. Membership in the WSG was voluntary and between 2003 and 2006, only two of the six faculty members chose to be replaced at the end of their two-year terms. Commitment to the initiative and interest in serving was thus high, and continuity of membership had the advantage of increasing the shared understanding of the contexts for the W-implementation. Though they each brought different levels of knowledge about and experience of teaching writing, all members were involved in teaching W-courses themselves.

Faculty Participation in W-course Development

Beyond the demonstration of ownership at the committee level, faculty participation in W-course development was crucial both to provide for the requirement to take effect in the Fall of 2006, and to transform the teaching and learning culture. From the start with 10 courses in the first full year from Fall 2002 through Spring and Summer semesters of 2003, expansion was sustained and encouraged, aided by the addition of Adrienne Burk to CWIL's consulting team in Fall 2003. In the following three semesters, Fall 2003 and Spring and Summer 2004, three of us worked intensively with 29 instructors and their 37 TAs in 32 courses from 13 departments, serving a total of 1846 students. Of the 37 TAs, 25 attended a 3-day pre-semester seminar. The number of W-courses per semester continued to increase. In the Fall of 2004, we worked with faculty in 12 courses, more of which were larger lower-division courses rather than the smaller upper-division courses in which faculty had felt more ready to experiment. Nearly 2000 students took these 12 courses taught by 11 faculty members, three of whom were teaching the W-course as a second or third iteration and one of whom taught two W-courses with smaller enrolments. By the beginning of Spring semester 2005, 44 W-courses had been developed, involving 88 TAs and 3992 students. An additional 14 W-courses were piloted in Spring and Summer 2005, five of which were repeat iterations. Thirty-nine TAs were involved and 1741 students. What all these numbers add up to is the commitment of 32 professors to W-course preparation and teaching, 12 of whom offered their W-course more than once during this part of the pilot period. They represented 31 departments from the FASS and the Applied and Physical Sciences.

With few exceptions, these W-courses had all been supported by CWIL to a greater or lesser degree, depending on the professor's expressed needs and interests. The level of support also depended on CWIL's resources. During the Spring and Summer of 2005, for instance, support was curtailed somewhat by staff absences on leave, and by the time taken to interview and hire prospective new consultants for CWIL and a new departmental assistant. As the implementation deadline of Fall 2006 became less of a shadowy and distant target, it was clear that faculty confidence in the level of support available to them needed to be maintained and that CWIL staffing correspondingly needed to be enhanced. The prospect of the deadline also meant that more departments began searching for volunteer faculty members to submit proposals for W-courses that would be offered when the requirement came into force, if not before. Between Fall 2005 and Fall 2006, the academic year leading up to the deadline, an additional forty professors joined the W-course initiative and offered a pilot W-course.

Fortunately, support for some course development and implementation devolved in a few instances to departments. In those cases, the nature of the demand for CWIL services was changed and departmental as well as individual faculty ownership of the W-initiative encouraged. The philosophy department, having led the way with the Steven Davis collaboration, continued to be inventive in its commitment to the teaching of writing and in taking ownership of its own disciplinary needs. Jodi Lough, CWIL's research assistant and herself a TA in philosophy, drew on her years of experience with CWIL to work closely with the department's TAs as their designated mentor. In 2005, she was hired as an instructor charged with supporting both faculty and TAs in the W-philosophy courses. The psychology department, also long committed to improving and supporting student writers, also hired instructors who would take responsibility to support faculty and TAs in that department as well as teach courses. CWIL faculty worked with them as needed to assist in course preparation and TA training. The English department enhanced their commitment to professionalizing their graduate students, and CWIL worked with them in designated training for TAs as well as with faculty designing their W-courses.

Faculty Workshop Participation

While W-course planning and support itself constituted substantial professional development, that work was usually preceded by and enhanced by workshop participation. Between Fall 2002 and Summer 2005, CWIL offered over 80 workshops in which about 250 faculty from 33 of SFU's 38 departments participated. These included the continually modified Writing-Intensive Learning series as well as sessions planned in response to requests for particular topics, like evaluation of writing, inviting ESL students into academic writing, and preparing W-course proposals. TAs were rarely involved in the faculty sessions but the faculty who were supervising their TAs in a W-course were consulted about the direction and focus of the TA workshops and participated in an orientation that helped to ensure some shared understanding of expectations and pedagogy. Such orientations were opportunities for the faculty member to take ownership of pedagogies they were adopting and to demonstrate to their TAs that the change in practice was a matter of their own choice.

Challenges to Ownership: Negotiation of Boundaries and Student Perceptions

Recognition of ownership was an important consideration not only for faculty but also for both the TAs and the students in a W-course. In the early months, we put so much energy into what Condon rightly names the "missionary" task of the first stage of working with faculty, that we overlooked the potential impact on the perception of students. Although we or the instructor took time at the first class to explain what was being undertaken and we invited completion of the student surveys, it was difficult to articulate the nature of the relationship between the faculty member and CWIL, and the changes in the course assignments and pedagogy. The surveys were clearly attached to CWIL and its research interests. But when we, rather than the course instructor, did the explaining about the university's W-initiative, it seemed as if we were intruding and were responsible for a significant change in the approach to teaching that students did not universally welcome. Neither we nor the instructors anticipated this problem of perception. Some instructors preferred us to come to class and explain the context for their pedagogical changes: we brought a clear understanding of that context as well as expertise on which they were relying to some extent and they also wanted us to be seen as members of their instructional team. It became clear, however, that it was not in anyone's interest that W-courses be labeled "CWIL" courses, either by students or faculty. Nor was it useful for the "writing component" as some faculty termed it, to be seen by students as an add-on. Our goal was for the use of writing and the instruction around writing to be seen and understood as an alternative way of teaching the course content.

Although they were taking on the challenge to use and teach writing differently, not all the instructors had a secure grasp on the concept of writing as a way of learning the course content. When they began, that recognition was often at the level of discourse rather than experience. The value for learning had yet to be demonstrated. Nor were many instructors in the habit of explaining the reasons for their teaching practice to students. It did not seem necessary to provide a rationale for lecturing or for setting questions or for using PowerPoint in their presentations since these were taken-for-granted methods and techniques. The use of writing for learning, however, and the emphasis on drafts and revision did require some justification, particularly in courses where students did not expect to write. Shifting responsibility away from us at CWIL on to instructors to articulate the context for the writing emphasis and explain their own motivation to their classes was another important, if small, step toward faculty ownership and student acceptance.

2. Administrative support: Strong philosophical and fiscal support from institutional administrators, coupled with their willingness to avoid micromanagement.

As the second constituent of the *sine qua non* for a writing program, philosophical and fiscal administrative support for the writing initiative and for CWILs role in it both inspired and enabled development during the pilot period. Support was anchored in two levels of governance, the office of the dean of arts and social sciences and, at the more senior level, in the office of the vice president academic.

Support at the level of the dean's office

The dean of the FASS, John Pierce, had inspired and established CWIL. He showed a strong commitment to and understanding of the principles behind the W-course initiative and, once we at CWIL had demonstrated that we were achieving the W-course targets agreed upon, he approved CWILs budget proposals, including the hiring of a departmental assistant and additional consultants, Adrienne Burk in 2003 and two others in 2004. His attitude on management might be summed up in the quote attached to his e-mail signature: "Organizations learn only through individuals who learn" (Senge 1990). He valued and trusted individual effort, encouraged careful reporting, and was open to hearing suggestions. As dean, he had relatively limited time to attend to CWIL and certainly did not micromanage. Nor, indeed, did Roger Blackman, associate dean of arts, one of the people to whom he delegated support for CWIL. Roger Blackman had long advocated for more attention to writing in the disciplines and fully understood what CWIL was attempting to do. Although, as mentioned earlier, CWIL was not formally constituted as a centre, the proposal for a centre, drafted by Blackman and eventually forwarded for discussion by the dean to the vice president academic, opened with a statement clarifying the mandate set out by FASS for CWIL. (See Appendix 11.)

> The Centre for Writing-Intensive Learning aims to *make the use of writing constitutive* of the teaching and learning culture in the faculty of arts and *to foster students' skills as writers.* The centre will *develop resources and strategies to support writing* as a means of learning and thinking in all disciplines, and *assist faculty on a by-request basis* in planning and offering writing instruction in their courses. In collaboration with faculty and departments, the centre will *monitor and assess the implementation* of new or modified approaches to the uses and teaching of writing. Information from such assessment will be used to influence future instruction and *to evaluate outcomes.* (emphasis added)

The statement makes clear that the dean acknowledged the interdependence of teaching and research for ongoing improvement in the teaching and learning of writing and also acknowledged that expertise was housed, although not exclusively, in CWIL. Roger Blackman's grasp of the complexity of the undertaking as well as commitment was also evident in his personal support. He was always ready at the end of the phone or at his desk to respond to questions, particularly around matters of university policy and politics. He served as mentor and guide through what to me, as a neophyte, were the mazes of the administrative machinery and I depended on him for impartial and reliable information and advice.

Support at the level of the vice president academic

As the person responsible for the overall curriculum initiative of which writing was part, John Waterhouse approved and provided substantial funding during the pilot stage. He established a new implementation committee composed of an appointed chair and five elected faculty members representing the five main faculties. This new UCITF was charged with ensuring a successful transition into all the new requirements, including writing, by serving as "an enabling structure." Support included funds that could be used for research and materials purchase and funds for UCITF members' participation in and travel to events and conferences that would assist them in accomplishing their mandate. The UCITF became responsible for identifying resources needed both for implementation and maintenance of the requirements and for requesting and distributing funds as needed for those resources.

In the case of the writing requirement, one of the needed resources was funding for additional TA hours. It was clear from the outset that TAs would need more time or fewer students if they were to provide the level of commitment needed for writing in a W-course. Before the UCITF was constituted, part of CWIL's budget was allocated to enable individual faculty members to buy the extra TA time they needed for their pilot W-courses. As the certification of courses proceeded, beginning formally in Spring 2004, the Task Force took over responsibility for funding TA support and developed standard policies about funding levels. They arrived at a formula to govern decisions that could be applied across all disciplines for the W-courses. They allocated an extra $75.00 per filled-seat in W-courses. The expectation of this policy was that departments would make a commitment to offer *x* number of W-courses in return for that support. What this meant is that by Fall 2006, course enrolments would largely be the basis on which decisions could be made about the number of TAs to be hired for a course, about the hiring of specialist writing instructors or about some other form of assistance to the instructor offering the W-course. CWIL would have no role in any such decisions that, following regular university procedures for distribution of funds, would be under the control of and channeled from the vice president academic through the faculty deans to departments. The effect of such fiscal decisions, however, appeared to ensure sustained commitment to the professional development work being done by CWIL to support faculty and train TAs.

Beyond ensuring adequate funding, John Waterhouse, through the UCITF, also provided administrative oversight. In Spring 2004, he appointed a director of curriculum who became the administrative intermediary from the vice president's office, charged with overseeing the implementation of all three strands of the new curriculum, the quantitative and breadth as well as writing dimensions. The mandate was very broad and included researching the outcomes of the implementation as well as encouraging its development and communicating its implications and requirements across the SFU campus and to the wider college community who would be sending transfer students. As well as continuing to serve on the UCITF in this role, the director also joined all the support groups for the three strands of the new curriculum, including the WSG of which I, as CWIL director, was a member. In that capacity, she was positioned to represent the vice president academic's philosophical commitment to the writing-intensive learning and genre-based approach to writing in W-courses, as defined in the criteria and as conceptualized by the WSG. She also represented the emergence of the larger institutional currents within which CWIL now needed to find its place.

Challenges at the level of administration

Managing the immensely complex logistical tasks associated with a curriculum change required new units of bureaucracy to overlay and mediate existing processes and lines of communication. Each unit had its own role and responsibilities and these had to be coordinated and communicated not only with the others involved in the curriculum implementation but also with those pre-existing and affected by the implementation. CWIL was one of those pre-existing units. In the two years since CWIL had been established, we had built a working unit, a clear identity, and a reputation for high quality performance and generally productive relations with faculty and administration. Sheltered in the faculty of arts and social sciences, CWIL had functioned fairly independently. Predictably, perhaps, once the necessary bureaucracy for the implementation became more actively involved, the environment in which we worked became more constrained. Improvisation was replaced with regulation and we had to re-construct and re-construe ourselves. The newly constituted WSG was charged to define and certify W-courses and recommend levels of funding. As well, the WSG was to make programs aware of different models for W-courses and to recruit instructors to offer W-courses. In encouraging faculty to develop pilot W-courses and working to build momentum for the W-initiative in FASS, CWIL had previously fulfilled both these latter roles in its first two years. At this juncture, however, the role of CWIL had to be clearly differentiated from that of the WSG as did the role of the WSG have to be differentiated from that of the UCITF which was the policy-making body.

The greater distribution of responsibility was both necessary and desirable. From the task force's point of view, it was important that any information passed onto departments be accurate and they wished to have control of that information. The task force, after all, was the body that would be accountable to both the administration and the faculty community. It was also a necessary step in expansion that more people take responsibility and ownership. Existing support services for writing in the engineering and business departments were validated anew. From the point of view of CWIL faculty, however, the task force's assumptions and perceptions of CWIL's role appeared incompatible with the original mandate set out by the dean in the faculty of arts and social sciences. This point of view proved a source of considerable tension and strain for CWIL faculty in the absence of formal changes in that mandate. For example, although CWIL had proposed W-criteria for FASS W-courses by late 2002, had played a key role in their refinement as members of the WSG, and had influenced their acceptance for the university at large, CWIL faculty were informed that they should not be communicating information about the criteria when explaining their own services in a venue such as a department meeting, unless accompanied by a WSG member who would respond to such questions. Adhering to this instruction was practically difficult and its implications troubling.

With the exception of the UCITF chair, Dennis Krebs, with whom we frequently consulted, members of the task force apparently viewed CWIL as one among other "service units" dedicated to W-course support. The support offered in the other units, specifically the business and engineering departments, was limited in the former to communication courses and an effective peer tutoring program, and in the latter to two particular writing and communication courses. In both departments, this support for student writing was led by highly qualified writing and rhetoric instructors, but their activities and goals were not at all comparable in either scope or scale to the kind of support for the writing initiative developed by CWIL. They were not embarked, either practically or philosophically, on an effort at cultural transformation in which W-course development was only a part, however significant. Dennis Krebs, UCITF chair, confirmed in an email message to the author on August 20, 2007 that he endorsed CWIL's concept of its role and its wide range of activities, as set out in the updated 2004 Draft Mandate (Appendix 10). He also recognized that some task force members' had a different understanding. The director of curriculum, for instance, in an email message to the author on February 1, 2007, explained that the UCITF had never interpreted CWIL's role in terms of the 2004 mandate. Since CWIL had no direct access to the UCITF and was not aware of conflicting interpretations of its role, the difference in perception was clearly a factor, though not articulated at the time, when misunderstandings later had to be negotiated.

The effects on CWIL faculty of these different perceptions had two dimensions. On the one hand, responsibility for promoting W-course participation was shifted to the WSG and the director of curriculum, whose goal was to ensure that an adequate array of courses would be available to students when the requirement took effect. CWIL's efforts to encourage that participation had always felt somewhat partisan and even tinged with an element of self-interest. It was important and helpful, therefore, to have others advocate for W-courses instead. But equally, the shift had the adverse effect of subordinating the academic argument and demonstration of the principles and purposes of writing-intensive learning to the pragmatic matter of recruitment to the initiative and the lining up of W-courses. Instead of being the spokespersons making the academic case for W-courses to individual faculty and taking a scholarly approach to writing and professional development, CWIL faculty were asked to act in a service role as mediators of the W-curriculum. Sensitivities around such a shift were heightened by the limited-term lecturer status of all CWIL faculty, which created a constant sense of job insecurity, by what CWIL faculty interpreted as a negating of their expertise in and knowledge of their discipline, and by a sense that the entrepreneurial spirit that had energized them was being dampened. Some frisson and turbulence can probably be expected, however, during such a complex process. Despite a few clumsy moves and occasions when more open communication would have been helpful at a personal level, we generally managed to avoid unproductive confrontations; CWIL faculty at this stage still felt confident in the administration's support for the overall direction of the implementation in which we were playing what we judged to be a significant and largely acknowledged if not well understood role.

3. Symbiosis with other institutional programs/missions

From the outset in 2002, CWIL made determined efforts, as described above, to establish connections across campus. Townsend notes that "the more cooperation and links a WI program has with other initiatives the better, assuming that WI program leaders keep the WI focus in balance." Such cooperation, she proposes, helps in "creating a curricular requirement that is tightly woven into the institutional fabric" (Townsend 2001, 243). Condon identifies the making of such links and collaborations with a third stage of development, cautioning also that coordinating with others should not mean losing sight of the W-program mission. Any coordinating should be for mutual benefit. He adds that a contribution to development can also be made by links with "other, similar programs at peer institutions to make common cause" (Condon 2006).

Unlike institutions which already had writing programs that a W-initiative would enhance, Simon Fraser had no such program. Therefore, the task for CWIL (and later in collaboration with the WSG and UCITF) was to assist in drawing attention to writing and to the new approach the university proposed to take in using and teaching it. We felt we had to move immediately into raising the profile of writing. That meant making the links which elsewhere could perhaps wait till a program was more fully realized. Over the next three years, post-launch, therefore, we continued and expanded our efforts to find compatible others with whom to make connections and collaborate. Among these were: Cheryl Amundsen with whom we collaborated on a proposal to enhance teaching and learning, the Consortium of the J. S. Knight Institute at Cornell, and the UCITF with which we consulted on new programs. Reaching for symbiosis was not an altogether straightforward process, however, and we experienced challenges.

Collaborating for enhancing teaching and learning: Cheryl Amundsen

One of the most effective projects on campus for enhancing teaching was that developed by Cheryl Amundsen, associate professor of education. Cheryl's intellectual association was with the Carnegie Scholarship of Teaching movement and through her collaboration with colleagues at McGill University, she had embarked on a program of research investigating how professors link what they know about the development of knowledge in their disciplines with what they do with students and "the process by which [professors] change and develop their thinking about teaching and learning, and subsequently link their thinking to practice" (Saroyan and Amundsen 2004, ix). She brought her program to Simon Fraser when she joined the faculty of education and invited me to attend her five-day workshop "Rethinking Teaching/Course Design" in Spring 2004. We had already met and discovered common ground in our approach to faculty development, neither of us persuaded of the value of single, injection-style workshops and both committed to long-term engagement. My participation in her workshop led to our discussing potential collaboration. Among our ideas was that we adapt her workshop model, in which groups of professors worked together in groups or cohorts to improve their courses and teaching, and have the focus on the development of W-courses. In early June, 2004, we met again and chatted excitedly over coffee about developing a university-wide centre, an Institute of Inquiry-Based Teaching, or Institute for Study of Teaching and Learning in Higher Education. Such an institute would include course development activities planned by and offered to faculty members from across the university. Associated research activities would focus on studying the processes that faculty were undertaking and the impact of those processes on learning and on understanding the ways of teaching in different disciplines. Always conscious of our anomalous institutional status, I saw such an institute as a potential umbrella home for CWIL that would embed our workshops and faculty mentoring in a context of reflective practice and research that could be institutionally recognized and legitimized.

Although we at CWIL became enthusiastic about this possibility, there were no precedents for such a centre and the concept initially garnered limited encouragement from the administration. We continued to exchange ideas with Cheryl, and in late summer and early fall 2004 discussed drafts of a formal proposal that Cheryl had taken to the next level of development with one of her colleagues in Education, Mark Fettes, at the invitation of the Task Force (UCITF) of which Mark was a member. That proposal was refined a few times in consultation with several interested groups over the next two years. In an effort to place CWIL on the institutional map, we chose to include the Institute concept in various other proposals we ourselves submitted to the vice president academic for coordinating writing activity across the campus. Although no firm commitment for an institute was emerging at that time, Cheryl did not abandon it as a possibility; she continued to voice the need for its role in enhancing attention to teaching at SFU. For us at CWIL, however, the process itself had enabled us to imagine and conceptualize a vehicle and future for CWIL that would position us as a university-wide resource in ways that seemed unavailable to us from our base in the FASS. If the structure could accommodate a resident and permanent unit, like CWIL, as distinct from a looser association of short-term seconded faculty, it would provide a context and opportunity for meeting with other colleagues interested in the study of teaching, and assert a scholarly identity for CWIL that would also be compatible with our more readily recognized service identity.

Making links beyond the institution: The Cornell Consortium

We were able to meet with colleagues who shared our interest in both teaching and writing through connection with another institution. Jonathan Munroe, director, invited SFU to participate in the J. S. Knight Institute Consortium in the Summer 2004. The institute brought together delegates from universities embarking on and developing writing in-the-disciplines programs to share ideas and practices and learn from each other and from the experience of faculty at Cornell. The request for participation was that three people holding different positions would represent the university: an administrator, a faculty member with an interest in writing, and a writing program director. SFU was well represented by professor Jon Driver, Dean of Graduate Studies; Dr. Barbara Frisken, who would replace Dennis Krebs as chair of the UCITF in Summer 2004; and myself, as director of CWIL. We joined representatives from nine other universities, including ones from the UK, Germany, and Holland, in four days of presentations and discussions of the purposes and practices associated with effective teaching of writing in the disciplines. Both Jon Driver and Barbara Frisken were in a position to influence the development of SFU's writing initiative at an administrative level. Both came away with a deeper understanding of the meaning of writing-intensive learning and with many ideas for how to support SFU's fledgling project. As Barbara wrote in her part of our joint report, "My general feeling was that writing-intensive classes are examples of active-learning where everybody must participate. It is important to de-emphasize the mechanics and emphasize writing as a way of learning" (Strachan, Frisken, and Driver 2004, 5). She also made recommendations about professionalizing the teaching by graduate students, hiring faculty-based writing instructors, and offering recognition for excellent W-course teaching. Jon Driver also reflected on classroom applications, observing that he "came away from the workshops re-energized to think about my own teaching" as well as making suggestions for strategies that might be adopted at SFU. (Strachan, Frisken, and Driver 2004, 2)

The link to Cornell afforded an opportunity to confirm the general effectiveness of the ways in which CWIL was contributing to the SFU writing-initiative. It enabled us to feel confident of eventual success in the overall project if we could help create the right conditions, conditions which would reflect the particularities of our context but which conformed to such principles as encouraging faculty ownership and arguing for strong administrative support. The presentations at the Institute further illustrated the outcomes of collaboration between the Knight Institute faculty and faculty from the disciplines. Some of the Cornell presenters, as Jon Driver noted, "reported that they were lukewarm about the idea to start with, but saw benefits to their teaching and their students' abilities and confidence that convinced them of the value of the 'writing in the disciplines' approach." Jon recommended that "SFU needs to find ways that will encourage faculty members to try this approach, and provide support that encourages experimentation within some limits of good practice" (Strachan, Frisken, and Driver 2004, 2). He thought the examples set by SFU faculty as well as examples from the other universities undertaking this kind of major curriculum change, would be encouraging and inspiring.

Collaboration on new programs and proposals: UCITF

What the Cornell experience reinforced was the need for other supporting units around campus for writing. It was decided by the UCITF and the WSG that these should include two additional elements: first, a pre-W course preparation for those students who qualified for entrance to the university but lacked a requisite level of language skills to benefit from W-courses; and secondly, a writing center to assist students with writing. We made considerable efforts at CWIL to be part of the planning process for these new initiatives. Kathryn Alexander served with faculty in education on the committee developing the FAL program proposal and a draft curriculum. We all worked, at the request of the director of Curriculum and of Barbara Frisken, chair of UCITF, on drafting a comprehensive proposal that would structure the teaching and learning of writing under a common theoretical and administrative framework. We reasoned that creating a coherent framework during the planning stage would ensure that W-course work being done with faculty by CWIL and the tutoring of students in a new writing center would be mutually reinforcing. We also believed that assessment of writing and scholarship in the teaching of writing (as sponsored perhaps by the institute proposed by Cheryl Amundsen) should be coherent with faculty-led, discipline-based writing.

Challenges to symbiosis

The vision of a coherent framework as embodied in our proposal stayed on paper. A decision came forward from the senior administration that separated service to students and service to faculty. The goal "*symbiosis with other institutional programs/missions*" would not readily be achieved in the formal structures being established. We learned that a student learning commons that would offer a comprehensive set of services to students was to be created in the library. It would include a computer lab, as well as spaces for workshops and consultations about writing. A director would be appointed to manage the commons overall and a coordinator would be hired specifically to manage writing support for students. The matter of service to support faculty brought CWIL's anomalous positioning into sharp focus. As mentioned earlier, CWIL had no formal status as a unit. We did not fit the requirements for an autonomous centre as defined in the university's policies for centers. However, the Learning and Instructional Development centre (LIDC) directed by a professor of education had been established with the following mission: "to collaborate with academic units and instructors, as well as other university services to create a world-class teaching and learning environment that provides outstanding educational experiences to SFU students" (LIDC Strategic Plan, 2005). We also were clearly engaged in faculty support and development. CWIL, however, took a more specifically disciplinary and academic approach to faculty development which differed from the more educationally guided approach taken by LIDC. While these approaches might be seen as complementary by the faculty, fulfilling different needs, CWIL felt they were philosophically distinct views of faculty development. LIDC did not share that perception which led to some feelings of disparity for CWIL faculty. The senior administration, however, working on the assumption that faculty support in all its forms would be more efficiently carried out under one administrative umbrella, re-located us from the FASS to the LIDC in Spring 2005. The decision was made jointly by John Pierce, dean of arts and social sciences, in recognition of CWIL's university-wide mandate and by the vice president academic, John Waterhouse. The outcomes of this arranged marriage would depend largely on the LIDC director; it remained to be seen whether the assumptions of the administration would prove correct. In terms of Condon's continuum at the 3rd stage, the move to LIDC sited CWIL for integration into as yet undefined "larger, other agendas" (Condon 2006).

The CWIL faculty, not wishing to lose sight of possible symbiotic relationships in the new structures that had been created, worked informally. We responded to discussion papers, attended open planning meetings, supplied resources, and shared our experience over coffee and lunch with the people designated to work with student writing in the proposed structure of the learning commons. Adrienne Burk established a collegial working relationship with Elaine Fairey who was appointed director of the learning commons and we all welcomed our colleague Amanda Goldrick-Jones when she was brought in from the University of Winnipeg to be coordinator of writing services for students. With these professional colleagues, we might be confident of a shared commitment to research-based thinking about writing and about the teaching of writing and of respect for expertise in the field.

The creation of centralized student writing services as well as the development of more in-house writing support at the department level (as mentioned above) meant that CWIL faculty could be collaborating and consulting with others across campus on their terms and in their spaces, thereby contributing to a spreading of expertise and encouraging increased faculty engagement with writing. One of the obstacles to increasing engagement, however, frustratingly familiar to people involved with professional development, is the reward structure at the university. Condon identifies "awards for writing and course development and motivational awards for faculty, departments" (2006) as another feature of the third stage, and this need for reward of some kind is next on Townsend's list as well.

4. A reward structure that values teaching

What SFU offered to faculty as extrinsic "reward" for W-course teaching took two forms: assistance from CWIL in planning and implementing the W-course and additional TA support. The formula for funding (see above) and the preferences of the department determined exactly how that support would be distributed, but it typically meant more TAs for large courses and, for the TAs, a reduced number of sections and slightly smaller sections. Funding was also made available for course development time. Time, often the commodity most sought by faculty, is available for W-course development from funds that can be used to hire a sessional instructor to replace the faculty member and to purchase course materials; extra money was also available for instructional support to TAs and tutor markers to relieve instructors of that responsibility.

The most hopeful sign on the horizon that could lead to some revisiting of the current, deeply embedded valuing of research over teaching would be the senate's approval of the formation of the Institute for the Study of Teaching and Learning in the Disciplines. If research into their teaching won the kind of recognition that research in their subject field was given during tenure and promotion reviews, faculty would be encouraged to view such research as having scholarly merit. In itself, that would be a significant departure from defining research only in terms of what it contributes to knowledge in the discipline. The possibility that the formation of the institute might foster a shift is encouraging.

Other forms that rewards or recognition might take were suggested by the W-faculty consulted for this book. They also expressed their views on the matter of the institutionally established reward structure. Some, indeed, would like to see restricted class size as a reward for teaching a W-course, another feature that appears in Townsend's list (See Chapter Seven).

5. A low student-to-W-instructor ratio, along with TA help if necessary

At SFU, everyone involved in the W-initiative recognized that class size had to be addressed effectively if instructors were to give adequate instruction and feedback on writing. The assigning of more TAs to large enrolment courses was the main approach taken to keep student–instructor ratios at a manageable level. Courses that are designated writing courses, as distinct from W-courses in the disciplines, do restrict enrolment to between 17 and 20 students per section. But the pilot period surfaced the complexity of enrolment patterns, particularly in the upper-division W-courses, and raised questions about the practicality of establishing firm and universal guidelines for W-class size. Unlike many US institutions, there has been no broad policy about class size adopted at SFU for W-courses. In large lower-division W-courses, the funds-per-seat approach has been taken for deciding on the size of tutorial sections. As of fall 2007, instructors teaching the upper-division W-courses, however, have to negotiate their own terms for support at the department level. Whatever decisions are and will be made with respect to instructor–student ratios, this element would not appear to be one that would threaten the future of the W-initiative, since both the precedent and rationale for class-size restriction have been established.

6. Regular internal assessment procedures combined with periodic external review

Townsend suggests that both internal and external assessment are essential components of a strong WI system and Condon foregrounds assessment at the third stage on his continuum of development. Assessment, he suggests, may take the form of faculty naming and articulating of outcomes, internal monitoring of student progress and achievement and carefully designed assessment processes, which include both formative and summative assessment (Condon 2006). Some departments, as part of their decision-making around W-course identification, articulated outcomes they thought important for student writing in their discipline. Such informal discussions have probably occurred more widely than we at CWIL were aware and may very well serve as the underpinning for W-course assignments in such disciplines as psychology and philosophy, which have defined their particular characteristics of good writing quite precisely. As has already been noted above, CWIL was intent from the outset on collecting baseline data for use in assessing the initiative at the program level as well as on documenting faculty and student responses to the W-course implementation. During the pilot period, however, we were not able to undertake a systematic program of assessment of student writing. We collected many sets of student papers, complete with assignment details, feedback on drafts and revision, notes on the classroom context and both instructor and student verbal and written observations about the assignment, and the writing process. Apart from drawing on some of this material for illustrative purposes during conference presentations, however, we did not engage in the kind of systematic analysis necessary to produce reliable assessment data. Such research required time not available to us. Nor, moreover, had we been successful in making the case that CWIL's practice and research should be linked in a reciprocal relationship.

CWIL was invited to contribute to but not take responsibility for writing assessment. The UCITF was, of course, concerned about the assessment of all three strands of the new curriculum requirements and asked the WSG to draft a proposal for assessing the writing strand. CWIL faculty contributed substantially to that draft through me as a member of the committee. The resulting WSG proposal distinguished two related and interdependent purposes for assessment of the writing requirement:

1. The instructional effectiveness of W-courses must be assessed, to determine whether W-courses improve student writing to a degree that meets faculty expectations.

2. The effectiveness of the W-program must be assessed, to determine the legitimacy of the commitment and expense associated with the new writing requirement (Writing Support Group 2005, 1–5).

With respect to the first of these purposes, the proposal emphasized the importance of ongoing, course, and class-based local assessment that reflects departmental norms and expectations. To assess program effectiveness, the proposal argued for the need "to compile data from a wide range of sources to serve as indicators of change in such areas as practice, development of skills and resources, and outcomes as measured by results in tests, surveys, and interviews with principle stakeholders" (Writing Support Group 2005, 1). The proposal then made 10 recommendations for collection and analysis of relevant sources of data and concluded with a summary of the existing instruments and data already available, the majority of which had been developed and compiled by CWIL, although, as noted earlier, not subjected to either qualitative or adequate quantitative analysis.

The UCITF appointed a committee to be chaired by Cheryl Amundsen to take on the development and implementation of an assessment plan.

The committee reviewed each of the support group proposals and in consultation with the WSG assigned a priority to each of the writing recommendations. After a year of development undertaken by Cheryl and Cathi Dunlop, the proposal was submitted to the director of curriculum in Spring 2006. As of January 2007, Cheryl reported in an email to the author that there had been no follow-up from the office of the vice president academic. At the course level, however, the pre- and post-surveys (see Appendix 9) used by CWIL and the W-faculty with whom we worked provided information about student reactions to the W-courses during the pilot period, information that supplemented the standard university course evaluation forms. The responses were entered into a database and summarized by course and across courses. Since CWIL faculty and the professors with whom we worked were interested in getting some feedback, these raw data offered interim indications of trends on specific topics. Statistical analyses followed in Summer 2007 by a team of researchers from within the LIDC (Groeneboer et al. 2007). A total of 3000 surveys were completed between Fall 2003 and Summer 2006. Of these, 1599 surveys were analyzed after data cleaning based on the following criteria: (a) all pre-course surveys could be matched with a post-course survey; (b) all responded to a question about the language used in the home; and (c) both pre- and post-surveys included a response to a self-rating of "overall writing skill." Answers to open-ended questions were coded into categories; academic term, level of course, and level of CWIL support were entered as additional data.

The study examined changes in student self-ratings of overall writing skill and specific skills pre- and post-course, and explored the relationship between the level of CWIL support of the course and student self-ratings of specific writing skills. The analysis showed: a highly significant increase in students' self-rating of their writing skills after taking a W-course ($P < 0.0001$); a highly significant increase in their self-ratings on specific writing skills such as summarizing or citing sources ($P < 0.0001$); and a pre-/post-difference in self-ratings on specific writing skills that was significantly higher in CWIL-scaffolded courses than in courses that received no scaffolding ($P < 0.011561$). The figure below shows the pre- and post-course means for self-ratings on specific writing skills in CWIL-scaffolded courses and in courses with no scaffolding. The ratings were based on a scale of 1–5 with 1 indicating least confidence and 5 indicating most confidence.

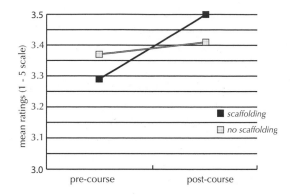

1. There was an average difference in self-ratings of overall writing skills from pre-course test to post-course test of $M = -0.308$ (SD = 1.1704), indicating a highly significant increase in self-ratings after taking a W-course, $t(1596) = -10.52$, $P < 0.0001$.

2. There was an average difference in the self-ratings of specific writing skills score from pre-course test to post-course test of $M = -0.189$ (SD = 0.71), indicating a highly significant increase in self-ratings after taking a W-course, $t(1260) = -9.44$, $P < 0.0001$.

3. The pre-/post-difference in self-ratings on specific writing skills was significantly higher ($P < 0.011561$) in CWIL-scaffolded courses ($M = -0.20607$, SD = 0.701655) than in courses that received no scaffolding ($M = 0.03361$, SD = 0.758374) (Groeneboer et al. 2007).

Given the effects of attitude and self-assessment on learning to write, these findings alone would seem to indicate the demonstrable value of W-courses and additionally the difference made by W-faculty support. Other sources of information for both CWIL and W-faculty about outcomes of the W-course development and implementation took the form of interviews, the substance of which has been reported in previous chapters.

At the institutional level, the matter of assessment had assumed a limited profile in the first stages of the curriculum implementation and, as of 2007, no commitments had been made on what kinds of program assessment might be undertaken. Townsend signaled the importance of both ongoing internal and external review and Condon echoed that dual focus in his call for institutional assessments, program accreditation, and a carefully designed process of assessment with "multiple, generative benchmarks" to ensure accountability (Condon 2006). On the matter of assessment, SFU appeared however, at the end of the pilot period, to have made no move toward fulfilling that requirement of a third stage of development, as defined by Condon.

7. Flexible but sound WI criteria

SFU arrived at a set of criteria for W-courses, as outlined in detail in Chapter Two. Condon associates the choosing of criteria with pilot course development at the second stage; at SFU, criteria were developed to ensure a level of W-course integrity that the W-course certification process was intended to confirm. They accommodated a degree of flexibility in application, particularly with respect to the amount and types of writing to be assigned and the characteristics of revision processes. The criteria also served to ground the program in principles of practice and appeared well established and accepted as distinguishing features of W-courses across all disciplines by the end of the pilot period.

Classroom and teaching level characteristics

As described above, the seven features that Townsend identifies with an effectively implemented writing requirement all fall within the purview of administration, whether at the level of the vice presidents or of the deans and departments. The administration constructs conditions that scaffold the W-initiative and demonstrates a level of administrative commitment that acknowledges faculty ownership and participation. The real evidence of effective writing-intensive teaching and learning, however, is to be found in individual classrooms. Townsend identifies these last three key characteristics in pedagogical terms that relate to what an instructor wants to teach, why and how. These characteristics embody principles that help prevent situations in which writing is treated as a "mere add-on for the sake of labeling the requisite number of W-courses" (Townsend 2001, 245).

8. The integration of W-assignments with course goals and an instructor's pedagogical methods

This characteristic of an effective writing program asserts the primacy of the instructor's own intentions with respect to the course material, and the need for compatibility between the instructor's preferred styles of presentation and the demands of writing instruction. Instructors whose only or principal method of teaching is lecturing may be unwilling or unable to accommodate integrating writing instruction, but the assumption underlying the criteria is that writing will be taught and not simply talked about. Previous chapters in this book have dealt with many examples of

identifying course goals and integrating those goals into writing assignments in ways compatible with how the instructor approaches teaching. By
the end of the pilot period, W-courses that met this requirement were well
established as the norm for consistency with this characteristic.

9 and 10. Faculty support characteristics: knowledgeable and diplomatic W-program personnel; patience and vigilance

In identifying these personal qualities, Townsend refers particularly to
those people whose expertise in the field of writing enables them to assist
faculty in planning and implementing their W-courses and in training and
mentoring their TAs. She suggests that these people need skills in interpersonal relationships and that they need, as do all the others involved in
the program's evolution, *patience and vigilance.* In the matter of these last
of Townsend's characteristics, I suggest that the chapters of this book have
demonstrated the extent to which we at CWIL, the people most directly
associated with faculty support in the classroom, were likely to be seen as
"knowledgeable and diplomatic" or "patient and vigilant." These descriptors do not, however, imply any particular process of development. They
are necessary constituents of successful relationships. From the point of
view of development, Condon proposes that supporting faculty at all the
stages requires the kinds of sensitivities and patience Townsend identifies,
but Condon also suggests that as the program moves into the third and
fourth stages, faculty support will change in its focus.

With a basis laid in course development at the first and second stages,
faculty support will devolve to other stakeholders who play a formal role in
local mentoring, and departments will seek out support rather than being
sought. That in itself puts the W-program personnel in a different relationship: in the fourth stage, others see the W-program as a model of professional development and seek advice so that they can apply the processes
to their own programs and generate similar strengths (Condon 2006).
Although by Fall 2006, both the philosophy and psychology departments
had largely assumed responsibility for W-faculty support, SFU had not
moved far beyond the second stage of development at the end of the pilot
period. The formation of an *Institute for the Study of Teaching and Learning
in the Disciplines* would offer potential for making substantial changes in
how professional development might be imagined and implemented at
SFU, and CWIL's practice also had the potential to attract imitation if the
writing initiative matured into the third and fourth stages of growth. But
both possibilities lay in an uncertain future. That the Senate Committee
on University Priorities (SCUP) unanimously approved the proposal for

the Institute in January 2007 was not of much consequence or consolation for CWIL. By that time, significant changes in CWIL's structure and functional mandate had already shifted the unit further away from what had been at best a tenuous link with an Institute.

LOOKING FORWARD: ASSESSING THE PROSPECTS

As the 2006 deadline for the writing requirement approached, there seemed to be good reason for optimism: An environment was emerging that was marked by the characteristics Townsend identifies as critical for overall program effectiveness. Cumulatively, all of Condon's Stage I and most of Stage 2's features had been accomplished with nascent features of Stage 3 in evidence. "Enlightened self-interest," Condon suggests, should spur programs to manage the third stage (Condon 2006).

Other influences are always afoot in such ventures, however, and optimism needs to be tempered, as Miller cautions, with the awareness that "every educational program [is] . . . the product of a series of complex, contradictory, compromised, and contingent solutions whose permanence is never assured . . . any effort at reform must be conceived of not as an isolated act but as an ongoing process that forever needs to be tended, monitored and nurtured" (Miller 1998, 8). Townsend provides evidence of that need in her report that "There is a history in the U.S. of writing programs being jeopardized . . . as a result of fiscal, philosophical, and/ or political [evolutions]. It's hard to imagine that good programs with solid reputations can be so vulnerable, but the harm that can be done is real and the case histories are revealing. The 2007 Conference on College Composition and Communication featured a session titled 'How Strong Programs with National Identities Fail' in which the demise of six such writing programs was outlined" (M. Townsend, personal communication, August 20, 2007).

When CWIL was moved to the LIDC, the sense of autonomy that we had previously enjoyed was lost as we became a part of a larger and more traditional arm of the university. CWIL faculty found it difficult to adapt to a more closely managed environment with different forms of accountability demanded. Since we had demonstrated successes in our practice and shown ourselves to be fiscally responsible, we were not comfortable with this change. In hindsight, I realize that my assumption, based on prior verbal assurances that things would continue more or less as before, was mistaken. The assurances I had been given were neither contractual nor formal; they were not an outcome of direct discussions between me, as director of CWIL, and the director of the LIDC; nor were they the result of consultations between me and the vice president academic who was responsible for making the decision about the move or between me and the associate vice president who was largely responsible for implementing the move. There is no way of knowing, of course, whether an explicit commitment to terms of the move could have been negotiated or whether such terms would have made a difference; in the event, as the consequences of the move became apparent, the lack of a documented and explicit commitment from the decision-makers certainly meant there were no formal avenues of recourse or appeal.

The move was not only administrative but also physical. We were moved into a specially built, self-contained space we had helped design. It was superbly equipped and physically quite superior to our previous somewhat cramped offices full of makeshift furniture scrounged from Central Stores. It was also, however, a sheltered cul-de-sac, well away from the thoroughfares along which faculty pass en route to their offices and meetings, a factor we would have to take into account in adjusting our practice and means of communication. With the change of location came a change of name. The Centre for Writing-Intensive Learning (CWIL) became the Writing-Intensive-Learning Office (WILO). In his discussions with the vice president academic about the shift of CWIL out of FASS, the dean had insisted on retaining the name and acronym for possible future designation of a writing centre that would be dedicated to research, as policy dictated a centre should be, and with an associated rather than a permanent cadre of faculty. While the cliché that "a rose by any other name will smell as sweet" may apply to roses, in these times of branding and name association, we felt the loss very acutely as a loss of part of our identity. We were also concerned about faculty response to the change. The name CWIL stood for their experience of support in writing; a change might augur the changes in level and quality of support that many had predicted would follow once the requirements took effect. A name change had to be accommodated, however, and we made lists and brainstormed and debated. After many hours and exchanges on names clever, cute and plain, we decided that retaining the WIL part was essential and the acronym with "office" was workable, if not witty.

As it turned out, the partners in this new relationship of WILO and LIDC discovered they had less in common than had been hoped or assumed. The changes of name and location were only the beginning of a series of unexpected changes. Accounting for what ensued necessarily entails making choices and judgments about what details to include, what decisions to foreground, and what perceptions and versions of events stand up to critical scrutiny. I am mindful, as I attempt this sketch of the period from June 2006 to September 2007, of Jane Austen's caution in *Emma* that "Seldom, very seldom, does complete truth belong to any human disclosure; seldom can it happen that something is not a little disguised, or a little mistaken." In recognition of the multiple perspectives at play and as a way of contextualizing the transition to LIDC and its consequences, I propose to begin by taking a somewhat indirect route. I will set out the rationale for an alternative to incorporating WILO within the LIDC and identify the elements I believe were overlooked by SFU in rejecting that alternative. For this purpose, I use as a point of reference, the experience of another institution faced with a similar choice.

When a decision about the location of a CWIL-type unit needed to be made at Miami University, Ohio, the university chose to create a centre independent of their excellent Centre for the Enhancement of Teaching and Learning (CELT). Paul Anderson, director of the Roger and Joyce Howe Center for Writing Excellence at Miami, whose program is ranked among the top sixteen in the country (Center for Writing Excellence 2006), describes the choice in terms of the university's belief in demonstrating the importance of writing and distinguishing the teaching of writing from generalized good teaching practice. He explains that

> the goal of improving the writing of our graduates is a high enough university priority that having our center for writing excellence separate from the CELT gives this goal special prominence. The goal of the CELT office is, more vaguely (but not less important), to foster better teaching. The most important benefit of having separate faculty support for writing is that it provides a focus on our aspirations with respect to writing that could not be obtained if it was just one more thing that the faculty development program offered. A separate writing program has given us a distinctive identity which has helped us immensely in our work to persuade faculty across the university to view writing as a central feature of a Miami education. Also, improvement of writing has an appeal to potential donors that the more general activity of a CELT does not have. The donors who gave my center $10.5 million dollars are passionate about the importance of writing in college and afterwards. They would not have been enticed to provide a gift to the less focused goals of the CELT office. Finally, while the goal is to see that all our graduates leave with a very high level of writing ability, the faculty development program is necessarily defined in terms of a faculty outcome: faculty will become better teachers. Of course, that faculty outcome benefits students. We want to assess those outcomes but not exclusively on an institution-wide basis by looking at what students can do. The real measures of instructional change have to focus on faculty behaviors. (Anderson 2007)

Anderson's reasons for insisting on a distinctive identity were echoed in CWIL's concept of their role. His observations about assessment correspond also to CWIL's multi-faceted efforts to help create the classroom conditions for improving writing and the climate for faculty development that engenders change in faculty behavior.

Administrators felt that the structural changes conceived for CWIL were both useful and sensible for the institution; combining multiple functions under a single unit no doubt promises a simpler administrative structure. However, these structural changes also changed the distinctive identity that, mindful of published research, CWIL had tried deliberately to develop. Assessment and research initiatives undertaken by CWIL for the previous four years, including student and faculty surveys, were now assisted by the staff in LIDC's division of Applied Research on Teaching. This support was perceived by WILO faculty as an unwelcome intrusion into their business. Program development and planning continued to be performed by WILO faculty; however, the logistical tasks of event advertising and direct communication with participants in workshops were now assigned to the LIDC Program Coordinators. This was a difficult adjustment for WILO faculty, who were accustomed to dealing directly with their own administrative assistant. The restructuring also led to WILO faculty feeling somewhat disabled as they adjusted to the changes in expectations and routines. Several of the logistical and budgetary tasks were now distributed among LIDC staff who handled similar functions for the other faculty development programs in the unit. Writing workshops and events were now part of chronological lists of all the LIDC events that included instruction on WebCT, advanced voice and presentation skills, or how to use blogs to enhance learning. WILO's responsibilities were redefined with a greater focus on service, such as running workshops for both instructors and TAs and consulting with individuals about their W-courses. Thankfully, WILO's engagement in academic activities, such as conference presentations, research and publishing, continued to be supported.

These outcomes were not immediately realized with the transfer of CWIL from FASS to LIDC in Spring 2005, but took place over the period from Spring 2005 to Spring 2007. The trend was set in motion in July 2005. Without implying any critique of the structural change that was implemented, it is relevant to note that each of these outcomes was a natural consequence of that change, and that each one concretely diminished the visibility of the unit as an individual entity with a distinctive, campus-wide mission. Diminishing the number of individual units on a given campus may in fact, be wholly desirable; it may be good administrative practice. But it will interest researchers in curricular change that even sensible administrative reorganizing may sometimes put curricular innovations in conflict with the research that informs them—in this case, for example, with the research that recommends a distinctive unit identity and continuity in leadership (Anderson 2007, Condon 2006, Miraglia and McLeod 1998).

According to university policy at the time, I was due to retire from the director position at the end of August 2005. I was invited to accept a 16-month post-retirement contract to write a book about the writing initiative and another faculty member from WILO was offered the post of acting director until a new director could be hired. Her decades of professional consulting and managerial experience, attuned to the demands of supporting the writing initiative over the past three years, made her the obvious choice for interim successor. We both accepted. Apart from doing whatever we both felt was needed to ensure a smooth transition, I removed myself from the day to day activity and the acting director worked with the WILO team that now included herself and four others: a highly recommended new departmental assistant, two newly hired consultants (one a new PhD with many years' experience in working with faculty on the teaching of academic writing, and one who had been with the unit since its inception and had developed strong faculty relationships); all of the faculty members, including the acting director, were on limited-term lecturer contracts. Over the next several months, the WILO faculty realized that they were now in a more "corporate" style administrative department rather than a faculty. WILO faculty did not immediately recognize that difference in style and its consequent demands, nor did the LIDC initially recognize a need for explicit orientation to its normalized corporate practices. In the absence of either explanation or consultation, coming to terms with the redefining of their role proved difficult for WILO faculty. Not unexpectedly, misunderstandings continued about WILO's new mandate.

The need for greater clarity about relationships in the LIDC led to a meeting in February 2006 among the associate vice president, the director of the LIDC, and the acting director to correct misperceptions, discuss policy issues and set out specific expectations. In June, 2006, after ten months of leading WILO, the acting director was asked to devote all her time to WILO's faculty service functions as a consultant and to step down from her administrative position. The director of the LIDC would assume the acting director role until a new director could be assigned. The unexpected shift in leadership had a ripple effect within the WILO faculty. They were puzzled by the timing during a period when candidates had just been interviewed for the director position and a new person was expected to assume leadership within a few months. One of the new lecturers, appointed September 2005 on a limited-term contract, decided to return to her former institution. The other new consultant, who regarded WILO's work as both "highly innovative and exciting" (personal communication, August 21, 2007), secured a tenure-track position in the faculty of education, wanting the security of such a position.

Consequently, in September, 2006, just as the new W-requirements were to take effect and a flurry of demands from faculty could be expected, WILO's team had been reduced from five full-time positions to three. The remainder of the workload was serviced through short-term appointments. The director of the LIDC appointed a new acting director. A professor from the faculty of education, the new appointee was selected because of her long career as a teacher of writing in the faculty of education, as a consultant who taught professional literacy in various industries, as an author of professional texts and creative writing (e.g., screen-plays, children's books, poetry, short stories). She had also participated in the successful initiation of the W-initiative's FAL program, stepping in to assist at a crucial point in August 2006 to facilitate its implementation. It was felt she would have the needed credibility with various faculties. The new acting director brought with her a new education perspective to the pedagogy and theory which had formed the basis of CWIL/WILO's practice. She also brought in two of her doctoral students, both senior PhD students in education, and a highly respected professor emeritus.

These staffing changes did not, of course, change the fact that the new W-requirements were in place, that W-courses needed to be offered, that existing W-faculty needed support and that new W-faculty and TAs needed to be prepared to offer what was intended to be an expanding range of courses; and, if writing was to become embedded across the disciplines and be naturalized into the teaching and learning culture, then more writing and writing instruction would need to appear at some level in many non W-courses, which would also mean ongoing mentoring and support of faculty. Clearly, the new strains attendant on a change of leadership as well as the ongoing strains attendant on the merger with LIDC needed to be resolved.

Negotiations had been underway over several months in late summer through the fall of 2006 with a candidate interviewed in June for the role of WILO director. The multi-layered search process was complicated, however, by agreements negotiated between the university and SFUFA (the faculty association) that governed how the director would be hired. The difficulty in hiring became evident when, despite the selection of a candidate who was considered outstanding by the WILO director Appointments committee and the director of the LIDC, no department or Faculty would agree to hire this person. It seems the departments saw no obligation to accept an unsought position in their ranks or a member they had not themselves selected. When it became clear by December 2006 that this would be a failed search and no new director hired, the WILO faculty with the support of SFUFA and the director of the LIDC presented a decentralized model. A proposal was also made by the faculty of education to house a centralized model in the faculty of education that would be called a "signature centre." The deans considered both models and voted to accept the decentralized model. The rationale was that they felt confident they could handle the W-mandate in their own faculties now that the initial work had been successfully completed.

While it may be argued that there were no necessary or inevitable outcomes of merging WILO into the LIDC, the rationale at Miami University for distinguishing support for writing from support for teaching in general indicates that there are differences in perception, in visibility, in priority, in confidence and in appeal to faculty that can occur in structures like this. It's possible that hiring a permanent WILO director like the candidate noted above, with a professional credential as a researcher in the field of writing-in-the-disciplines, coupled with successful administrative experience, would have reaffirmed the distinctive identity and purposes of a unit dedicated to supporting the writing initiative, even within the LIDC umbrella (difficult as others' experience suggests this may be). In WILO's case, however, no such permanent director appointment could be made.

As of January 2007, the former acting director had resigned from the university and the departmental assistant for WILO had been reassigned to other duties. On July 9, 2007, Senate received a preliminary report prepared by the director of university curriculum and institutional liaison on the implementation of the new curriculum. The report stated that "The resources of the Writing Intensive Learning Office are now being redistributed to the faculty deans' offices. This will further integrate support for writing-intensive learning into the disciplines." The "resources" referred to appear to be mainly in the form of funding for instructors who will be hired by individual departments to help support their W-courses. The faculty of science, for instance, has awarded a one-year lecturer, science W-support contract, beginning in September 2007, to a recent graduate in biology with previous experience supporting W-courses. The faculty of health sciences has hired a W-instructor for an eight-month position with the possibility of extension. As of Fall 2007, positions for two new W-consultants in the faculty of arts and social sciences had not been filled. As we approach the end of this story, one can only hope the various Faculties will bring the optimism and goodwill to the W-initiative that was began in CWIL and continued in WILO, and that the vision of the initiative will not be lost.

The work reported in this monograph speaks to widespread faculty commitment and expertise. Turnover in administrative roles, and thus of perceived priorities in planning and development, is a condition of life in a university. The always anomalous institutional positioning of CWIL left it vulnerable to widely differing interpretations of its role and functions and, like so many similar units elsewhere, vulnerable to dismantling. To the list of ten characteristics of strong programs identified by Townsend, I think two others need to be added. In their analysis of surveys of what they termed "mature programs"—those that had been sustained over at least a ten-year period—Miraglia and McLeod point to "strong, consistent program leadership" as a key factor (1997 p.48). Miraglia and McLeod report that "fully two-thirds of the enduring programs have had either the same WAC director or only two directors in the past decade. . . . An enduring program. . . is very much the product of a pioneering, persevering, and creative leader" (55–56). The administration at SFU did not feel that there was a need for a new and permanent structure to establish a secure status for a director whose responsibility would be to ensure continuity of effort, vision and purpose. They felt that these responsibilities would be well accomplished through a faculty-centric model, supported by a director of university curriculum and a faculty member who will chair a cross-faculty committee and serve as a coordinator. Decentralizing in the sense of creating and developing local practices and expertise is, on the one hand, an essential criterion for successful transformation of a culture of teaching and learning. On the other hand, decentralizing without also retaining a hub makes impossible the kinds of synergies that develop when people share in a common enterprise and have common points of reference, whether in a team at the center or as associates spread across the campus. To consistent leadership, I would add a second factor: consistent staffing with highly qualified permanent faculty. Short-term hiring and turnover of faculty means loss of experience and continuity, a loss that can weaken an initiative as surely as a frequent turnover of leadership, if to a lesser degree.

Chris Anson comments in his account of events at a writing program at the University of Minnesota, "What strikes me . . . is how easily all the things that have taken so much negotiation, planning and hard work are dismantled" (Anson 2002, 168). As the upper echelons at SFU weigh current priorities, prospects for the future of the initiative appear uncertain. At the grassroots level, however, where W-faculty teaching in classrooms is to be found, the conditions still exist for hope that SFU may eventually become a stellar example of a successful writing initiative like Miami University and the many others where writing in the disciplines is visible and effective across the university.

EPILOGUE

*In an epilogue, the writer may step out of role and round out or comment
on the main action. The epilogue is an after-word, peripheral.*

Chris Anson's comment on "how easily all the things that have taken so
much negotiation, planning and hard work are dismantled" goes on to
qualify the sense of "heartbreak" with the reminder that "in spite of the
politics and hierarchies in which we work as administrators of writing
programs, it is the human moments, the connections we make and the
lives we touch and improve, the ways we live and work *in* and *through* our
places in higher education that really matter" (Anson 2002, 168). He is
quite right, of course. Those of us who had the pleasure of working with
SFU faculty and engaging in stimulating discussions about writing and
teaching can feel only a sense of gratitude for those opportunities. That
does matter. As individuals, we and the faculty we worked with, as well as
the students in their classes, all gained from those connections and the
sense that there were lives we touched and improved. As individuals, however, we also have a great sense of loss. As one of my colleagues poignantly
described it, "our little centre was always touching a nerve or boundary
somewhere—that was the nature of our work. When we moved, we were
embarked on a daily and steady march over the edge and no one would
stop it from happening." One of the administrators involved put it down
to a "basic lack of trust and the intransigence of individuals representing
various competing interests." We all see from a different vantage point.

A project as ambitious as the one launched at Simon Fraser needed to
be nurtured and tended. A vision fades when we shift our gaze or turn
our backs. It may not be lost entirely, of course. In writing this book, I
hope I leave evidence of what is still possible. The future will depend on
who cares to come forward and take up the challenge of halting a drift
toward token compliance and of cultivating a scholarly interest in teaching writing.

But nothing is guaranteed. It will not be easy or simple.

In any case, a new story is about to begin with new actors in new
roles. . . .

APPENDIX 1
A Proposal for the Development of Undergraduate Writing-Intensive Courses at SFU

Universities that have implemented successful writing-intensive programs have insured that the university community (a) understands the value of writing as a fundamentally important tool for learning, especially as it relates to the acquisition of knowledge in disciplines and the cultivation of critical thinking abilities, (b) is receptive to recommended initiatives and (c) collaborates in the creation of the program. Successful writing-intensive programs tend to possess the following features:

- They are adequately funded.

- They are widely supported by faculty, students, and administrators.

- They are phased in relatively slowly, over a period of at least 3 years. There are no quick fixes; a long-term commitment is necessary.

- Participation by faculty is voluntary.

- The distinctiveness of writing in different disciplines is respected.

- Departments are actively involved in the process, deciding how great an emphasis to place on the acquisition of critical thinking and writing abilities in their disciplines and whether to focus on the development of such abilities in lower or upper division courses.

- The effectiveness of initiatives is assessed at appropriate times.

A Proposal

1. A Task Force consisting of experts on writing, including representatives from the Centre for Writing-intensive Learning, will be created to design and implement a university-wide program aimed at enhancing the verbal and critical thinking skills of SFU students by focusing on writing abilities.

2. Types of Course: The Task Force would focus on initiatives directed at developing or refining discipline-specific writing-intensive courses (see endnote).

3. Types of Instructor: Writing-intensive courses or tutorials could be taught by three types of instructor: faculty, dedicated Writing Instructors, and TAs.

Faculty. Faculty from the English department currently offer writing-intensive courses such as English 199. Faculty from other departments, such as philosophy and engineering, have offered discipline-specific writing-intensive courses. To enlist the assistance of additional faculty, members of the Task Force could meet with representatives of Programs, Departments, Schools, and Faculties (e.g., Deans, chairs, Undergraduate committees) to describe successful writing intensive programs from other Universities, to discuss the structure of writing-intensive courses, to identify faculty interested in helping develop them, to identify the existing courses most conducive to restructuring, and to explore the possibility of developing new courses. Faculty might teach the writing-intensive component of their courses or collaborate with Writing Instructors (see below) to build writing-intensive components into their courses. Members of the Task Force would discuss with each unit possible problems with implementing a writing-intensive requirement and the most appropriate form such a requirement might take.

Dedicated Writing Instructors. Patterned after the model writing-intensive philosophy course developed by Steven Davis and Wendy Strachan, dedicated Writing Instructors with appropriate training could be hired to teach writing-intensive tutorials in relatively large courses in disciplines. Regular faculty would teach two-hour lectures and the Writing Instructor would teach a one-hour tutorial. A dedicated Writing Instructor would have an advanced degree in the discipline in which writing-intensive courses were taught, as well as training in teaching writing.

Teaching Assistants. Graduate student TAs might also be trained to teach discipline-specific writing-intensive tutorials in relatively large courses in place of Dedicated Writing Instructors.

4. Resources: The university would have to allocate sufficient funds to implement writing-intensive courses (see below). Faculty interested in creating and teaching writing-intensive courses should be offered incentives such as administrative support, teaching reductions, professional development allowances, and credit toward merit increments in salary. Resources also would have to be allocated to train TAs.

5. Training: Experts on writing from the Centre for Writing-intensive Learning and elsewhere could prepare resources designed to help faculty develop writing-intensive courses and, when appropriate to train instructors (faculty, Writing Instructors, TAs) to teach such courses effectively. TA s might hone their writing abilities and their competence to teach writing-intensive tutorials in graduate courses. TA training courses might be taught jointly by faculty from the Centre for Writing-intensive

Learning and discipline-based faculty. Experts might offer assistance such as the following:

- Training Seminars
- Workshops
- Summer institutes on writing
- Pre-course planning in the semester before the writing-intensive course is offered
- Ongoing mentoring and in-course consultation during the first semester

6. Costs: Currently, the Centre for Writing-intensive Learning has a budget. This budget probably would have to be increased. If direct entry students were required to take two writing-intensive courses, with students from other post-secondary institutions required to take one, enrollments in writing-intensive courses would be approximately 8,000 per year (3000 direct entry students x 2 W courses plus 2000 transfer students x 1 W course). At 15 students per tutorial, 533 writing-intensive tutorials per year would be required. If all writing-intensive tutorials were taught by TAs paid at normal salaries in courses currently offered in disciplines, it would cost the university only the amount necessary to train the TAs to teach writing. However, it is improbable that TAs could handle the marking and office hours connected with a writing intensive course within the number of hours in the present TSSU contract. They probably would have to be allocated additional hours. If all tutorials were taught by Writing Instructors with a course load of 24 tutorials per year, we would need 22.2 Writing Instructors to teach writing-intensive tutorials. If these instructors were paid $40,000 per year (the beginning salary for lab instructors), the total salary for writing-intensive instructors would be $888,000 per annum, plus benefits, and this amount would increase as the Writing Instructors climbed the salary step system. But the incremental cost of writing-intensive tutorials would be substantially less than this. First, it is unlikely we would need this many Writing Instructors. Some writing intensive courses could be taught by faculty without Writing Instructors, and the tutorials in other writing-intensive courses could be taught by TAs. Second, even if all writing-intensive tutorials were taught by Writing Instructors, approximately $666,250 would be saved from the TA budget (533 tutorials divided by 4 contact hours times $5,000). Thus, the incremental cost of hiring Writing Instructors to replace TAs to teach writing-intensive tutorials would begin at approximately $222,000 per annum, plus benefits.

Although it would be more expensive to employ Writing Instructors than to employ TAs to teach writing, employing Writing Instructors has several advantages over employing TAs. As examples, we would expect Writing Instructors to be more highly trained than most TAs, and to stay at SFU longer, thus allaying the need for the kind of ongoing training we would have to offer TAs.

7. Assessment: After writing-intensive courses have been developed and offered, they should be assessed.

Endnote

The movement known as "writing across the curriculum" (WAC) has evolved throughout its 30-year history. Early on, its advocates emphasized writing as a tool for learning in potentially every context. More recently, some theorists have emphasized the particulars of different contexts and the different demands those particulars place on writers." (Hilgers, Hussey & Stitt-Bergh 1999,. 331). "WAC typically emphasized writing processes (prewriting, drafting, revising, editing) and products (journals, learning logs) that could be adapted to any course. . . . More recent studies of learning and the rise of cognitive science shifted attention from general cognitive skills to skills functioning in contextualized ways (Detterman & Sternberg 1993; Perkins & Salomon1989; Petraglia 1995). . . . Practitioners shifted attention from general goals and general processes to the particulars that define situations as unique. . . . Thus, "writing across the curriculum" seemed to shift toward "writing in specific contexts" or disciplines (WID). (p. 318)

Writing-intensive courses may assume several forms: (a) courses offered by the English Department, such as SFU's English 199, (b) discipline-specific writing courses offered by departments designed to foster writing and critical thinking abilities while teaching the content of courses.

Successful writing-intensive courses have been found to have the following features:

- Writing is associated with critical thinking, inquiry/problem-posing and problem solving through assignments that require arguments.

- Students write multiple drafts and receive feedback on each draft.

- Students are trained in critical reading.

- Students are encouraged to write in a variety of forms and lengths, to a variety of audiences

- Samples of target genre are available for discourse analysis: recognition of typical structures, modes of reasoning, use of evidence and technical language, modes of audience address.

- Resources such as journal articles are made available to instructors to illustrate alternative approaches to, and applications of, writing in the discipline.

- Writing-intensive courses or tutorials are relatively small to permit adequate feedback.

APPENDIX 2
Pre-Course Questionnaire

1. Listed below are reasons students might enroll in this course. Please indicate how important *each* reason was for you.

		Not at all Important	Somewhat Important			Very Important
a.	personal interest	1	2	3	4	5
b.	recommendation of advisor or other faculty member	1	2	3	4	5
c.	recommendation of a classmate	1	2	3	4	5
d.	requirement for graduation in major	1	2	3	4	5
e.	fit with schedule	1	2	3	4	5
f.	other (please describe)	1	2	3	4	5

Other: _____

2. Which topic or topics on the course outline are particularly interesting to you?

3. What other economics courses have you taken?

4. What is your major (or most likely major)?
minors?

5. How many S. F. U. and/or transfer credit hours do you have?

		below 20	21–30	31–40	41–60	61 plus
5a.	S. F. U. Hours					
5b.	Transfer Hours					

6a. Do/did you speak mainly English in your childhood home?
Yes_____ No_____

6b. If no, what language do you use most of the time?

7. Compared to other students at this university, how do you rate your writing skills overall? (no decimal points)

Poor			Adequate					Excellent	
1	2	3	4	5	6	7	8	9	10

8. In general, how do you rate yourself on the following writing skills?

		Need lots of help	Struggle with this	Feel okay	Fairly confident	Very confi-dent
		1	2	3	4	5
a.	deciding on a topic and focus					
b.	researching material for the paper					
c.	avoiding procrastination					
d.	voicing my own opinions appropriately					
e.	using correct grammar and punctuation					
f.	organizing the paper with my data					
g.	editing and rewriting drafts					
h.	quoting effectively					
i.	summarizing others' ideas					
j.	paraphrasing things in my own words					
k.	developing a strong argument					
l.	writing introductions with a clear thesis					
m.	writing good conclusions					

Please describe and comment on your previous experience with writing at the university or in high school—problems, interests, etc. (use back of paper as needed).

APPENDIX 3
In-class Memo Assignment and Peer Review Guide

Econ 355, professor Don DeVoretz

You have been asked by your boss, Mr. Peter Harder who heads Canada's aid programme (CIDA) to outline an argument to justify why your country is deserving of a portion of Canada's $100 billion aid package. Using one economic, social, demographic indicator shown in the movie *Year of Living Dangerously* outline a case for your country. The basic components in this argument are:

1. A clear description, which outlines why your country is poor, but deserving. This would involve use of one economic, social and demographic indicator shown in the movie but also a discussion to demonstrate what positive features of your country, good gov't, health indicators, exports, education, or low population growth that indicates a capacity to use the aid. State exactly what the indicators are; for example health would be life expectancy, infant mortality rate, etc.

2. Outline what specific forms of aid to alleviate what are the weak points of your economy as noted in your indicators. For example, my country has a high infant mortality rate; this would imply that it is poor but that health aid could alleviate this problem. Use at least four types of aid: education, health, agricultural, policing, water, resource conservation, etc. to illustrate your country's specific needs.

3. Once you establish what type of aid is required, explain the connection between this form of aid and your country's future prospects of development.

4. Conclusion: Tie together your indicators, your country's plight and a full description of the aid package in the final paragraph and make a recommendation to Peter Harder. The recommendation is for a specific form of aid, for a specific period of time and for a specific amount. Use 500 word maximum.

PEER REVIEW PROCESS

Note: *The proposal assignment #3 asks you to make is similar to one you will be asked to respond to on the mid-term. Use this time in the tutorial to see how to improve the way you are presenting the issues you need to address and to make sure that you understand how to explain your reasoning and be convincing to someone who, in this case, can give money to your country.*

Step One: As reader working with a partner

Take on the role of Mr. Peter Harder: you get this memo on your desk and you know what you look for in such memos. How convinced are you that this is a good case for your attention?

Read through the paper once to get an overall impression of what the writer is talking about and how they are making the argument to request aid. Underline the most interesting or most powerful or best-worded sentence in the paper.

Read again and identify each of the following indicators that the writer is meeting the demands of the assignment: (you could put a check mark or write a note in the margin)

- One economic, social and demographic indicator

- Reason country is poor but deserving – do reasons make sense?

- Positive features that indicate capacity to use aid – are these really positive?

- Specific forms of aid to assist – are these explained?

- Statement of connection between form of aid and need of country and why/how aid will help – do you fully understand how it will help?

- Explanation of how aid will further country's development – is development stressed here? Do you agree?

- Recommendation to Peter Harder based on summary of aid package requested – specific time and amount

In the role of Peter Harder, talk to the writer about this memo: what questions or problems did you have in following their thinking? What gaps and leaps did you have to make that need to be filled in? What did you disagree with or want to challenge? What made it unconvincing?

Step Two: As Writer

Now that you have met with the boss about your memo, write some notes underneath your memo to say what specific changes you would make if you were going to revise this memo: what would you do to improve your argument and be more convincing so that he's willing to look at it again? Think about rearranging some parts, adding important details, giving more or better reasons, taking out irrelevant information, being more clear about the connections and how parts fit together, being concise and clear, using topic sentences in paragraphs or transition sentences etc.

An excellent memo and notes will include all the points listed above and be clear and well-argued. The notes may point to lapses in the argument, note additional info to include etc., or suggest rearrangements – and thus show awareness of what to do in a revision.

A good memo and notes will include most points and show a logical argument, though may be incomplete but the memo will indicate what needs to be done so it's likely the memo will move up a grade when revised.

A satisfactory memo and notes will attempt to make an argument and include some of the points but not be very convincing and the memo will not show clear evidence of how changes will be made to improve.

APPENDIX 4
Econ 355 Assignment Questions Summary

professor Don DeVoretz

Question 1. Based on what you see in the feedback, what are 4 or 5 ways you can improve in the next assignment?

Seventy-one students replied to this question. Some provided only one response, others provided up to five. For the sake of brevity, all of the responses were compiled together and the percentages were calculated based on an average of 2.5 responses per student.

	#	%
Be more concise/specific/clear	33	18.1
Better links/transition/flow/connections/organization	25	13.7
More details/data/research	24	13.2
Expand ideas/explanation/develop thoughts	22	12.1
Effective argument/supporting evidence/relevance	19	10.4
Grammar/language/vocabulary/sentence structure	14	7.7
More preparation time/read more	12	6.6
Proof read/draft	10	5.5
Improve introduction	7	3.8
Improve conclusion	6	3.3
Consult with TA	5	2.7
Assignment related particulars	5	2.7

Question 2. How does writing affect understanding and knowledge of economic content?

Sixty-five of 71 students responded to this question. As the numbers indicate, most students believe that writing has a significant positive affect in their understanding and knowledge of economic content. Samples of students comments are located below.

	#	%
Significantly	54	76.1
Somewhat	7	9.9
Not at all	4	5.6
No response	6	8.5

Significantly:

- "Writing is good in that it forces you to accumulate your knowledge and present full-rounded arguments. economics students don't do enough papers!"

- "Writing makes me think more. When I am asked to write on a topic, I would research on the topic, therefore would gain more knowledge."

- "Writing is a key tool used to express the fundamentals of economic theory. Without an understanding of how to structure a paper, one lacks the ability to express his/her viewpoint."

- "Helps in improving academic writing skills. Most econ courses don't do a lot of writing which means that writing skills can be out of practice, making it difficult to express thoughts in an argumentative fashion. Writing with feedback allows the opportunity to practice this skill."

- "Writing I find to be very helpful in economics. Without constant work, the concepts can pass me by. By doing regular writing assignments, I fell up to date with the course. Also, it helps to organize my thoughts in my head to make sure I truly do understand. It is easier to think I understand than actually write about it."

Somewhat:

- "Not much other than how the writer might mean different things the we readers, and assumptions must be clear in arguments."

- "Writing in this class does affect our understanding of econ, but not a lot. Picking an individual country to work on is complicated enough, writing an argument based on it is even worse."

- "Writing has no effect on my understanding of economics, I understand what I read. But it helps me explain economics in a clear manner so other people may understand myself."

- "Personally, I think the writing assignment counts too much of the total marks. However, these assignments help me to prepare the other courses final essays and give me an idea to write a good paper."

- "Sometimes it's just not that easy to express my understanding of economics with perfect writing skills."

Not at All:

- "It doesn't help me at all. Instead, it takes more time away from understanding and reading the text."

Question 3. Any suggestions/comments? 28/71 responded to this question

	#
Assignments require too much time	8
More experience for writing is gained	6
Don't like to write/writing assignments	5
Feedback is good	4
Marking unfair	3
Make the topics more understandable	2

Suggestions/comments:

- "The question could be more straight forward (or the topic). Sometimes it requires too much time to try to figure out what exactly to write according to the topic."

- "The feedback is useful and I learn to construct a logical paper."

- "There is always a word limit on the paper, but the things required for the paper are so much that almost impossible to put it into the limit."

- "The comments on the paper are sometimes helpful; however, it would be better to have a guideline on what the expectations are for the paper."

- "Assignments ask for too much when they are only suppose to be 500 words – hard to include all info and develop it in only 500 words."

- "More uniform marking scheme. I cannot tell how to evaluate my writing. This is very subjective marking."

- "Spending too much time to read and do research. Reduce the number of assignments."

- "The writing assignment's topic is not very hard. But the marking is quite difficult. Since a lot of Econ classes don't require writing a paper, we actually don't get practice with writing before. Everybody get perfect mark in Assignment 1 from one TA, whereas the other TA didn't give out full mark for the same assignment. So, I think the marking is not fair."

- "These writing assignments aren't very difficult, but are really time-consuming, since lots of research is required."

- "There are too many writing assignments. With full-load of courses, it is difficult to keep up and still be able to present a paper that is considered good, especially when researching into a country that may be little known about. Maybe have less papers, longer number of pages."

- "Excellent ideas. Keeps the students involved with the course."

- "I think the writing assignments take up way too much of our tutorial time. I found that it would have been helpful to discuss more of our readings in tutorials."

APPENDIX 5
Survey Data from Third Year W-Course, Economic Development, Economics 355

Information presented in this Appendix is collated from surveys carried out in the ECON 355 course taught by Dr. Don Devoretz in the Fall of 2003. The class consisted of 106 students, including 63 whose first language was not English.

SURVEY QUESTION	Self-Rating	Pre-Course Survey		Post-Course Survey	
		# of Responses	Rating x # of Responses	# of Responses	Rating x # of Responses
Compared to other students at this university, how do you rate your writing skills overall?	1.0 Poor	1	1.0	0	0
	2.0	1	2.0	0	0
	3.0	5	15.0	6	18.0
	4.0	7	28.0	6	24.0
	5.0 Adequate	32	160.0	13	65.0
	6.0	14	84.0	10	60.0
	7.0	20	140.0	15	105.0
	8.0	9	72.0	11	88.0
	9.0	2	18.0	3	27.0
	10.0 Excellent	1	10.0	2	20.0
	TOTAL	92	530.0	66	407.0
	AVERAGE RATING		5.76		6.17

Based on the rating scale above, 92 students self-rated their writing skills at an average of 5.76 at the start of the course. At the end of the course, 62 students rated their writing skills at an average of 6.17, a change of 7.1 percent.

PRE- COURSE AND POST-COURSE SURVEYS

Students were asked the rate themselves on twelve specific writing skills before and after the course on a range from 1 "Needing a lot of Help" up to 5 "Very Confident." .The results were weighted by the number of students responding in each category and then averaged for the number of students responding to each question (appendix 5). The results are summarized:

In general, how do you rate yourself on the following writing skills?

	Pre-course	Post- Course	Percent Change
1. Editing and rewriting drafts	2.70	3.24	0.199
2. Getting papers in on time	2.91	3.29	0.165
3. Paraphrasing things in my own words	3.02	3.48	0.153
4. Writing good introductions	2.90	3.20	0.122
5. Writing good conclusions	3.0	3.33	0.111
6. Voicing my own opinions appropriately	2.93	3.26	0.11
7. Making an argument effectively	2.87	3.15	0.098
8. Using correct grammar and punctuation	2.85	3.12	0.096
9. Summarizing others' ideas	3.17	3.50	0.09
10. Deciding on a topic and focus	3.05	3.29	0.076
11. Spelling	3.20	3.44	0.076
12. Organizing the material for the paper	3.25	3.49	0.075
13. Avoiding procrastination	2.65	2.71	+ 2.4%

In general, how do you rate yourself on the following writing skills:	Rating	Pre-Course Survey		Post-Course Survey	
		# of Responses	Rating x # of Responses	# of Responses	Rating x # of Responses
(1) Editing and rewriting drafts	1.0 Need lots of help	9	9.0	1	1.0
	2.0 Struggling	27	54.0	12	24.0
	3.0 Feel okay	39	117.0	29	87.0
	4.0 Fairly confident	14	56.0	18	72.0
	5.0 Very confident	2	10.0	6	30.0
	TOTAL	91	246.0	66	214.0
	AVERAGE RATING		2.70		3.24

Students indicated a self-assessed average improvement of 19.9 % (from 2.70 to 3.24)

In general, how do you rate yourself on the following writing skills:	Rating	Pre-Course Survey		Post-Course Survey	
		# of Responses	Rating x # of Responses	# of Responses	Rating x # of Responses
(2) Getting papers in on time	1.0 Need lots of help	5	5.0	1	1.0
	2.0 Struggling	21	42.0	8	16.0
	3.0 Feel okay	44	132.0	31	93.0
	4.0 Fairly confident	19	76.0	16	64.0
	5.0 Very confident	2	10.0	10	50.0
	TOTAL		265.0		224.0
	AVERAGE RATING		2.91		3.39

Students indicated a self-assessed average improvement of 16.5% (from 2.91 to 3.39)

	Rating	# of Responses	Rating x # of Responses	# of Responses	Rating x # of Responses
(3) Paraphrasing things in my own words	1.0 Need lots of help	3	3.0	1	1.0
	2.0 Struggling	22	44.0	12	24.0
	3.0 Feel okay	40	120.0	17	51.0
	4.0 Fairly confident	24	96.0	26	104.0
	5.0 Very confident	3	15.0	10	50.0
	TOTAL	92	278.0	66	230.0
	AVERAGE RATING		3.02		3.48

Students indicated a self-assessed average improvement of 15.3 % (from 3.02 to 3.48)

	Rating	# of Responses	Rating x # of Responses	# of Responses	Rating x # of Responses
(4) Writing good introductions	1.0 Need lots of help	9	9.0	5	5.0
	2.0 Struggling	24	48.0	14	28.0
	3.0 Feel okay	35	105.0	18	54.0
	4.0 Fairly confident	15	60.0	21	84.0
	5.0 Very confident	9	45.0	8	40.0
	TOTAL	92	267.0	66	211.0
	AVERAGE RATING		2.90		3.20

Students indicated a self-assessed average improvement of 10.2% (from 2.90 to 3.20)

In general, how do you rate yourself on the following writing skills:	Rating	Pre-Course Survey		Post-Course Survey	
		# of Responses	Rating x # of Responses	# of Responses	Rating x # of Responses
(5) Writing good conclusions	1.0 Need lots of help	8	8.0	3	3.0
	2.0 Struggling	14	28.0	8	16.0
	3.0 Feel okay	44	132.0	26	78.0
	4.0 Fairly confident	22	88.0	22	88.0
	5.0 Very confident	4	20.0	7	35.0
	TOTAL	96	276.0	66	220.0
	AVERAGE RATING		3.00		3.33

Students indicated a self-assessed average improvement of 11.1 % (from 3.00 to 3.33)

(6) Voicing my own opinions appropriately	1.0 Need lots of help	5 5.00	5.0	0	0.0
	2.0 Struggling	26	52.0	14	28.0
	3.0 Feel okay	36	108.0	26	78.0
	4.0 Fairly confident	20	80.0	21	84.0
	5.0 Very confident	5	25.0	5	25.0
	TOTAL	92	270.0	66	215.0
	AVERAGE RATING		2.93		3.26

Students indicated a self-assessed average improvement of 11.0 % (from 2.93 to 3.26)

(7) Making an argument effectively	1.0 Need lots of help	8	8.0	5	5.0
	2.0 Struggling	26	52.0	14	28.0
	3.0 Feel okay	36	108.0	21	63.0
	4.0 Fairly confident	14	56.0	18	72.0
	5.0 Very confident	8	40.0	8	40.0
	TOTAL	92	264.0	66	208.0
	AVERAGE RATING		2.87		3.15

Students indicated a self-assessed average improvement of 9.8 % (from 2.87 to 3.15)

In general, how do you rate yourself on the following writing skills:	Rating	Pre-Course Survey		Post-Course Survey	
		# of Responses	Rating x # of Responses	# of Responses	Rating x # of Responses
(8) Using correct grammar and punctuation	1.0 Need lots of help	10	10.0	5	5.0
	2.0 Struggling	22	44.0	12	24.0
	3.0 Feel okay	37	111.0	23	69.0
	4.0 Fairly confident	18	72.0	22	88.0
	5.0 Very confident	5	25.0	4	20.0
	TOTAL	92	262.0	66	206.0
	AVERAGE RATING		2.85		3.12

Students indicated a self-assessed average improvement of 9.6 % (from 2.85 to 3.12)

(9) Summarizing others' ideas	1.0 Need lots of help	0	0.0	0	0
	2.0 Struggling	20	40.0	12	24.0
	3.0 Feel okay	40	120.0	20	60.0
	4.0 Fairly confident	28	112.0	23	92.0
	5.0 Very confident	4	20.0	11	55.0
	TOTAL	92	292.0	66	231.0
	AVERAGE RATING		3.17		3.50

Students indicated a self-assessed average improvement of 10.0% (from 3.17 to 3.50)

(10) Deciding on a topic and focus	1.0 Need lots of help	4	4.0	1	1.0
	2.0 Struggling	19	38.0	9	18.0
	3.0 Feel okay	42	126.0	31	93.0
	4.0 Fairly confident	22	88.0	20	80.0
	5.0 Very confident	5	25.0	5	25.0
	TOTAL	92	281.0	66	217.0
	AVERAGE RATING		3.05		3.29

Students indicated a self-assessed average improvement of 7.6 % (from 3.05 to 3.29)

In general, how do you rate yourself on the following writing skills:	Rating		Pre-Course Survey		Post-Course Survey	
			# of Responses	Rating x # of Responses	# of Responses	Rating x # of Responses
(11) Spelling	1.0 Need lots of help		2	2.0 334	0	0
	2.0 Struggling		17	34.0	12	24.0
	3.0 Feel okay		37	111.0	22	66.0
	4.0 Fairly confident		33	132.0	23	92.0
	5.0 Very confident		3	15.0	9	45.0
	TOTAL		92	294.0	66	227.0
	AVERAGE RATING			3.20		3.44

Students indicated a self-assessed average improvement of 7.6% (from 3.20 to 3.44)

(12) Organizing the material for the paper	1.0 Need lots of help		1	1.0	2	2.0
	2.0 Struggling		16	32.0	4	8.0
	3.0 Feel okay		38	114.0	26	78.0
	4.0 Fairly confident		33	132.0	26	104.0
	5.0 Very confident		4	20.0	7	35.0
	TOTAL		92	299.0	65	227.0
	AVERAGE RATING			3.25		3.49

Students indicated a self-assessed average improvement of 7.5 % (from 3.25 to 3.49)

(13) Avoiding procrastination	1.0 Need lots of help		6	6.0	5	5.0
	2.0 Struggling		27	54.0	16	32.0
	3.0 Feel okay		48	144.0	35	105.0
	4.0 Fairly confident		8	32.0	6	24.0
	5.0 Very confident		0	0.0	1	5.0
	TOTAL		89	236.0	63	171.0
	AVERAGE RATING			2.65		2.71

Students indicated a self-assessed average improvement of 2.4 % (from 2.65 to 2.71)

ADDITIONAL POST-COURSE QUESTIONS

Question 1: There are anticipated advantages for taking a course that pays attention to writing as well as content. Please indicate whether you generally agree or disagree with the following:

MAJORITY POSITIVE RESPONSES	Valid Responses	% Yes	% No
1. Getting feedback showed me what I needed to do to improve my paper	64	93.8%	6.2%
2. Getting feedback on my writing before it's graded made sense to me	63	88.9%	11.1%
3. Rewriting and revising helped me figure out what I was saying	63	88.9%	11.1%
4. By writing, I got to explain complex ideas clearly and make them my own	63	85.7%	14.3%
5. Writing gets me engaged in the subject matter more than just listening to the lecture	62	69.4%	30.6%
6. Short, informal writing exercises helped me focus on concepts and explore topics	61	68.9%	31.1%
7. Feedback showed me my ideas are good but I need more direction on technical matters like grammar, punctuation and citation practices	62	67.7%	32.3%
8. Working with classmates was both worthwhile and enjoyable	48	64.6%	35.4%
9. I need time to figure out my ideas so more time for the in-class writing would have been beneficial	56	58.9%	41.1%
MAJORITY NEGATIVE RESPONSES			
10. It was more work, but worth doing because I felt more confident	58	41.4%	58.6%
11. I found it useful to get feedback from my classmates	53	34.0%	66.0%
OVERALL		70.3%	29.7%

The responses to these questions indicated an overwhelming positive response from the students on the benefits of feedback, revising and collaborating in the writing process. Students appeared to recognize that the process helped them understand and learn better through writing. Majority negative responses were only expressed at the added work required and in the value of the feedback experience from classmates.

Question 2: Your opinions of the writing-intensive process are important to us. Please indicate whether you generally agree or disagree with the following:

	Valid Responses	% Yes	% No
1. The writing-intensive process gave me skills I can apply to other courses	61	68.9%	31.1%
2. I think that the writing emphasis worked well in this course	61	60.7%	39.3%
3. The emphasis on writing in this course improved my writing skills	58	55.2%	44.8%
4. I think the writing emphasis would be better in another course in my area	48	43.8%	56.3%
5. The writing focus in the course was well-timed for me in my program	58	39.7%	60.3%
6. I would like to take another writing-intensive course because I saw my writing improve with this approach	58	13.8%	86.2%

Responses to this question indicate an appreciation of the skills learnt but also a shortage of enthusiasm for the work involved. A reluctance to the W-element appears evident and this emphasizes the hurdles involved to get students to buy into the process enthusiastically.

Question 3: Please describe other resources that were particularly helpful to your development as a learner/ writer this semester: friends, email responses from TA or prof, class discussion, library workshop etc.

Responses are tabulated below. Some students indicated more than one resource as helpful:

Resource	# of Responses Indicating the Resource as Helpful
T/A	39
Friends	14
E-Mail responses	13
Class Debate	12
professor	9
Internet	6
Library & Library Workshops	6
Tutorials	4

| Specific Guidelines | 2 |
| Other | 5 |

Students indicated the TA's as being the most helpful resource by a significant margin, thus validating the considerable input made by CWIL/ WILO to make sure they were well- trained for the job. The value of peer input, communications and group participation in the process also appears to have been recognized by the students. It is interesting that the professor's input appears to be rated much lower than that of the TA's.

Question 4: Please comment on how you feel about writing.

Some students had more than one comment on how they felt

Comment	# of Respondents
Time Consuming	12
Help Understand Subject	12
Good to do /great	9
Writing is Good / Enjoyable	7
A Necessity / Important	7
I Feel Confident	7
Help Organizing	4
Was Hard	4
Too much work	4
Improves writing skills	3
Don't like it / Not good at it	3
Waste of time	2
Writing Improved	2
Other (5)	5

Question 5: Taking into account where you are in your program, what would you like to see changed or added in a course that has a writing intensive approach? If you can, please make a suggestion that would have increased your learning in the course and or improved your writing of the major assignments.

Some students had more than one comment on how they felt

Suggested Changes	# of Respondents Advocating Change
Fewer Assignments	14
Give more credits for course	7
Clearer instructions from Prof /TA	6
Make assignments worth more	5
More group discussions	5
More help from TA	3
Have drafts reviewed	3
Have special classes on writing prep	2
More Feedback	2
Other (12)	12

APPENDIX 6
Categories for Analyzing Students' Written Responses

Thinking Strategies (adapted from Bloom's Cognitive Taxonomy)

Knowledge T1	Comprehension T2	Application T3	Analysis T4	Synthesis T5	Evaluation T6
Recall information; recount facts; quote or copy; reproduce; describe	Understand meaning; re-state information in own words; interpret, extrapolate; explain; paraphrase; interpret	Use or apply knowledge; put theory into practical effect/ example, construct; react; respond	Interpret elements/ principles/ structure; identify relationships; quality/ reliability of components; identify parts and functions of a process; measure, test, experiment	Develop new unique structures/ systems/ models/ approach/ ideas; creating thinking/ operation; propose solutions or new approaches	Assess effectiveness of whole concepts in relation to values, viability; critical thinking with comparisons and review; judgment relates to external criteria that is evaluated

Writing Strategies

Structure W1	Style W2	Mechanics W3	Authorship W4
Organized; focused; transition; central thesis/argument	Tone; originality; economy/effective use of words (appropriate use of terminology/technical language)	Spelling; grammar; sentence structure; punctuation	Ownership of ideas and language; writer is engaged with the task; ideas are writer's own or writer speaks ideas in own 'voice'

Course Content Errors

Lack of understanding of concepts E1-E5	Lack of writing skills E6-E7	Answer is disorganized E8-E10
E1. Oversimplification E2. Incorrect context E3. Errors of fact E4. Meaningless information included E5. Logical errors	E6. Incorrect word use E7. Awkward wording	E8. Vague E9. Irrelevant information is included E10. Answer is incomplete – a fuller explanation is required

Learning Strategies (adapted from Bigg's Structure of Observed Learning - SOLO)

Pre-structural L1	Unistructural L2	Multi-structural L3	Relational L4	Extended Abstract L5
The response is not appropriate. The student has not understood the question/point	One or a few aspects of the question picked up but understanding is nominal; (a) simple naming, terminology; (b) focusing on one conceptual issue in a complex case (only one feature is given serious consideration)	Several aspects of the question are learnt but are treated separately; (a) disorganized collection of items, 'shopping list'; (b) 'knowledge-telling' a strategy used in essay-writing in which the student 'snows' the marker with masses of detail, often using a narrative genre inappropriately but with the desired effect; (c) simple list, which may nevertheless be adequate for some purposes, while (b) may well address abstract content and be quite impressive in its way, although in most cases the structure is simplified and wrong	The components are integrated into a coherent whole with each part contributing to the overall meaning; (a) understanding, using a concept that integrates a collection of data; (b) understanding how to apply the concept to a familiar data set or to a problem [(a) is a declarative understanding, (b) functioning, which requires (a) for the application to work	The integrated whole at the relational level is re-conceptualized at a higher level of abstraction. This enables generalization to a new topic or area, or it is turned reflexively on oneself – understanding as transfer/ transformative or meta-cognitive (a) relating to existing principle, so that unseen problems can be handled; (b) probably the highest level in most undergraduate work, with (b) a surprising bonus if it occurs. (b) is often called 'post-formal,', the sort of understanding required to do postgraduate research

APPENDIX 7
Questions for structured interviews

PROFESSIONAL BACKGROUND (COULD BE DRAWN FROM CV)

1. Education

2. Teaching experience

3. Service activity

4. Publications

SELF AS WRITER

What is your own background as a writer? What knowledge of writing do you bring or what experience that equips you for this work? Any reading on writing or on teaching writing that you've done either before or during the process? Research that has been interesting or useful to you and in what ways?

> How would you describe yourself as a writer – both as an academic and other?
>
> What helps you to write?
>
> What is typical of your own process as an academic writer?
>
> How would you define writing and what is entailed in writing?
>
> How much do you write a day? Or do you write everyday?
>
> What impact, if any, has teaching the W-course had on your own writing and research?

WRITING IN THE DISCIPLINE

> Do you support the direction the university has taken with respect to where writing is to be taught? What do you find convincing about the WID thrust of the new curriculum? What do you see as problematic? Do you think that learning to write in your discipline could as well be learned in a composition class or might be better taught by the English department and by people with particular expertise in teaching writing? Why or why not?

What role/purpose does written material and writing fulfill in your discipline – in the profession?

What is characteristic of writing in your discipline? What are typical features of writing in your discipline?

What do you think is most important to emphasize in working with student writers in your discipline?

Self as teacher

What kind of image do you have or yourself as a teacher – a metaphor – are you a mechanic, accountant, gardener, doctor, nurse, tour guide . . .

What do you think is your job as a teacher? How would you define your role as a teacher? To what extent does it include teaching students to write in your discipline? To what extent do you find this acceptable or not?

What impact has the W aspect had on your teaching and thinking and planning for the W-course and in other courses – if any? Why or why not?

How does what you teach and the way you teach reflect your own learning and writing experience – or does it?

As a learner – what helps you to learn new and complex material?

How does taking on and offering a W-course make you feel about yourself as a teacher? Does it affect how you think of yourself or see yourself?

Could you identify two or three key insights that the W-teaching has brought you?

RELATIONS WITH CWIL /WSG

How does the process of working with someone on your syllabus affect your thinking and teaching practice?

What questions do you have for me as someone charged to work with faculty?

How can the institution/WSG encourage ongoing reflection about and revision of W-courses?

What has helped you develop as a W-faculty member? Do you find it is useful to read accounts by others in your discipline? Have you any interest in writing such accounts yourself?

Would you be receptive to peer evaluation of teaching? By whom?

What do you want to improve in your W-course and why?

Self as member of department

What reactions do you get from colleagues when you describe your W-course or the W initiative or CWIL? How do people respond?

What support have you had or do you need from the department?

Would you be interested in mentoring other new W-faculty? What would allow you to do that without being stretched too far?

Teaching the W-course

A. Criteria

How have the criteria for W-courses and the application of them affected your interest and commitment to the W-initiative? For those in early pilots, what was your relation to the criteria?

How important are the criteria? To what extent do you think them necessary or not? How do you think the implementation of the criteria in W-courses should be monitored or should it?

In what respects is the process for certification and the completion of forms different in kind and quality from what happens internally when you submit a course outline?

B. Relation to Course Content

How have you accommodated the writing along with the content you want to teach?

Are there constraints that W imposes on the way time is used and/or effects on flexibility for teaching?

How does it affect your understanding or appreciation of your own course material/discipline?

How have you interpreted the requirement to teach professional and disciplinary genres? How does this work for you?

What is the nature of the tradeoff, if there is one, between delivery/presentation of content and student writing activity

C. Relation to TAs/Effects on TAs

How does the W-aspect affect your relationship with the TAs – is this an advantage or not?

Do you see this experience as offering career development for a future academic/teacher?

How much involvement/direction have you found you need to have with the TAs? Or would you plan to have in another iteration of your course?

what are some of the key issues for you in the selection and assignment of TAs to the course?

D. Relation to Students/Effects on Students

How do you think writing might have an impact on students sense of themselves as thinkers and writers? - (something that points to the idea C Murray mentions of an authorial self).

How does it change your relationship with students – if it does?

What do you see to be or hope is the value of the writing for the students in your course?

What impact do you think W has had on student literacy? What would you include in a concept of literacy?

What do you think motivates students? - desire for excellence or for grades or are those the same thing?

What have you learned from students about the W?

What do you think students have most difficulty with in your course?

How do you handle shifting student expectations? How do students' expectations affect what you do – their preconceptions about how they learn in the class?

What have you found challenging about marking student writing – if you are doing it yourself?

APPENDIX 8
Arts Faculty Survey

Name_____ Department_____

Student Writing in the Faculty of Arts: a Survey of Views and Practices

1. Please indicate your views about student writing in your discipline by marking the following as either "1" for major problems "2" as somewhat of a problem and "3" as a negligible problem.

__a. knowledge of discipline-specific structure and conventions

__b. grammar, usage, punctuation, spelling, and mechanics

__c. selecting an appropriate topic

__d. knowledge of generic structures and conventions of academic writing

__e. sentence structure and style

__f. researching

__g. addressing an appropriate audience

__h. ESL

__i. focus and organization

__j. logic, quality of argument, supporting claims

__k. other (please specify):

2. Typically, what percentage of your students grades' is determined by their written work, including essay examinations:

__ in first year courses?

__ in second year courses?

__ in upper division courses?

3. What purpose(s) do writing tasks serve in your courses? Please check all that apply.

__Evaluate students' learning (for grading)

__Assess students' learning so you can focus later classes on their needs

__Demonstrate know-how specific to your discipline

__Encourage students' to think and/or learn independently

__Other (please state):

4. To what extent does the quality of students' writing (as distinguished from the "content") affect your students' grades?

5. What types of writing do your students do? (Check all that apply.)

__a. papers involving significant secondary (library) research

__b. critical/opinion papers

__c. research reports

__d. lab reports

__e. book reviews

__f. summaries (of readings)

__g. journal entries

__h. in-class essay examinations

__i. take-home essay examinations

__j. quizzes that require full-sentence answers

__k. other (please specify) _____

6. Who sets the assignments?

__instructor (i.e., you)

__teaching assistant

__someone else (please specify) _____

7. Has the type of writing you assign changed over your years at SFU?

__ Yes

__ No

If yes, is that because (check all that apply)

__a. your workload has increased (or decreased)

__b. ESL students' skills

__c. transfer students' skills

__d. increased incidence of plagiarism

__e. other (please specify)_____

8. Typically, how much time do you spend helping students develop their writing for assignments? ___ hours per course

9. Typically, how much time do you yourself spend grading and/or commenting on students' finished papers? ___ hours per course

10. Please rank the following eight items according to their importance as criteria for your evaluation of student writing:

__a. grammar, usage, punctuation, spelling and mechanics

__b. vocabulary (including knowledge of discipline-specific terms)

__c. discipline-specific conventions

__d demonstrated knowledge of course content__e.original insights

__f. logic / quality of thought, argument, and/or support for claims

__g. organization and coherence

__h. other (please specify)_____

11. Which of the following do you do, or have done by your teaching assistant? Please check any that apply and if something is done by a teaching assistant, please indicate with TA.

__a. beyond making the assignment, do you spend time in class helping students understand and approach writing tasks?

__b. do you state explicit goals/criteria you will use to evaluate the writing?

__c. do you show students models of good writing by professionals?

__d. do you show students models of good writing by other students?

__e. do you show students examples of your own writing?

__f. do you confer with students while they are in the process of writing?

__g. do you respond to drafts?

     __ orally

     __ in writing

__h. do you have other students respond to drafts?

    __ individually

    __ in small groups?

    __ in tutorial/lab discussions?

__i. do you have other students read and/or respond to students' finished writing?

    __in tutorial or lab discussions

    __in small groups

__j. do you write comments on the margins of students' writing?

__k. do you write comments at the end of students' writing?

if so, how long is a typical comment?_____

__l. do you comment on students' finished writing orally (i.e., in conference)?

__m. do you comment on the writing (as distinguished from the "content")?

__n. do you have students revise after you comment?

Any other comments?
Many thanks for your help!

APPENDIX 9
Post-course Questionnaire

In this course, you probably had opportunities to write both formally and informally, and may have been given feedback on drafts of your papers to help you revise. Whether this approach to writing is typical or untypical of your course-work at SFU, you will have had some reaction to the process: you may have noticed effects of writing on your learning and understanding of the content, and/or your confidence in talking about what you've read and understood. Your answers to the following questions will help us in planning writing activities in other courses:

1. There are anticipated advantages for taking a course that pays attention to writing as well as content. Please indicate whether you generally agree or disagree with the following:

		Mostly Yes	Mostly No	N/A
a.	By writing, I got to explain complex ideas clearly and make them my own	1	2	3
b.	Getting feedback on my writing before it's graded made sense to me	1	2	3
c.	Rewriting and revising helped me figure out what I was saying	1	2	3
d.	Feedback showed me my ideas are good but I need more direction on technical matters like grammar, punctuation and citation practices	1	2	3
e.	Getting feedback showed me what I needed to do to improve my paper	1	2	3
f.	I found it useful to get feedback from my classmates	1	2	3
g.	I need time to figure out my ideas so more time for the in-class writing would have been beneficial	1	2	3
h.	Writing gets me engaged in the subject matter more than just listening to the lecture	1	2	3
i.	Working with classmates was both worthwhile and enjoyable	1	2	3
j.	It was more work, but worth doing because I felt more confident	1	2	3
k.	Short, informal writing exercises helped me focus on concepts and explore topics	1	2	3

2. Your opinions of the writing-intensive process are important to us. Please indicate whether you generally agree or disagree with the following:

		Mostly Yes	Mostly No	N/A
a.	The writing focus in the course was well-timed for me in my program	1	2	3
b.	I would like to take another writing-intensive course because I saw my writing improve with this approach	1	2	3
c.	I think that the writing emphasis worked well in this course	1	2	3
d.	I think the writing emphasis would be better in another course in my area	1	2	3
e.	The writing-intensive process gave me skills I can apply to other courses	1	2	3
f.	The emphasis on writing in this course improved my writing skills	1	2	3

3. Please describe other resources that were particularly helpful to your development as a learner/ writer this semester: friends, email responses from TA or prof, class discussion, library workshop etc.

4. Please comment on how you feel about writing.

5. Taking into account where you are in your program, what would you like to see changed or added in a course that has a writing intensive approach? If you can, please make a suggestion that would have increased your learning in the course and or improved your writing of the major assignments.

6. Compared to other students at this university, how do you rate your writing skills overall?

Poor				Adequate				Excellent	
1	2	3	4	5	6	7	8	9	10

7. In general, how do you rate yourself on the following writing skills:

		Need lots of help	Struggle with this	Feel okay	Fairly confident	Very confident
a.	Deciding on a topic and focus	1	2	3	4	5
b.	Researching material for the paper	1	2	3	4	5
c.	Avoiding procrastination	1	2	3	4	5
d.	Voicing my own opinions appropriately	1	2	3	4	5
e.	Using correct grammar and punctuation	1	2	3	4	5
f.	Organizing the paper with my data	1	2	3	4	5
g.	Editing and rewriting drafts	1	2	3	4	5
h.	Quoting effectively	1	2	3	4	5
i.	Summarizing others' ideas	1	2	3	4	5
j.	Paraphrasing things in my own words	1	2	3	4	5
k.	Developing a strong argument	1	2	3	4	5
l.	Writing introductions with a clear thesis	1	2	3	4	5
m.	Writing good conclusions	1	2	3	4	5

Thanks for your help!

APPENDIX 10
Draft: CWIL Mandate, January 2004

To help make the use of writing an integral part of the teaching and learning culture across the university. To provide instructional support for writing-intensive courses; to conduct research on writing-intensive learning. To be a source of guidance/expertise/information/ consultation/ assistance/training for those who want to create writing-intensive courses. To serve as a source of information about how to design and offer high-quality, academically-effective writing courses.

What this means in practice is that CWIL faculty:

- meet with instructors who may be interested in offering W-courses or in simply revising a writing assignment

- mentor such instructors both during and after the implementation of a W-course to provide ongoing professional development

- train and mentor TAs attached to W-courses through pre-semester and during-semester workshops and meetings

- provide information and expertise to the Writing Support Group

- offer examples of writing-intensive courses from other universities

- offer sample course outlines, syllabi, writing assignments, handouts

- offer faculty workshops, seminars, brown bag lunches

- house resources such as books, articles, web sites, databases, descriptions of models from other universities pertaining to the design and assessment of writing-intensive courses

- document and assess current and developing practices in the teaching of writing across the university

- offer guidance about the assessment of student writing

- offer guidance about the assessment of writing-intensive courses

- conduct and publish research on the design and assessment of writing-intensive courses and on models and contexts for effective writing-intensive learning

- at the behest of programs, provide an evaluation of the expertise in writing instruction possessed by instructors those programs are considering hiring

- coordinate and collaborate with other units (Bridge Program, HCCC, Continuing Studies, Coop Programs etc.) to help develop resources and services for improving student writing practices and products and enhancing the climate in which students function as writers.

- research and develop workshops and provide consultation on specialized genres of writing such as SSHRC Doctoral applications

STRUCTURAL ORGANIZATION OF CWIL

- director
- "Steering committee" with representatives from all Faculties
- "Facilitators" (at present two: KA, AB)
- Administrative Assistant(s)
- Research Assistants
- Associates: these might include faculty and others who have an interest and commitment to W-learning – participation could depend on the functions or role of the associates.

MANDATE OF THE WRITING SUPPORT GROUP

- Defining W courses
- Certifying W courses
- Recommending funding for W courses
- Making programs aware of different models for W courses (CWIL might provide information on a range of models)
- Recruiting instructors to offer W courses
- Organizing the development of Foundational Writing Courses

The director of CWIL or a designate should be a member of the Writing Support Group and whatever successor body follows it.

APPENDIX 11
Constitution for the Proposed Schedule A centre

Centre for Writing-Intensive Learning (CWIL),
Faculty of Arts, Simon Fraser University

PURPOSE

The Centre for Writing-Intensive Learning aims to make the use of writing constitutive of the teaching and learning culture at Simon Fraser University and to foster students' knowledge and skills as writers. The centre will develop resources and strategies to provide instructional support for writing-intensive courses and conduct research on writing-intensive learning. The centre will assist and collaborate with faculty in planning and offering W-courses that meet the criteria for the new curriculum requirements. The centre will collaborate with faculty and departments to research and assess the implementation of new or modified approaches to the uses and teaching of writing. Information from such assessment will be used to influence the future design of high-quality, academically-effective writing courses.

GOVERNANCE

The centre will be governed by a steering committee consisting of the director of the centre and seven members appointed by the Dean of arts who will serve for two year terms: a representative from the Dean of arts office, one faculty member from each of the following: English department, Science faculty, Education faculty, social sciences, and two members from outside the university: one from the provinces colleges or articulation committees and one public figure involved in education. The steering committee determines policy for the centre and approves new initiatives and programs. A management committee consisting of the Dean of arts and the director of the centre will oversee fiscal operations of the Center and make strategic decisions.

The affairs of the centre shall be administered by a director, who will be appointed by and report directly to the Dean of arts as required by Simon Fraser University's Policies and Procedures for Schedule A centres and Institutes. The director will serve as an advocate for the centre's interests, will have signing authority on behalf of the centre for all accounts, contracts, and agreements of the centre, and will supervise all employees of the centre. The director will prepare an annual report to submit to the Dean at year-end.

FUNDING

The centre will be funded jointly by the faculty of arts and the vice president academic. It will use the operating budget of its predecessor, the Centre for Research in Writing, which was previously administered by the English department. As the activities of the centre require increases in staff and materials, further resources will be sought.

STAFF

Director: The term of the director shall be 3 years, with the possibility of renewal for a further term. The director reports to and is evaluated for salary review by the Dean of arts and the director's academic home department.

Limited term lecturers: In the first year, a lecturer will be appointed for an initial term of two years with the possibility of renewal. The director will hire additional lecturers as the centre requires, in consultation with a committee, and be responsible for supervision and allocation of duties.

Departmental Assistant: The DA reports to and is evaluated by the director.

Research Assistant: RAs will be appointed as required. At least one RA will be sought for the first semester of operation of the centre and an additional RA in the second and subsequent semesters as required.

Future staffing will depend on the needs identified by the director in consultation with the Dean of arts and the steering committee.

ACTIVITIES OF THE CENTRE

Faculty will fulfill the following responsibilities:

- Meet with instructors who may be interested in offering W-courses or in simply revising a writing assignment

- Mentor such instructors both during and after the implementation of a W-course to provide ongoing professional development

- Train and mentor TAs attached to W-courses through pre-semester and during-semester workshops and meetings

- Provide information and expertise to the Writing Support Group

- Offer examples of writing-intensive courses from other universities

- Offer sample course outlines, syllabi, writing assignments, handouts

- Plan and offer workshops, seminars, summer institutes, departmental retreats, and other forms of training sessions for faculty and TAs for W-course development, assessment, and revision.

- House resources such as books, articles, web sites, databases, descriptions of models from other universities pertaining to the design and assessment of writing-intensive courses

- Document and assess current and developing practices in the teaching of writing across the university

- Offer guidance about the assessment of student writing

- Offer guidance about the assessment of writing-intensive courses

- Conduct and publish research on the design and assessment of writing-intensive courses and on models and contexts for effective writing-intensive learning

- At the behest of programs, provide an evaluation of the expertise in writing instruction possessed by instructors those programs are considering hiring

- Coordinate and collaborate with other units (Bridge Program, HCCC, Continuing Studies, Coop Programs etc.) to help develop resources and services for improving student writing practices and products and enhancing the climate in which students function as writers.

- Research and develop workshops and provide consultation on specialized genres of writing such as SSHRC Doctoral and Master's scholarship applications

- Establish links with other institutions (e.g. Cornell Knight Institute) to enhance the profile of Simon Fraser University and to collaborate on research and implementation projects.

Proposal submitted by:
Wendy Strachan, PhD
Director, Centre for Writing-Intensive Learning
Simon Fraser University

APPENDIX 12
Stages of Writing Program Development—Notes from a
Presentation at Simon Fraser University, June 6, 2006

Bill Condon, Washington State University
Presentation developed with
Carol Rutz, Carleton College.

Used by permission.

Problematizing
Problems are early-stage. Difficulty getting established, ghettoizing of writing, resource scarcity. Moving to third stage involves WAC in serving institution-wide agendas.

First Stage
There's a problem—or interest. Missionary work. New goal: Infusing writing throughout students' experience. Writing is everybody's job. Moving beyond inoculation. Writing to learn. Typically one person's vision. Early success depends on person's energy and charisma.

Articulate your own vision—local!

Faculty understand differences between learning to write and writing to learn. Accept role in student learning with regard to writing.

Buy-in from faculty, admin, other key players/stakeholders

Second Stage
Minimal administrative existence or implementation. Faculty development. Missionary work. Others learn to serve our agenda. Course and assignment development, responding to writing, grading. Enlisting the apostles. Usual suspects.

Marginal. Self-contained. Still dependent on founder. Essentialist and administrative.

You clearly HAVE stakeholders.

Functions and leadership begin to differentiate and become embodied.

People with mapped workloads (important transition!)

Build a model of relationships within program and of program within larger institutional and social contexts.

Name. Presence. Identity.

Listen to others' representations of your program.

Indicators chosen in participatory process. Hermeneutic circle.

Continual change—no stasis. Incremental improvement, guided by careful processes for change.

Create reliable, continual archives of materials, policies, evolution of program—history.

Scholarship in area recognized as valuable within institution and in higher education.

Budget!

Ability of key players/founders/vision people to let go, to stop being exhausted, to hand off pieces of program or whole program to others.

Third Stage

Integration into larger, other agendas. Institutional assessment, accreditation, accountability. Faculty development in larger context (LTC, CTLT).

Program begins to become indispensable.

Writing Studio, Junior portfolio. Expansion beyond Faculty development. Focus on outcomes and student progress/achievement. Instructional support. Role in IR. Play into institutional needs. Gain institutional support. Creation of greater presence: both in effect and in personnel. Collaboration among units directly associated with writing and more broadly. Theory becomes more robust. Program becomes more dynamic. Naming outcomes, letting faculty articulate them.

Awareness of theoretical framework underlying program efforts (e.g., sustainability theory). Use framework to identify and track indicators for sustainability and improvement.

Carefully design assessment process. Multiple, generative benchmarks.

Formative as well as summative assessments. Don't fossilize program by limiting its assessments.

Ability to coordinate with other efforts and preserve program mission.

Awards for writing, for course development, etc.

Motivational awards for faculty, departments.

Collaborating with other campus initiatives and programs for mutual benefit.

WAC starts to come to program—see program as resource that they can access, that belongs to stakeholders.

Being willing to let some of it go—hand over program outcomes to others who can use them for their own purposes.

Avoid mission creep(s). Prioritize response to demands from stakeholders in WAC program.

Unite with other, similar programs at peer institutions. Make common cause.

Upper administration recognizes validity of our assessment practices, seeks advice from consultants in our field.

Fourth Stage

Driving change. Alliance with other curricular initiatives. Feeds into improvement.

Begin to have signature pedagogy (Shulman). Institutional identity congruent with activities. Move beyond usual suspects. Becomes widely valued resource. Full theorizing of program(s).

WSU: CT project. Become pattern for other initiatives (Math). Invitations into departments and programs. Extreme expansion of WAC workshops.

CC: Assessment now taken in stride. Don't need to "sell" assessment any more. Patterning new initiatives on existing, valued writing model. QR, visuality. Double helix.

Assessment—program, SLOs, faculty attitudes and expectations, curriculum (mapping), etc.

Written history or record(s) of program origins and development. Make it *accessible*.

Use accumulated history as source for benchmarks.

Others see your program as model, seek advice so that they can apply your processes to their own programs to generate similar strengths to your own.

Scholarship in area recognized as valuable within institution and in higher education.

Stages are cumulative, not linear. All go on at once, Programs may stop at any stage, but they don't leave off one when they move to the next. Enlightened self-interest should spur programs to reach third stage WAC at least. Is evolution to fourth stage inevitable? Maybe not. Need to go beyond capacity, to overwork to get there. Then program can build capacity to get relief.

REFERENCES

Ackerman, John M. 1993. The Promise of Writing to Learn. *Written Communication* 10(3): 334–370.

Ad Hoc Curriculum Committee. 2001 Reviewing and Developing Undergraduate Curricula at SFU: a Discussion Paper. [cited December 28, 2005]. http://www.sfu.ca.proxy.lib.sfu.ca/ugcr.

———. Final Report of the Ad Hoc Curriculum Committee. 2002 [cited December 28, 2005]. http://www.sfu.ca.proxy.lib.sfu.ca/ugcr. http://www.sfu.ca/ugcr/files/ucc_final.pdf

Ad Hoc Senate Committee. Penultimate Report of the Ad Hoc Curriculum Committee. 2002 [cited December 28, 2005]. http://www.sfu.ca/ugcr.

Applebee, Arthur N. 1984. Writing and Reasoning. *Review of Educational Research* 54(4): 577–596.

———. 1984. *Contexts for Learning to Write: Studies of Secondary School Instruction*. Norwood: Ablex.

Arnason, Ulfur. 1998. Response. *Journal of Molecular Evolution* 46: 379–381.

Arnold, Matthew. 1853. The Scholar-Gypsy. In *The Oxford Book Of English* Verse:1250–1900., ed. Arthur Quiller-Couch, 751. Oxford: Oxford University Press. 1919.

Bangert-Drowns, Robert L., Marlene M. Hurley, and Barbara Wilkinson. 2004. The Effects of School-Based Writing-to-Learn Interventions on Academic Achievement: a Meta-Analysis. *Review of Educational Research* 74(1): 29–58.

Barnett, Robert W., and Jacob S. Blumner. 1999. *Writing Centers and Writing Across the Curriculum Programs: Building Interdisciplinary Partnerships*. Contributions to the Study of Education. Vol. 73. London: Greenwood Press.

Bawarshi, Anis S. 2003. *Genre and the Invention of the Writer*. Logan, Utah: Utah State UP.

Bazerman, Charles. 1997. The Life of Genre, the Life in the Classroom. In *Genre and Writing: Issues, Arguments, Alternatives*, Eds. Wendy Bishop, Hans Ostrom, 19–26. Portsmouth: Boynton/Cook.

BC Liberal Party. BC liberal party platform, 2001 http://www.bcliberals.com/.

Beach, R. 1989. Evaluating Writing to Learn: Responding to Journals. In *Encountering Student Texts: Interpretive Issues in Reading Student Writing.*, eds. B. Lawson, S. Ryan and W. R. Winterowd. Urbana: NCTE.

———. 1979. The Effects of Between-Draft Teacher Evaluation Versus Student Self-Evaluation on High School Students' Revising of Rough Drafts. *Research in The Teaching of English*. 13: 111–119.

Bean, John C. 2001. *Engaging Ideas: the professor's Guide to Integrating Writing, Critical Thinking, and Active Learning in the Classroom*. San Francisco: Jossey-Bass.

Beaufort, Anne, and John A. Williams. 2005. Writing History: Informed or Not by Genre Theory? In *Genre Across the Curriculum*. Eds. Anne Herrington, Charles Moran, 44–64. Logan: Utah State University Press.

Berkenkotter, Carol, and Thomas N. Huckin. 1995. *Genre Knowledge in Disciplinary Communication: Cognition/Culture/Power*. Hillsdale: L. Erlbaum Associates.

Berthoff, Ann E. 1978. *Forming, Thinking, Writing: the Composing Imagination*. Hayden English Language Series. Rochelle Park: Hayden Book Co.

Bishop, Wendy, and Hans Ostrom, eds. 1997. *Genre and Writing: Issues, Arguments, Alternatives*. Portsmouth: Boynton/Cook.

Blackman, Roger. 2002. Centre for Writing-Intensive Learning. Memo to John Waterhouse, vice president academic.

Blaney, Jack P. 2000. Revised "Values and Commitments" Document. Memorandum, Office of the President.

———. 1999. Values and Commitments Statement. Memorandum, Office of the President.

Bruner, Jerome. 1986. *Actual Minds, Possible Worlds*. Cambridge: Harvard University Press.

Burkland, J., and N. Grimm. 1984. Students' Response to Our Response. Paper presented at Conference on College Composition and Communication, New York.

Candlin, Christopher, and Ken Hyland. 1999. *Writing: Texts, Processes, and Practices*. Applied Linguistics and Language Study. New York: Longman.

Center for Writing Excellence. 2006. *U.S. News and World Report Ranking*. http://www.units. muohio.edu/cwe/.

Charney, Davida H., and Richard A. Carlson. 1995. Learning to Write in a Genre: What Student Writers Take from Model Texts. *Research in the Teaching of English*. 29 (1): 88–125.

Christie, Frances. 1999. *Pedagogy and the Shaping of Consciousness: Linguistic and Social Processes*. Open Linguistics Series. London: Cassell.

Christie, Frances, and J. R. Martin. 1997. *Genre and Institutions: Social Processes in the Workplace and School*. Open Linguistics Series. London: Cassell.

Coe, Richard. 2002. The New Rhetoric of Genre: Writing Political Briefs. In *Genre in the Classroom: Multiple Perspectives,*. ed. Ann M. Johns, 197–210. Mahwah: Lawrence Erlbaum Associates.

Condon, William, and Diane Kelley-Riley. 2004. Assessing and Teaching What We Value: the Relationship Between College-Level Writing and Critical Thinking Abilities. *Assessing Writing*. 9: 56–75.

Cope, Bill, and Mary Kalantzis. 1993. *The Powers of Literacy: A Genre Approach to Teaching Writing*. Critical Perspectives on Literacy and Education. London: Falmer.

Crowley, Sharon. 1998. *Composition in the University: Historical and Polemical Essays*. Pittsburgh Series in Composition, Literacy, and Culture. Pittsburgh: University of Pittsburgh Press.

Davis, Steven. May, 2002. A Proposal for the Development of Undergraduate Writing-Intensive Courses at SFU. . http://www.sfu.ca/ugcr/files/ucc_final.pdf

Dench, Sarah. 2007. Preliminary Report: Implementation of Undergraduate Curriculum Changes: Paper S.07–85 Spring 2007. Simon Fraser University Senate. http://www.sfu.ca/Senate/meeting_summaries/Sum_0707.html

Devitt, Amy J., Mary Jo Reiff, and Anis S. Bawarshi. 2004. *Scenes of Writing: Strategies for Composing with Genres*. New York: Pearson/Longman.

Dias, Patrick. 1999. *Worlds Apart: Acting and Writing in Academic and Workplace Contexts*. Rhetoric, Knowledge, and Society. Mahwah: Lawrence Erlbaum Associates.

Farris, Christine, and Christopher M. Anson. 1998. *Under Construction: Working at the Intersections of Composition Theory, Research, and Practice*. Logan: Utah State University Press.

Freedman, Aviva. 1993. Show and Tell? The Role of Explicit Teaching in the Learning of New Genres. *Research in the Teaching of English*. 27: 222–251.

———. 1994. *Learning and Teaching Genre*. Portsmouth: Boynton/Cook Publishers.

———, and Peter Medway. 1994. *Genre and the New Rhetoric*. Critical Perspectives on Literacy and Education. London ; Bristol: Taylor & Francis.

Fullan, Michael. 1993. *Change Forces: Probing the Depth of Educational Reform*. New York: Falmer.

———. 2003. *Change Forces with a Vengeance*. London: Routledge Falmer.

Fulwiler, Toby, and Art Young, eds. 1990. *Programs That Work: Models and Methods for Writing Across the Curriculum*. Portsmouth: Boynton/Cook.

Gagan, David. 1998. Statement of Purpose. Memorandum, Office of the vice president academic. http://www.sfu.ca/vpacademic/accountability/purpose.html.

Geisler, Cheryl. 1994. *Academic Literacy and the Nature of Expertise: Reading, Writing, and Knowing in Academic philosophy*. Hillsdale: Lawrence Erlbaum Associates.

Geller, Anne Ellen. 2005. What's Cool Here? Collaboratively Learning Genre in biology. In *Genre Across the Curriculum.*, eds. Anne Herrington, Charles Moran, 83–105. Logan: Utah State University Press.

Gere, Anne Ruggles, and Eugene Smith. 1979. *Attitudes, Language, and Change.* Urbana: NCTE.

Gerson, Carole. 1996. Supplementary Course Fees for 100-division Courses. Memo to English Department Faculty and Sessionals ed.

Giddens, Anthony. 1984. *The Constitution of Society: Outline of the Theory of Structuration.* Cambridge: Polity Press.

Giltrow, Janet. 1998. Reading and Writing in Cross-Cultural Situations: Request for Ethics Approval. Ethics Request Form, Simon Fraser University.

———. 1997. writing centre Submission to Departmental Review Documentation. English Department, SFU.

———, and Michele Valiquette. 1994. Genres and Knowledge: Students' Writing in the Disciplines. In *Genre and Education.* eds. Aviva Freedman, Peter Medway. Portsmouth: Heinemann. 47–62.

Graff, Gerald. 1992. *Beyond the Culture Wars: How Teaching the Conflicts Can Revitalize American Education.* New York: Norton.

Gragson, Gay, and Jack Selzer. 1990. Fictionalizing the Readers of Scholarly Articles in biology. *Written Communication.* 7(1) (January): 25–58.

Grant, B. December, 2000. Terms of Reference and Membership - Ad Hoc Senate Committee to Review and Develop the Undergraduate Curriculum. Senate Minutes S.00–112. http://www.sfu.ca/Senate/meeting_summaries/archives-Senate/SenateMinutes00/Mins_1200.html

Griffin, C. Williams. 1982. *Teaching Writing in All Disciplines.* New Directions for Teaching and Learning. Vol. 12. San Francisco: Jossey-Bass.

Groeneboer, C., W. Harris, N. Payne, and M. Whitney. 2007. Writing-Intensive Course Study Report. (Forthcoming at http://www.sfu.ca/lidc)

Grumet, Madeleine R. 1988. *Bitter Milk: Women and Teaching.* Amherst: University of Massachusetts Press.

Hargreaves, Andy, and Michael Fullan. 1992. *Understanding Teacher Development.* New York: Teachers College Press.

Haviland, Carol Peterson, and Edward M. White. 1999. How Can Physical Space and Administrative Structure Shape Writing Programs, writing centres, and WAC Projects? In *Administrative Problem-Solving for Writing Programs and Writing Centers.*, ed. Linda Myers-Breslin. Urbana: NCTE.

Herrington, Anne, and Charles Moran. 2005. The Idea of Genre in Theory and Practice: an Overview of the Work in Genre in the Fields of Composition and Rhetoric and New Genre Studies. In *Genre Across the Curriculum.*, ed. Anne Herrington, Charles Moran. Logan: Utah State University Press.

———. 1992. *Writing, Teaching, and Learning in the Disciplines.* Research and Scholarship in Composition. Vol. 1. New York:

Hilgers, Thomas L., Edna Lardizabal Hussey, and Monica Stitt-Bergh. 1999. 'As You're Writing You Have These Epiphanies': What College Students Say about Writing and Learning in Their Majors. *Written Communication.* 16(3): 317–353.

Hillocks, George Jr. 1987. Synthesis of Research in Teaching Writing. *Educational Leadership.* 44(May): 71–82.

———. 1982. The Interaction of Instruction, Teacher Comment, and Revision in Teaching the Composing Process. *Research in the Teaching of English.* 16: 261–277.

Huber, Mary Taylor, Morreale, Sherwyn P. Carnegie Foundation for the Advancement of Teaching, and American Association for Higher Education. 2002. *Disciplinary Styles in the Scholarship of Teaching and Learning: Exploring Common Ground.* Washington: American Association for Higher Education.

Hyland, Ken. 2004. *Genre and Second Language Writing.* In *Teaching Multilingual Writers,* ed. Diane Belcher, Jun Liu. Ann Arbor: University of Michigan Press.

Hyland, Ken. 2000. *Disciplinary Discourses: Social Interactions in Academic Writing.* Applied Linguistics and Language Study. New York: Longman.

Johns, Ann M. 1997. *Text, Role, and Context: Developing Academic Literacies.* The Cambridge Applied Linguistics Series. New York: Cambridge University Press.

Johnston, Hugh. 2005. *Radical Campus: Making Simon Fraser University.* Vancouver: Douglas & McIntyre.

Jolliffe, David A., and Ellen Brier M. 1988. Studying Writers' Knowledge in Academic Disciplines. In *Writing in Academic Disciplines: Advances in Writing Research.*, ed. David A. Jolliffe. Vol. 2, 35–88. Norwood: Ablex Publishing.

Kapor, Mitch. 2005. Content Creation by Massively Distributed Collaboration. UC Berkeley Distinguished Lecture series. http://www.ischool.berkeley.edu/about/news/pressreleases/kapor11092005

Kipling, Kim, and Richard John Murphy. 1992. *Symbiosis: Writing and an Academic Culture.* Portsmouth: Boynton/Cook Publishers.

Klein, Julie Thompson. 1996. *Crossing Boundaries: Knowledge, Disciplinarities, and Interdisciplinarities.* Knowledge, Disciplinarity and Beyond. Charlottesville: University Press of Virginia.

Knoblauch, C. H., and L. Brannon. 1984. *Rhetorical Traditions and the Teaching of Writing.* Upper Montclair: Boynton/Cook.

Krebs, Dennis. 2007. CWIL Revised Mandate January 2004. Personal communication February 20, 2007.

Kvale, Steinar. 1996. *Interviews: an Introduction to Qualitative Research Interviewing.* Thousand Oaks: Sage Publications.

Kynard, Carmen. 2005. "Getting on the Right Side of It": Problematizing and Rethinking the Research Paper Genre in the College Composition Course. In *Genre Across the Curriculum*, ed. Anne Herrington, Charles Moran. Logan: Utah State University Press. 128–151.

Land, R. E., and S. Evans. 1987. What Our Students Taught Us about Paper Marking. *English Journal.* 76: 113–116.

Langer, Judith. 1992. Speaking of Knowing: Conceptions of Understanding in Academic Disciplines. In *Writing, Teaching and Learning in the Disciplines.* ed. Anne Herrington, Charles Moran. New York: MLA. 69–85.

Latour, Bruno. 1987. *Science in Action.* Cambridge, Massachusetts: Harvard University Press.

Lave, Jean, and Etienne Wenger. 1991. *Situated Learning: Legitimate Peripheral Participation.* Learning in Doing. Cambridge: Cambridge University Press.

Lea, Mary R., and Brian V. Street. 1998. Student Writing in Higher Education: an Academic Literacies Approach. *Studies in Higher Education.* 23(2): 157.

Lee, Virginia S. 2000. The Influence of Disciplinary Differences on Consultations with Faculty. In *To Improve the Academy: Resources for Faculty, Instructional and Organizational Development.*, eds. Matthew Kaplan, Devorah Lieberman. Vol. 18. Bolton: Anker Publishing. 278–290.

L'Eplattenier, Barbara (ed). 2004. *Historical Studies of Writing Administration: Individuals, Communities, and the Formation of a Discipline.* West Lafayette: Parlor Press.

Light, Richard J. 2001. *Making the Most of College: Students Speak Their Minds.* Cambridge: Harvard University Press.

Lillis, Theresa Turner, Joan. 2001. Student Writing in Higher Education: Contemporary Confusion, Traditional Concerns. *Teaching in Higher Education.* 6(1). 57–68

Little, Joseph. 2001. Book Reviews. *Journal of Business and Technical Communication.* 15(1) (January): 116–118.

Lough, Jodi. 2003. Writing Resources in the Faculty of Arts (SFU). Report prepared for CWIL. http://www.sfu.ca/lidc/wilo

Lynch, C., and P. Kleman. 1978. Evaluating our Evaluations. *College English.* 40: 166–180.

Madigan, Robert, Susan Johnson, and Patricia Linton. June, 1995. The Language of Psychology: APA Style as Epistemology. *American Psychologist.* 50(6): 428–436.

Mailloux, Steven. 1998. *Reception Histories: Rhetoric, Pragmatism, and American Cultural Politics.* Ithaca, N.Y.: Cornell University Press.

Manguel, Alberto. 1996. *A History of Reading.* New York: Penguin.

McLeod, Susan. 2001. The Pedagogy of Writing across the Curriculum. In *A Guide to Composition Pedagogies*, eds. Gary Tate, Amy Rupiper and Kurt Schick, 149–164. New York: Oxford University Press.

McLeod, Susan H., and Eric Miraglia. 2001. Writing Across the Curriculum in a Time of Change. In *WAC for the New Millennium*, ed. Susan H. McLeod, Eric Miraglia, Margot Soven and Chris Thaiss, 1–27. Urbana: NCTE.

Miller, Carolyn R. 1994. Rhetorical Community: the Cultural Basis of Genre. In *Genre and the New Rhetoric*. eds. Aviva Freedman, Peter Medway, 67–77. Taylor & Francis.

———. 1984. Genre as Social Action. *Quarterly Journal of Speech*. 70.2: 151–167.

Miller, Richard E. 1998. *As If Learning Mattered: Reforming Higher Education*. Ithaca: Cornell University Press.

Miller, Susan. 1995. *In Loco Parentis: Addressing (The) Class*. ed. Jane Gallop. Vol. 17, 155–164. Bloomington and Indianapolis: Indiana University Press.

Miraglia, E., and S. McLeod. 1997. Whither WAC? Interpreting the Stories/Histories of Enduring WAC Programs. *Writing Program Administrators Journal*. 20(3): 46–55.

Monkman, Leslie, Ronald Bond, Ina Ferris, and Richard Gruneau. March 1997. Report of the committee to Review the Department of English, Simon Fraser University.

Monroe, Jonathan. 2003. *Local Knowledges, Local Practices: Writing in the Disciplines at Cornell*. Pittsburgh: University of Pittsburgh Press.

———. 2002. *Writing and Revising the Disciplines*. Ithaca: Cornell University Press.

Muir, Cam C., Birute M. F. Galdikas, and Andrew T. Beckenbach. 1998. Is There Sufficient Evidence to Elevate the Orangutan of Borneo and Sumatra to Separate Species? *Journal of Molecular Evolution*. 46: 378–381.

Newell, George E., and Peter Winograd. 1989. The Effects of Writing on Learning from Expository Text. *Written Communication*. 6(2): 196–217.

Parker, Robert, and Vera Goodkin.1987. The Consequences of Writing: Enhancing Learning in the Disciplines. Upper Montclair: Boynton/Cook.

Paul, Danette, and Davida Charney. 1995. Introducing Chaos (Theory) into Science and Engineering: Effects of Rhetorical Strategies on Scientific Readers. *Written Communication*. 12(4): 396–438.

Paul, Danette, Davida Charney, and Aimee Kendall. 2001. Moving Beyond the Moment: Reception Studies in the Rhetoric of Science. *Journal of Business and Technical Communication*. 15(3): 372–399.

Penrose, Ann M. 1989. *Strategic Differences in Composing: Consequences for Learning Through Writing*. Berkeley, CA; Pittsburgh: Center for the Study of Writing.

Prior, Paul A. 1998. *Writing/Disciplinarity: Sociohistoric Account of Literate Activity in the Academy*. Rhetoric, Knowledge, and Society. Mahwah: Laurence Erlbaum Associates.

Reeves, Carol. 1990. Establishing a Phenomenon: the Rhetoric of Early Medical Reports on AIDS. *Written Communication*. 7(3): 393–416.

Rivers, William E. 1994. Studies in the History of Business and Technical Writing: a Bibliographical Essay. *Journal of Business and Technical Communication*. 8(1): 6–57.

Rouse, Joseph. 1990. The Narrative Reconstruction of Science. *Inquiry*. 33: 179–196.

Russell, David R. 2002. *Writing in the Academic Disciplines: a Curricular History*. 2nd ed. Carbondale: Southern Illinois University Press.

Rutz, Carol, and Jacqulyn Lauer-Glebov. 2005. Assessment and Innovation: One Darn Thing Leads to Another. *Assessing Writing*. 10(2): 80–99.

Saroyan, Alenoush, and Cheryl Amundsen, eds. 2004. *Rethinking Teaching in Higher Education: from a Course Design Workshop to a Faculty Development Framework*. Sterling: Stylus.

Segall, Mary T., and Robert A. Smart, eds. 2005. *Direct from the Disciplines: Writing Across the Curriculum*. Portsmouth: Boynton/Cook Heinemann.

Shen, Andrea. 2001. FAS communications interview with Nancy Sommers. *Harvard Gazette*. http://www.hno.harvard.edu/gazette/2000/10.26/06-writing.html

Shulman, Lee S. 1987. Knowledge and Teaching: Foundations of the New Reform. *Harvard Educational Review*. 57(1): 1–22.

Simpson, Murray S., and Shireen E. Carroll. 1999. Assignments for a Writing-Intensive economics Course. *Journal of Economic Education.* 30(4): 402–410.

Sitko, B. 1992. Writers Meet Their Readers in the Classroom: Revising after Feedback. In *Constructing Rhetorical Education* eds. M. M. Secor, D. Charney, 278–293. Carbondale: Southern Illinois University Press.

Smagorinsky, Peter. 1991. The Writer's Knowledge and the Writing Process: a Protocol Analysis. *Research in the Teaching of English.* 25(3): 339–364.

Sommers, Nancy. 1982. Responding to Student Writing. *College Composition and Communication.* 33: 148–156.

———. 1980. Revision Strategies of Student Writers and Experienced Adult Writers. *College Composition and Communication.* 31(4): 378–388.

Stevenson, Michael. 2001. The President's Agenda: SFU at 40. http://www.sfu.ca/pres/files/presidents_agenda.pdf.

Strachan, Wendy M. 1990. Toward Understanding Literacy: Disarming the Appeal of a Theoretical Eclecticism in Teaching Practice—an Analysis of Disciplinary Perspectives. Unpublished Dissertation. Simon Fraser University.

———, and Steven Davis. Spring, 2000. Learning to Write in philosophy: Developing a Writing Intensive Course. http://www.sfu.ca/ugcr.

Straub, Richard. 1997. Students' Reactions to Teacher Comments: an Exploratory Study. *Research in the Teaching of English.* 31(1): 91–119.

Sullivan, Dale L. 1996. Displaying Disciplinarity. *Written Communication.* 13(2) (April): 221–250.

———. 1991. The Epideictic Rhetoric of Science. *Journal of Business and Technical Communication.* 5(3) (July): 229–245.

Swales, John M. 1990. *Genre Analysis: English in Academic and Research Settings.* eds. Michael H. Long, Jack C. Richards. Cambridge: Cambridge University Press.

———, and Stephanie Lindemann. 2002. Teaching the Literature Review to International Graduate Students. In *Genre in the Classroom: Multiple Perspectives.*, ed. Ann M. Johns, 105–120. Mahwah: Lawrence Erlbaum Associates.

Thaiss, Chris, ed. 1983. *Writing to Learn: Essays and Reflections on Writing Across the Curriculum.* Portsmouth: Boynton/Cook.

———, and Terry Myers Zawacki. 2006. *Engaged Writers: Dynamic Disciplines.* ed. Charles I. Schuster. Portsmouth: Boynton/Cook.

Townsend, Martha. 2001. Writing Intensive Courses and WAC. In *WAC for the New Millennium* eds. Susan H. McLeod, Eric Miraglia, Margot Soven and Christopher Thaiss, 233–258. Urbana: NCTE.

———. 1997. Integrating WAC into General Education: An Assessment Case Study. In *Assessing Writing Across the Curriculum: Diverse Approaches and Practices.* eds. Kathleen Blake Yancey, Brian Huot, 159–172. Greenwich: Ablex.

Tynjèalèa, Pèaivi, Lucia Mason, and Kirsti Lonka. 2001. *Writing as a Learning Tool: Integrating Theory and Practice.* Studies in Writing. Vol. 7. Dordrecht and Boston: Kluwer.

Undergraduate Curriculum Implementation Task Force. 2003. Request to Departments for Response to Draft Criteria for WQB Courses. http://www.sfu.ca/ugcr/WQB_Requirements/

Van der Gaag, Tanya. 2003. Writing in Undergraduate Courses: Weight in Grading Assigned to Writing as Specified on Course Outlines Faculty of Arts (Fall 2002). http://www.sfu.ca/lidc/wilo

Vygotsky, Lev S. 1978. *Mind in Society: the Development of Higher Psychological Processes.* eds. Michael Cole et al. Cambridge: Harvard University Press.

Waern, Y. 1988. Thoughts on Text in Context: Applying the Think-Aloud Method to Text Processing. *Text.* 8(4): 327–350.

Waldo, Mark. 1996. Inquiry as a Non-Invasive Approach to Cross-Curricular Writing Consultancy. *Language and Learning Across the Curriculum.* Volume 1(3): 6–22.

———. 2004. *Demythologizing Language Differences in the Academy.* Mahwah: Lawrence Erlbaum Associates.

Wallace, Ray, Alan Jackson, and Susan Lewis Wallace. 2000. Reforming College Composition: Writing the Wrongs. *Contributions to the Study of Education.* Vol. 79. Westport: Greenwood Press.

Walsh-Bowers, Richard. 1995. The Reporting and Ethics of the Research Relationship in Areas of Interpersonal Psychology, 1939–89. *Theory & Psychology.* 5(2): 233–250.

Walvoord, Barbara E. Fassler and Lucille P. McCarthy. 1990. *Thinking and Writing in College: a Naturalistic Study of Students in Four Disciplines.* Urbana: NCTE.

———, and NCTE. 1997. *In the Long Run: a Study of Faculty in Three Writing-Across-the-Curriculum Programs.* Urbana: NCTE.

Waterhouse, John. 2000. Request for an Ad Hoc Senate committee to Review and Develop the Undergraduate Curricula. Memorandum to Senate committee on Agenda and Rules. http://www.sfu.ca/Senate/meeting_summaries/archives-Senate/SenateMinutes00/Sum_1200.html

Werner, Warren W. 1989. Models and the Teaching of Technical Writing. *Journal of Technical Writing and Communication.* 19(1): 69–82.

Wertsch, James V. 1998. *Mind as Action.* New York: Oxford University Press.

White, Edward M. 1989. *Developing Successful College Writing Programs.* Paperback 1998 ed. Maine: Calendar Islands. 1998.

———. 1990. The Damage of Innovations Set Adrift. *AAHE Bulletin.* 43(3): 3–5.

———, William Lutz, and Sandra Kamusikiri. 1996. Assessment of Writing: Politics, Policies, Practices. *Research and Scholarship in Composition.* Vol. 4. New York: Modern Language Association.

Williams, Joseph, and Gregory G. Colomb. 1990. The University of Chicago. In *Programs That Work: Models and Methods for Writing Across the Curriculum.* eds. Toby Fulwiler, Art Young, 83–113. Portsmouth: Boynton/Cook Heinemann.

Writing Support Group. March 2005. Proposal: Assessment of the Writing Component of the Curriculum Initiative. Submission to the UCITF, Simon Fraser University.

Xu, Xiufeng, and Ulfur Arnason. 1996. The Mitochondrial DNA Molecule of Sumatran Orangutan and a Molecular Proposal for Two (Bornean and Sumatran) Species of Orangutan. *Journal of Molecular Evolution.* 43: 431–437.

Young, Art, and Toby Fulwiler, eds. 1986. *Writing Across the Disciplines: Research into Practice.* Portsmouth: Boynton/Cook.

INDEX

ABOUT THE AUTHOR

WENDY STRACHAN's teaching and research interests reflect a lifelong dedication to writing as a means of learning across the curriculum K-university. Over a period of fifteen years, she was director of National Writing Project sites in Asia, Athens and Europe before joining the faculty in the English department at Simon Fraser University and later taking on the development of the Centre for Writing-Intensive Learning as its director. Her research interests in the social contexts of genre acquisition and the conditions that support faculty in making pedagogical change have been published as articles, book chapters and hundreds of conference papers and presentations both nationally and internationally. *Writing-Intensive* is her first book.